D1028905

CIGAR ALMANAC

FIRST EDITION
1980

by
LEW ROTHMAN

Published by

EDUCATION SYSTEMS & PUBLICATIONS
195 Cortlandt St., Belleville, New Jersey 07109

Library of Congress Cataloging in Publication Data

Rothman, Lew. 1945
  Lew Rothman's Cigar almanac

  Includes index.
  1. Cigars. 2. Cigars — Catalogs. I. Title.
II. Title: Cigar almanac.
TS2283.R67   678'.73   79-22161

First Printing

Dedication

To my partner and wife LaVonda, my family, my friends, my co-workers, and all the people who love me (may all six of them live and be well).

Additionally, much of the knowledge I have accumulated about cigars is due to years of interrogation of the following people:

Harry Brolin
Dan Blumenthal
Frank Llaneza
Irving Kramer

All my knowledge of business is directly accountable to my father, Jack Rothman.

I have learned absolutely nothing from Marvin Shermer, but he did drive me to work for a long time (therefore, unbeknown to him I was able to get to work earlier and learn things from the people on the list which does not contain his name).

Contents

Foreword

Cigar smokers, in fact and fiction, are normally pictured as the elite of society. The successful businessman, the shrewd lawyer, the famous politician. They're supposed to be smart. Therefore, once you've read this book from cover to cover you should never have to ask a question about cigars again. Don't skip a word, a punctuation mark, as a rigorous two hour exam will follow. Those failing will be required to return this valuable book, and will *not* receive their money back. It's the price they pay for being stupid, and we don't want stupid people ruining the overall reputation of cigar smokers — right?

There is a much closer affinity between the buyer and seller of cigars than exists between any other group of consumers and vendors. Both have a strange love for this mysterious cylinder of rolled tobacco leaves. When cracking open a new box of cigars, I myself get as excited as my customer does to fondle and examine the product within.

It's like opening a pound of coffee, hearing that telltale hiss — that aromatic explosion that shocks my senses alive and makes my taste buds go into overdrive. Considering the fact that I sell about a million cigars a week, this has to be a marvelous product indeed to produce this same reaction in me over and over again, day after day, year after year. Smokers thrill to every nuance of the cigar — its feel, its texture, its bouquet, its wrapper shade, its degree of oiliness, they even delight in the styles and variations of the packaging. Just the exotic name of a product can start a smoker dreaming of memorable moments past.

> "Hoyo de Monterrey de Jose Gener,
> Excalibur I, SunGrown, Rich Maduro,
> packed twenty to a Spanish Cedar Boite
> Nature Chest."

That's the title of just one size of one brand, yet it instantly makes the cigar connoisseur cognisant of the following facts:

This cigar is a descendant and recipient of all the knowledge, pride and tradition of one of the oldest and most respected of the family owned Cuban Cigar Firms Hoyo de Monterrey de Jose Gener.

It is their finest product — Excalibur.

It is their largest size — the No. I.

It is a 7¼ inch cigar with an immense 54 ring size.

It is being presented in its most attractive shade — the rich, dark, oily Maduro.

It is encased in a heavy chest of aromatic Spanish cedar to enhance even further its own natural bouquet.

It is going to be one of the most expensive cigars you have ever bought.

You won't give a damn — because it'll be worth it.

The Cigar Almanac is the real and simple exploration of every feasible question the cigar smoker can reasonably ask.

In the ensuing pages and pictures you will find simple answers to your questions, a guide to most popular cigars sold in this country, descriptions of each as to size, cost, quality, method of manufacture, etc. You will also find copious quantities of baloney in order to make the book have enough pages to warrant the price you paid for it.

I have always believed in satisfying the public's desire to get their money's worth. Therefore, if you, after reading this book, do not feel you have gotten your money's worth, call me and I will send you some more pages at no extra charge.

The cigar industry today

Cigars sales in this country have eroded dramatically in the last decade, from 9 billion cigars annually to 4½ billion. This erosion can be traced to a number of obvious factors, among which are the decline of cigars as a status symbol, the hesitancy of cigar manufacturers to increase retail prices, the change in ownership of cigar manufacturers from family to corporate businesses, the influence of marketing and packaging experts, and the demise of the cigar as a profitable sale item for the retailer. These factors in themselves, and in interaction among themselves, have crippled the unit sales of cigars nationally, and if left unchecked will continue to cast a shadow of doom and dismay over what is basically a fine consumable sales item that has become an institution the world over.

The cigar has always been, until the past decade, the symbol of success. The wealthy banker, the railroad tycoon, the successful politician, the mafia chieftain — wherever power was concentrated in an individual, that man invariably was a cigar smoker. For generations young men on the way up emulated these successful men and became cigar smokers while climbing and battling through the ranks to reach the top of their chosen profession. Today, while this is still true to a degree, the cigar is no longer the strong symbol of success it once was. As a result the number of new smokers entering the buying market has been distinctly lower than necessary to replace those who have left by virtue of disuse or death. The cigar industry will have to lay back and wait for a smoker of such dynamic personality and popularity to come along that young men, in the emulation of this cigar chomping champion, will once again flock to cigar counters across the nation, and breathe new life into this industry.

A second factor to consider in the decline of the cigar industry was the hesitancy during the 1960's of cigar manufacturers to increase prices during a decade of constant inflation. During this decade they found their profit margins eroding, and attempted to offset this erosion by introducing new technological improvements such as homogenized tobacco leaf, which in effect reduced the quality of their products. They proliferated the number of sizes and packings they offered for sale, which watered down an already weakening market. They invaded en masse new merchandising outlets such as drug chains, supermarkets, etc., thereby weakening the traditional corner cigar store. This in turn created massive return problems from outlets which had no provisions for keeping cigars in saleable condition, and placed inferior merchandise in the hands and mouths of the consuming public. Additionally, the sale of cigars was removed from the auspices of a knowledgeable tobacconist and put in the hands of the checkout girl in the local supermarket. The cigar smoker to a great extent was no longer the purchaser, his wife was, and the excitement of choosing his day's supply of cigars and the comraderie that existed in the little corner cigar store began to fade. The manufacturers, in resisting price advances, proliferating products and outlets,

1

reducing cigar quality, and slashing sales forces, found themselves on a treadmill running faster and faster to stay in the same place. They became resigned to stagnation and erosion and turned their sights away from growth in units sold to the new goal of market share. Sales personnel were prodded to make more stops, place more sizes in racks and cases and open new accounts. The inevitable result came in the 1970's. When the dust settled, many manufacturers had shut down or been gobbled up by their competitors, volume was way down, the corner cigar store was a relic of the past, and the future held so little promise that it made the past decade of turmoil look as if it had been the glory years.

During these years, and the decade prior, ownership of cigar manufacturing companies moved from the family level to the "Corporate Giant" level. Policy is now made by lawyers and accountants, many of whom have never seen a cigar, rather than 2nd, 3rd, and 4th generation cigarmen. The policy of "the bottom line" came into the cigar industry with shattering force. Leaf buyers were now told ahead of time by corporate officers somewhere above how much they could spend per pound of tobacco, production costs were not determined by how much it cost to produce a cigar of a certain quality, but what quality cigar could be produced for a fixed price. Pride of product as a whole began to suffer, as it was replaced by increased emphasis on "the bottom line".

With volume marketing and the decline of profits, packaging experts became more important and more numerous. Flavored cigars, aromatic cigars, 5-packs, 4-packs, 3-packs, 6-packs, 7-packs, twin packs, convenience packs, pack racks, pack bars, bonus cigar packs, fresh packs, vac packs, assorto packs, plastic packs, economy packs — there was no end to the number of new items hitting the marketplace. The figures for the year ending in 1977 revealed a 50% decrease in cigar consumption in the previous seven years. The manufacturers were now aware that although their marketing geniuses had shuffled the deck a thousand times, the hand they dealt remained the same.

Last, and most significant in the demise of the cigar industry, was the growing reluctance of the surviving cigar stores to prominently feature and promote cigars. The cigar lost its position as a major source of income due to the expansion of accounts by the manufacturers into chain drug stores and supermarkets, and due to the gradual, but constant, increases in the wholesale list price of cigars, while retail prices were held down by outright chicanery on the part of the manufacturers.

Cigars now bore tags such as 26 cents or 2/27 cents, and these suggested retails were reflected in the wholesale list price of cigars to the retailer. The manufacturers were well aware that the shopkeeper was not going to charge his customer 26 cents for the cigar that was previously a quarter. In fact the manufacturer made it impossible by prepricing the merchandise at 26 cents, 4 for $1.00. In so doing he took a very small slice of profit from the retailer, while allowing the consumer to go on purchasing merchandise as if no price rise had occurred. This little trick was played on the retailer over and over and over for twenty years and is still being done today. The cumulative effect was an average 18% margin of profit from retail to wholesale list price on most domestic merchandise, even less when using suggested 5-pack prices. The result has been the disappearance of cigar displays in windows, the disappearance of open box displays in cigar cases, the disappearance of the cigar cases themselves, the removal of cigar racks from top of counter to behind the counter, the disappearance of any vestige of desire on the part of the retailer to sell an item so lacking in profit margin by comparison to any other item consuming an equal amount of display space of his shop.

The one bright spot in the entire industry is the high priced imported cigar. It's the big ticket item the retailer wants, and although the profit margin is not immense, it is almost double that of the domestic cigar. That single bright spot, which accounts for a mere 4% of cigar sales, now appears to be reaching its zenith. Hopefully, the cigar industry will not pin its hopes for the future on this 4% golden thread. Hopefully the industry will wake up, find a champion, a deliverer, to reinstate the cigar as a status item, return to the days of quality products, and let the quality of its product insure a healthy retail price, throw out the influences of the so called marketing men, limit their merchandise to the tobacconist rather than the supermarket, and build into the retail price of their cigars an honest profit for the retailer in return for his anticipated promotion and display of what is possibly his greatest potential source of income — that being the legendary symbol of manhood, the sign of status, the enjoyable, exciting, consumable cigar.

The cigar distribution game and how it affects the price you pay for your cigars

From the Source it goes like this:

1. The cigar factory is owned by the manufacturer, or has a working agreement with one or more importers.

2. The manufacturer or importer either sells and distributes the cigars himself, or selects various franchised distributors throughout the country to distribute the product to cigar stores throughout various areas of the country. Many times the larger cigar stores are able to purchase cigars directly from the manufacturer or importer, even though they are located within the realm of a distributor.

3. Several large chains of tobacco shops exist, where the chain purchases cigars from the manufacturer or distributor and then re-distributes the merchandise to its member stores.

4. The point to bear in mind is that intermediary profits are made every time another party enters the chain of distribution between your cigar store and the original source of production.

So have a heart. If you're buying from a store in Little Rock, Arkansas and paying full price for your cigars, bear in mind that the dealer there may actually be making less per cigar than the rock bottom, crash discount, volume cigar store in New York. His location and volume predetermine that he will simply have to pay more and charge more for his products. He is not a thief, he's just trying to make a perfectly legitimate profit — and you'll see just how little that is in the section describing the cigars you purchase and their wholesale prices. The small retailer is actually the backbone of the cigar industry, providing availability of products in non-metropolitan areas.

For God's sake don't buy cigars in supermarkets, and drugstores, diners, and luncheonettes. These vendors often charge very low prices, using tobacco products as loss leaders to bring you into their shops with the hope that you'll buy something profitable while you're in there. These people know absolutely nothing about the product and have no facilities whatsoever to keep your cigars fresh and palatable.

You want to buy cigars? Go to a cigar store. You want to buy a turkey go to a supermarket. If you persist in buying cigars in supermarkets, then most of your cigars will be turkeys.

Remember — the cheapest source for quality cigars is the store that purchases its product in the most direct manner. However, the only source for quality cigars is a tobacconist, a specialist in keeping his product in peak smoking condition regardless of the price he may charge for those products.

What makes you want to smoke a cigar?

You take out a cigar, remove the cellophane, smell it — it's got an aroma that nothing else on earth has. (If I could only make a cigar that smelled as good after it was lit, as before, every woman in America would love me, the Pope would declare me a Saint, and the Queen would knight me.) Now you bite off the tip, the best cigar cutter ever made is the one you were given — your teeth. It makes a perfect cut, and prepares you taste buds for what is to come. It's like the smell that hits you when you walk into a chinese restaurant - it gets your juices flowing. Then you strike a match (I personally like a lighter that makes a loud "click" when I snap the cover closed — does that sound weird??) and slowly rotating the cigar, and slowly puffing, wait for the flame to "leap" across from your match to your cigar (never let a flame touch the cigar itself - it leaves carbon deposits. Yech!) The end of your cigar momentarily shows a puff of flame immediately dying out. You then look at the glowing end, gently blow on it, it glows bright orange-red and is perfectly lit. AAHHH!

If you did that right it took 30 seconds. But during that 30 seconds I guarantee you, you were at absolute peace with the world. *"Gibraltar may crumble the Rockies may tumble", but* no matter what was going on around you, you'd have been unaware.

Sometimes I think if I just lit new cigars over and over all day I'd get so relaxed, so loose, that all they'd find left of me was a pile of loose jello in my chair surrounded by hundreds of "just lit" cigars. How on earth can anyone who doesn't imbibe in cigars know the feeling of lighting up a great, aromatic, solid cigar?

Lighting a cigar can be a weapon. You're in a heated debate. The other guy comes back at you with something that dumfounds you. Now, do you sit there with a stupid look on your face? NO! You hastily pull out a big cigar — you can't talk while you light it — the cigar gives you a look of importance, self assuredness, affluence PLUS it gives you at least 30 seconds to figure out some outrageous bullshit which is going to make the other guy look like a jerk!! Hopefully, he doesn't smoke cigars, otherwise he'll do the same thing to you. Then you'll throw away your cigar, light a new one, he'll throw away his, and so forth — and before you know it you'll both waste all these perfectly good cigars on some dumb argument.

Cigars can give you courage. Even if they don't, they'll give you something to do with your hands so that other people won't know you're nervous.

Cigars can give you a look of affluence — people think people who smoke big cigars have money — or at least they must have had some money before they bought the big cigars. Remember, a big cigar becomes a little cigar after it's been smoked for a while.Carry a big cigar in your pocket and people will assume that the little one you're smoking was originally bigger!

Cigars have MACHO.

Cigars relax your nerves, curb your appetite, and provide a unique taste sensation. A nice cloud of cigar smoke will shield your eyes from harsh lights - and keep the bugs away on a summer night. Cigars turn pussycats into men, and men into noblemen.

5

Keeping your cigars fresh

1.DON'T BE A DOPE. Cigars are perishable. Pretend they're tomatoes. When you go to the vegetable store, you look at all his produce and you see these fantastic juicy red tomatoes, the best you've seen in years. What do you say to the man (bearing in mind next week's batch of tomatoes may not be so good)? "Hey! These tomatoes are fantastic. Gimme 600 pounds!"

No. You don't say that cause you're not a dope. You buy 600 pounds and sure as hell you'll throw out 598 pounds of rotten tomatoes next week!

The same is true of cigars. BUY WHAT YOU CAN REASONABLY EXPECT TO CONSUME IN A 15-DAY PERIOD, and with the few little tricks that follow, you'll have 100% fresh cigars everytime.

2.In order to keep your cigars fresh, you have to buy them fresh.

How do you know they're fresh when you buy them?

Well, you could ask the shopkeeper, "Mister Shopkeeper, are these cigars fresh?" What do you think he's going to say? "No, don't buy in my store cause all my merchandise is dead stale!" No, I don't think he'll say that. So that doesn't work.

Second, you could ask him to open the box before you purchase it. But that is unfair to the shopkeeper. How would you like it if he handed you a previously opened box for you to purchase, knowing another customer had already rejected the box?

Instead, do the following and you'll get fresh cigars 99% of the time.

    A.   Go to a shop that sells a lot of cigars and turns its inventory frequently.

    B.   Check out his humidor. Cigars are supposed to be stored at about 65⁰ Farenheit and 68% humidity. Many shops control the humidity, ONLY A SUPERIOR CIGAR STORE REGULATES THE TEMPERATURE as well. If a store's humidor is not cool, the humidor is worthless.

    C.   With a dark cloth, or just your hand, wipe the surface of the box you wish to purchase. If you find a lot of white stuff, don't buy that box. Minerals settle out of the air in a humidor. It's sort of a chalky, limy, powdery stuff. If the boxes are powdery they've probably been there a long time or the stock clerk has a terrible case of dandruff. If they're clean, the cigars probably have just arrived.

    D.   Many boxes are coded by date on the bottom by the manufacturer. If you see 1278, you know it's December 1978. J76 means January 76. There are many codes, but they're all simple to figure out if you just look at them for a minute, and are not a complete dummy.

    E.   If the box is dirty or all beaten to hell, or the seal is broken, don't buy it, whatever price you're paying. You're paying for good, clean merchandise. Would you buy a tomato with a footprint on it for the normal going price?

F.   If the box has cellophane around it, make sure the cellophane is loose. The absence of moisture makes cellophane contract, therefore, a box with tight cellophane will often contain stale cigars.

G.   If you're buying a cigar in a bundle, give it a squeeze. The entire package should be resilient. If you give it a squeeze and hear a cacophony of crunching, snapping noises, like someone is munching potato chips at a Broadway show, you know that you don't want those cigars.

3. Okay, now you've bought what you believe to be a reasonably fresh box of cigars, but you're afraid to take them out of the shopkeeper's humidor because they'll get stale in the ½ hour it takes you to get home. Horseshit. Tomatoes, bananas, lettuce, anything you name, will show no sign of deterioration for at least 24 hours or so.

So relax. You don't have to run home and shove your cigars in a vacuum sealed can. They're just not that perishable. They'll last at least a week with no care at all.

Here's what to do:

A.   First take out enough cigars for the day. You don't want to spend your day unwinding wrappings off of mummified cigars six or eight times a day.

B.   Take the home humidor you spent 50 Bucks for, and throw it in the garbage can.

C.   Put your cigars (in, or out of the box) in a zip lock Baggie, or whatever you call those plastic bags you can seal over and over again. Mush out the excess air before you close it up.

D.   Throw the bag in the bottom of your refrigerator or in a plastic vegetable box, or both.
Now, what did that accomplish?

1.   Your cigars are now in an environment where the air exchange has been reduced to almost zero. That's the function of the bag and box.

2.   Due to the lower temperature of the refrigerator, the evaporation rate has been drastically lowered. Therefore, your cigars will not lose their moisture as readily.

3.   The lower temperature will also stop your cigars from getting wormy. (The tobacco beetle, the larva from which is found in cigar leaf, cannot incubate below 67°F.).

4.   The air-tight bag will protect your cigars from smelling like last night's shrimp scampi — and will protect tomorrow's salad from smelling like last night's stogie.

And that's it - That's all you have to know about storing cigars. Don't believe anything else and you'll be O.K.

How to refreshen cigars

Stale cigars can be brought back to life. They'll never be as good as they originally were but they can be brought back into acceptable smoking condition. The only requirement is *patience*. It takes a few weeks for a cigar to become stale. It takes a few months to bring it back. You wouldn't expect a broken leg to heal in the same amount of time it took to break it, you can't loose weight as fast as you can gain it. Similarly you can't cure a dry cigar overnight.

To refreshen a dry cigar or box of cigars:

1.   Put the whole works in a ziploc bag which you have previously punctured many, many,many, many times (this means more than one or two holes).

2.   Put that ziploc bag containing your cigars into a larger ziploc bag which contains a *wrung out* slightly moist sponge.

3.   Close the larger bag, throw it in the bottom of the refrigerator and *forget them* for at least a month.

4.   Check them after a month. If still stale put them back for another month.

This method can only fail if you are an idiot. If you *are* in fact an idiot, you're going to do one of several things:

1.   You're going to punch the holes in the outer bag, thus sealing your cigars in the competely dry inner bag.

2.   You're going to punch holes in both bags, allowing the moisture in the outer bag to escape, rather than penetrate the inner bag where your cigars are.

3.   You're going to put a wringing wet sponge instead of a *wrung out* sponge in the outer bag. This is going to create a superhumid environment and turn your cigars into something with the texture and consistency of a cheese blintz.

4.   You're going to open the bag *every five minutes* to check your cigars. Therefore, you're going to let the moisture escape, squeeze the life out of your cigars, and ruin a lot of ziploc bags.

5.   You're going to open the bag *every six minutes* and still do all of the above.

Do yourself a favor — have patience. Ever see the stretch marks women get during pregnancy? They occur because the skin cannot possibly stretch as fast as the abdomen is expanding. This is particularly true of women who do not have pliant, oily skin, and it is not uncommon for expectant mothers to use lubricants on their skin during pregnancy. Although I wouldn't go so far as to compare expectant mothers with a stale cigar, there is an analogy to be drawn here.

Most of the weight of a cigar is in the body or filler of the cigar. This filler is then covered by the binder and wrapper. The wrapper is a very thin, silky smooth, pliant, highly elastic piece of tobacco — much like a woman's skin. On a stale cigar that wrapper becomes rigid and dry.

9

In the process of trying to refreshen your cigars, if you try to bring them back too fast, you will do so by overhumidifying them (not wringing out the sponge enough). The filler of the cigar will absorb moisture and expand too fast for the delicate wrapper to contain it. The result: the wrapper will tear just like a woman's skin. Your cigars will be ruined, shot, gestorben, morte, messed up and worthless.

Next you're going to try to *unruin* the overmoist cigars by drying them out. Now the filler is going to contract faster than the wrapper, which will become very loose and wrinkled. Possibly the wrapper will peel off. Your cigars will take on the appearance of the people in the Dannon Yogurt ads. At this point you will commence to realize the value of patience in refreshing cigars.

You never, never, want to touch anything moist with your cigars — they will absorb water incredible fast. I believe the paper towels used on television ads to absorb water are probable made of white cigars. Wet cigars are ruined cigars.

Once you successfully refreshen cigars, smoke them immediately. A refreshened cigar, for some reason unknown to me, will go stale again much much quicker than a cigar which has never been stale.

In summation, follow the guidelines laid out here, have patience, patience, patience. When the cigars are ready, pounce on them and smoke them immediately.

Questions and Answers

Q.   Sometimes the cellophane on my cigars looks brown. How come?

A.   There are many types of cellophane cigar tubes, varying mainly in thickness. The thickest of which is called "140", the thinnest "220". These numbers refer to the total number of square inches of cellophane per pound. Naturally, the more expensive hand -made cigars are covered by "140". This heavier cellophane has greater moisture retention to keep these high priced cigars fresh, and has greater resistance to "cockling". (Don't get your hopes up — cockling has nothing to do with sex.) Cockling refers to the cellophane wrinkling and ruining the smooth "look" of the cigar.

All cigar wrappers contain a certain amount of oil in the wrapper, maduro cigars generally being the most oily. If you get a box of cigars with brown cellophane, most likely the cigars have been in that box an unusually long period of time, and the "oil" from the cigar has permeated the cellophane wrapper.

Occasionally you will buy a box of cigars and the cellophane tubes appear yellow. This indicated that the cellophane was old or yellowed before the cigars were packed.

Cigars having either brown or yellow cellophane, if kept in a proper humidified environment, are just as good as if the cellophane were crystal clear. If your cigars have any other color of cellophane besides yellow, brown or crystal clear, call the Department of Health.

Q.   Sometimes when I buy a box of cigars that are packaged in cedar boxes, I notice some kind of sticky sap-like substance on the wood or cellophane of the cigars. What is that substance?

A.   It's sap.

Sometimes the cedar used in these boxes is not dried out. The box is then loaded with cigars and placed in a cold humidor. The coldness makes the wood condense, the condensation causes the sap to ooze out from between the fibers of the wood, the sap makes you ask this question. Got it?

Q.   On the bottom of domestic cigar boxes I always see "TP 12345" or TP followed by some number. What does that mean?

A.   TP means TOBACCO PRODUCTS, and every factury must put its number on every box of its products. For example, any box of cigars bearing "TP 102" is a product of Villazon and Co., a Tampa, Florida manufacturer. If there is no number, it means that the cigars were imported into the United States, and our government does not have the authority to demand this identifying code to be placed on products.

Q. Dealers sometimes refer to the boxes of cigars I buy as 1/40th or 1/20th. vus is dus?
A. 1/40th of 1000 (the standard unit for cigars), for those of you who have not mastered long division, is a box of 25 cigars. 1/20th therefore is 50 cigars.

Q. What's "B X T"?
A. Some kind of "scientific" cellophane used by the American Tobacco Company that's supposed to keep cigars fresh.

Q. What's "Stay Fresh", "Fresh-loc", "Vac-pac", "Flavor-gard" and other terms I see on packages of cigars?
A. Same answer as above, only the cellophane was named by different scientists.

Q. What's a fuma?
A. A crudely made cigar, rolled by hand from the table cuttings of long filler cigars. They are twisted closed at the top, rather than being hand capped or flagged.

Q.Q.Q. What's a table cutting, a cap, and a flag?
A.A.A. Handmade cigars are usually made by ring size, then cut to the appropriate length desired. The piece that is cut off is the table cutting. Essentially it is a short piece of long filler. (That's still better than a long piece of short filler, but that's another story).

A cap is a round piece of tobacco used to close up the head of the cigar.

A flagged cigar is the mark of a real oldtime craftsman. When the wrapper is stretched onto the cigar, it is done in such a manner as to leave a somewhat rectangular piece of tobacco remaining at the head of the cigar. This piece is then fashioned and molded around the head of the cigar. A cigar made in this manner is less likely to peel. Some of the prominent brands of cigars still flagged are Partagas, Santa Clara, Macanudo, and Ramon Allones.

Q. Does a long ash mean a cigar is good?
A. Do cattle with long tails make tastier steaks than those with short tails?

Q. Is it good to have a long ash on a cigar?
A. NO! NO! NO! NO! NO! A long ash hinders the passage of air to the cigar, makes it burn unevenly, and usually gives the smoker a stiff neck from trying to balance it on the end of his cigar. Long ashes make people cross-eyed, get clothes, carpets, and sofas dirty, and if allowed to get long enough, become, for a period of time, the cigar smoker's only reason for living.

Q. Why do many people dislike cigar smokers?
A. Who cares?

Q. How come everyone gets mad if I leave my used cigar butts in the ashtray?
A. I'll bet you don't flush the toilet either.

Q. What does an expensive boite-nature cedar box do for cigars?
A. It improves the appearance and raises the cost.

Q. What does a glass tube do for the cigar?
A. It raises the cost astronomically - but it really keeps a cigar fresh. It's also handy to save dimes in, when it's empty.

Q. What is a marriage room?
A. A place where cigars are married. Cigars readily absorb odors, flavors tastes etc. After

manufacture they are ribbon-tied in bundles of 50 to 100, uncellophaned, and put into a temperature and humidity-controlled cedar room. After a period of time they "marry". This does not necessarily mean that two coronas marry and produce a little cigarillo. It means that all the cigars in the room absorb each other's bouquet and taste characteristics, creating a uniformity of taste and aroma among all the cigars in the marriage rooms. This helps create uniformity in the particular brand of cigar you are buying, so that boxes of cigars, regardless of size, bearing the same trademark will not differ materially in taste.

Q.   How come the taste of major brands of cigars remains relatively constant, yet the taste of cigars from small manufacturers seem to vary week to week?
A.   It's simple. The big manufacturers buy tremendous amounts of tobacco at a time. Then rather than waiting until that supply is exhausted, they slowly but constantly blend new tobacco purchases into their existing tobaccos. In this way, the taste of their cigar changes so slightly that the smoker cannot distinguish any change at all.

Small manufacturers buy tobacco as they need it. Often, subsequent purchases of tobacco were not even grown in the same country as the prior purchase. As a result their product changes radically in taste from one time to another. This is expecially, absolutely, and positively true in the case of these tiny hand made cigar shops located in major U.S. Cities.

Q.   Are you saying that here in the good old U.S.A. the little guy doesn't have a chance?
A.   Yup. Most cigar leaf is contracted for before it is grown. The major manufacturer takes the farmer's whole production. The tobaccos that the big manufacturer don't want are sold to leaf brokers who,in turn, sell it to smaller manufacturers and even smaller leaf brokers. The smaller manufacturers get the best tobaccos of the batch that wasn't good enough for the big manufacturers.

By process of elimination this leaves only the worst tobaccos. They are sold by the small leaf brokers.

Now — the little-hand made cigar shop wants to buy tobacco. Where does he get it?. From the small leaf broker, naturally.

If this little shop can pay quickly, he can get the very best of the tobacco that no one else wanted. If the little shop can't pay quickly he gets the worst of the tobaccos. It's that simple. The only raw material available to him is the stuff nobody else wanted. Additionally there is no guarantee for him of availability of tobaccos from any particular country. Therefore, although he's been using Dominican filler for the last two weeks, he may very well have to switch to Mexican, or Honduran because no Dominican was available when he needed it.

You can't get prime beef from a scrawny 8-year-old cow, and regardless of the skill of the little cigar maker, you can't get a fine uniform cigar from a man who has no access to the raw material.

Q.   My little hand made cigar man still makes me an all Havana cigar from tobaccos he bought before the embargo. What do you say to that?
A.   You are an idiot.

Q.   Every cigar I buy is stale. when I pinch the head it cracks wide open. Why?
A.   In the movie "King Kong vs. The Son Of Godzilla" a similar complaint was discussed. Godzilla found that although every human he found to eat was nice and soft, when he pinched their heads they cracked wide open.

You don't pinch the heads, you gently squeeze the body of the cigar to determine freshness.

Q.   When I open a box of uncellophaned cigars they smell fantastic. How come the cellophaned cigars don't provide me with the same aromatic impact?
A.   Ever been in a gymnasium locker room? Clothes make the difference.

Q.   What makes a cigar mild?
A.   There are two primary factors — the tobaccos used and the size of the cigar.

13

Although cigars from different countries may actually be blends of tobaccos, not necessarily from the nation of manufacture, for the purpose of simplification, we will talk in terms of country of origin. In order of their general mildness I would rate cigars as follows from mildest to strongest:

1.	United States	6.	Canary Islands
2.	Phillipines	7.	Brazil
3.	Jamaica	8.	Mexico
4.	Dominican Republic	9.	Cuba
5.	Costa Rica	10.	Honduras
		11.	Nicaragua

In order of brands you know, I would rate them as follows — again from mildest to strongest:

1.	GENERAL CIGAR CO. PRODUCTS	26.	CUESTA REY
2.	WM. PENN	27.	PERFECTO GARCIA
3.	BROOKS	28.	F.D. GRAVE
4.	R.G. DUNN	29.	TOPSTONE
5.	MARSH WHEELING	30.	PEDRO IGLESIAS
6.	CONSOLIDATED PRODUCTS	31.	HOYO EXCALIBUR
7.	BAYUK PRODUCTS	32.	SANTA CLARA 1830
8.	AMERICAN CIGAR CO. PRODUCTS	33.	VALDEZ
9.	U.S. TOBACCO PRODUCTS	34.	SUERDIECK
10.	DOMINICANA	35.	DANNEMANN
11.	TABACALERA	36.	MOCHA
12.	MACANUDO	37.	TE AMO
13.	ROYAL JAMAICA	38.	FLOR de MEXICO
14.	JAMAICA HERITAGE	39.	ORNELA
15.	PRIMO DEL REY	40.	CARL UPMANN
16.	DON DIEGO	41.	CHIVIS
17.	PARTAGAS	42.	MADRIGAL
18.	PALOMINO	43.	EL CAUDILLO
19.	DON MIGUEL	44.	CASA COPAN
20.	SIBONEY	45.	BANCES
21.	FLAMENCO	46.	BELINDA
22.	DON MARCOS	47.	HOYO DE MONTERREY
23.	H. UPMAN	48.	PUNCH
24.	MONTECRUZ	49.	JOYA DE NICARAGUA
25.	BERING	50.	COUNT CHRISTOPHER

The second factor affecting the mildness of the cigar is its physical size. The shorter and thinner a cigar is, the stronger it will be. The longer and thicker the cigar is, the milder it will be. When a cigar is short and thin it burns fast, giving you a hot and comparatively strong smoke. A big thick cigar on the other hand will burn slower. The lit end being far from your mouth allows the smoke to cool several hundred degrees before it reaches you. Additionally, the large volume of tobacco the smoke passes through actually filters the cigar. Therefore, the smoke from the big cigar is cleaner and cooler, and consequently milder.

Mildness, then, is to the greatest degree regulated by the two above factors — and you may in fact discover that a very tiny cigar from a place known for manufacturing mild cigars can often be stronger than a large cigar from a place known for manufacturing heavy or strong cigars.

Q. Sometimes the wrapper on my cigar flakes or peels off. How come?
A. There are many possible reasons, the major ones being:

— The cigar is stale and brittle.

— The cigar has a Cameroon wrapper, which is by nature smooth, silky, and dark brown. However it is also thin and brittle.

— The cigar has been stored in a home humidor, and you, like every other cigar smoker I have known, have over-humidified your cigars to the point where they look like brown dumplings. Then the filler expands and blows the damn wrapper off the cigar.

Q. Lots of tar comes out of the end of my cigars. Why?
A. Either you've discovered a new source of fuel oil for the United States, or you're gumming the hell out of your cigars, getting them too wet and creating what you refer to as a "tarry" substance.

Q. When I chew on my cigar, I get a lot of little pieces in my mouth. Why?
A. When I chew on my Burry's chocolate chip cookies I get a lot of little pieces in my mouth too. But strangely, if I don't chew on my cookies, they don't turn into little pieces. Hmm?

Q. My wife says my cigars stink.
A. She's right.

Q. When I relight my cigar it tastes yuchy. How come?
A. There's a lot of stale smoke in there. Blow backwards through the cigar before you lay it down to expel this smoke. Upon relighting it you'll find the degree of yuchiness greatly reduced.

Q. I notice soft spots in my cigars. Why?
A. They are improperly rolled, the filler tobaccos not having been laid in properly. Change brands.

Q. I notice little spots on my cigars. What are they?
A. They are one of two things. Either the cigar has rain spots (light spots created by drops of rain remaining on the tobacco leaf, which then magnify the sun's rays and bleach light spots on the leaf), or your glasses are dirty.

Q. The little spots are moving!
A. That's the tobacco beetle, a tiny lady bug-like bug sometimes referred to as worms.

Q. Sometimes I can't get any smoke through my cigars. What should I do?
A. Gently massage the cigar between your palms to break up the filler tobaccos. If this fails, return them to your tobacconist.

Q. What's the best buy in a cigar?
A. The best made cigar at the lowest price, regardless of whether or not you've ever heard of the brand name.

Exploring the Myth of the Cuban Cigar

Americans have a great fondness for anything illegal, unobtainable, or uneconomical.

Cuban cigars cannot be brought into this country for purposes of resale. There has been an embargo on trade with Cuba since 1961. Recently, the law has been changed and now allows Americans to bring in 100 cigars of Cuban origin, providing the proper duties are paid at customs.

Now, here comes the big catch. We have laws in this country protecting trademarks. Most pre-embargo factories in Cuba were either owned by American cigar companies, or exclusively dealt with American distributors. Every brand of Cuban cigar you've ever heard of did, and still does, belong to an American firm, many of whom are now producing cigars in countries other than Cuba, and bearing the former famous Cuban brand names. What does all this mean?

It means that you cannot bring any Cuban cigar into this country that bears any trademark that you have ever heard of, because these brands belong to American companies. You can't bring in MonteCristo, Romeo & Julietta, Partagas, Upmann, Ramon Allones, Hoyo de Monterrey, Punch, Larranaga, etc. All you can bring in is Juan Valdez Stogies or a similar unknown name.

Next, Cuban cigars are no big deal. Many of the brands now imported from Jamaica, Honduras, Mexico, Spain and the Dominican Republic are equal to, if not superior to, their Cuban counterparts.

When Castro came to power, most of the knowledgeable cigar manufacturers hightailed it out of Cuba, and over the years have re-established their factories in other countries.

If you've ever been in the Army, Marines, etc. you'll understand what I'm about to say. The Army buys the best food available. It enters the back door of the mess hall as grade A provisions, and it ends up on your tray as the worst inedible crud imaginable.

Let's look at Cuban tobacco for a minute. Great tobacco fields take time, patience, and money to develop. The soils must be treated scientifically to yield a similar crop of tobacco year after year. In pre-embargo Cuba, wealthy American firms took exacting and painstaking care of those fields to create a uniformity and continuity of taste in their products. After the embargo, the economically unstable and currency poor Castro regime could not afford the time, patience or capital to keep up these tobacco fields. Whatever tobacco grew on these fields was quickly harvested, manufactured into a finished product and sold for cash. A great cigar takes infinite patience to make. The fields must be coaxed to produce the most product. The leaves of the plant must be picked as they mature, not as fast as they grow. The tobaccos must be cured, not rushed to the point of manufacture. The cigars must be made by skilled, experienced rollers and supervised by experts, not rolled by unskilled workers and supervised by comparative amateurs. Finally, they must be selected and aged in cedar marriage rooms before packaging for sale, not rammed into boxes and instantly shipped abroad.

Essentially it takes knowledge and money to make a fine cigar. Post embargo Cuba had neither.

At the time of the embargo, no one knew it would last forever. Therefore, it was several years before factories producing quality cigars began to spring up in the countries previously mentioned. Additionally, it was several more years until the expertise of the manufacturers began to "bear fruit" and produce good quality cigars. The result was that Americans, from approximately 1962-1967, found that there wasn't a really good cigar available in the U.S. and their fond remembrances of the Cuban cigar became even fonder. That was the beginning of the myth. Today, these far flung factories are making fine products, and although the Cuban cigars are still good, they are not better.

Some Questions about Cuban Cigars

Q. How come the cigars I bring back from Europe are always stale?
A. Most Europeans like dry cigars. America is almost unique in its use of the moist cigar.

Q. How come they cost so much?
A . 1. Because dopes like you are willing to spend $3.00 for a "50-cent cigar to reminisce".
2. Most European countries have extraordinarily high duties on tobacco products.

Q. A friend of mine bought me some Cuban cigars from Canada called "Reas". They were only about 75 cents a cigar. They came packaged in aluminum foil. Why are they so cheap?
A. They're not cheap. The same quality cigar sells for 15 cents in the U.S. You're buying a short filler, homogenized cigar for the price of a hand made cigar just because it has some scrap Cuban filler in it.

Q. What do you think the impact of Cuban cigars will be, if and when they can legally be sold in the U.S.?
A. For the first few months people will buy them, thereafter their sales will diminish to a very minuscule amount.

Q. Why?
A. They'll be fantastically expensive. The prices out of Cuba are very high, the duties coming into the U.S. will be extremely high as compared with other cigar exporting nations, royalties will have to be paid to the American companies who own these trademarks in the U.S. and reparations will have to be made to the American companies whose factories and plantations were seized in the early 1960's.

I would estimate that an average box of 25 cigars, lonsdale shape (6¼ inches x 42 ring gauge) would cost the consumer about $75.00. Cigar smokers may be fanatics in their devotion to a good cigar, but, they are not crazy. A man smoking 50 cigars a week would have to spend $7.800.00 a year on cigars! That's absolutely insane.

Q. They say the finest tobacco in the world comes from Cuba. True or false?
A. ROT! Where does it cost more to grow tobacco — in some crummy valley in Cuba, or in the Connecticut River Valley where land is a couple of thousand dollars an acre, and where American labor is used and paid for? Fads come and go. Right now a Cameroon wrapper from Africa is in great demand, but for my money Connecticut is No. 1. When Cuba was at its peak, many a box of Cuban cigars bore the inscription "Grown from Connecticut seed". Americans have just gotten out of the habit of buying anything from America.

Do you know that all those super expensive English tobaccos and cigarettes are made from tobaccos grown right here in this country? We send our tobaccos to England — pipe tobacco is not my field — the English, Irish, Danish, etc. do something to it, maybe add "love potion #9", put it in a can (the Europeans absolutely kill us when it comes to making an attractive package) and then ship it back here. Then millions of dopey American pipe smokers run out and buy their own domestic tobaccos for over $1.00 per ounce. It's unbelievable!

Q. Where did all those famous cigar manufacturers go to after fleeing Cuba?
A. Menendez and Garcia of Montecrisco and H. Upmann fame went to the Canary Islands, Spain. Ramon Cifuentes of Partagas went to Jamaica. The Palicio family delegated its trademarks to Villazon & Co. of Tampa, Florida, and Honduras American Tobacco (an arm of Villazon) in Honduras. (Rey del Mundo, Belinda, Punch, Flor de Palicio, Flor del Mundo, Calixto Lopez, La Escepcion, Hoyo de Monterrey, Bauza, etc.)
Many minor manufacturers fled to Miami, some retired, some passed away.

How much should you spend for a box of cigars?

As little as possible, but enough for the shopkeeper to stay in business. The cigar store operator is disappearing as fast as the cigar store Indian, because of the very slim profit margins on most cigars.

The wholesale price of cigars 45 cents each and up is approximately 75% of the retail price. In other words a dollar cigar costs the shopkeeper 75 cents each. Cigars selling for 20 cents to 45 cents yield approximately 20-24% for the shopkeeper, and those under 20 cents give him only about 17% profit. So don't think you can buy a $1.00 cigar for 50 cents — it can't be done.

In addition to the above, your cigar dealer will get a discount from the wholesale list price of from 2 to 18% generally, depending on his volume of sales. This factor allows a high volume discount shop to retail its merchandise for much less than the full price shop, and yet make essentially the same profit per cigar as the full price, lower volume shop. Whether or not your favorite cigar store discounts its merchandise is most often dictated by its geographic location. Stores in big cities, with a large potential market, can conceivably achieve the high volume necessary to earn these additional discounts from the manufacturers. Small towns are lucky just to have a tobacconist. Why discount cigars if you're doing business in Shmigegee, Pa.? Even if every soul in town bought cigars in a shop there, it would never attain the volume necessary to make discounting profitable.

So all of the above boring logic boils down to the following:

If you want the convenience of buying in a local shop, you're going to have to pay a little more for your cigars. What's the big deal anyway — it's only money.

As a general rule, your local store should give at least 5% off on a box of cigars, a moderate size store 10% off, and a big discount shop 20 to 25% off.

Consult the wholesale listings in the back of this book for the correct cigar retail price, as many small shops tend to raise the true retail price of many cigars well above the manufacturer's suggested retail prices. These are the guys you don't want to buy from. To charge full price is one thing. To invent inflated retail prices is another thing.

Charge cards cost the dealer 2½ to 5% of the gross sale. In many local stores you'll get a better price for cash. In most discount shops you'll find charge cards are not honored. There is simply no room for the dealer to absorb these charges, given his slim margin of profit.

Buy where you're appreciated. Cigar stores run by individual proprietors warrant to an extent your satisfaction with the purchased product, greet you with respect, are anxious to give you a product which will make you a satisfied customer. Stores run under absentee ownership, staffed by kids, chain stores, drug stores etc. really don't care about you or your purchase. The people who work in these stores don't have a feel for the business, or for which brands satisfy certain characteristics the cigar smoker is looking for.

Part of your purchase price should be for the expertise you receive from your tobacconist, and the warranty he or she gives you to your satisfaction with the product purchased in that paticular shop. There are today many women tobacconists. These girls really know their product better than most of the men, out of sheer self defense. True, they may not smoke cigars, but then R.H. Macy did not to my knowledge wear ladies' lingerie. That didn't stop Macy from being the world's foremost buyer and seller of that product. So give the ladies a chance. I believe you'll be quite surprised at their indepth knowledge of this business.

Save 50%! Buy a box get a box free! 2/3 OFF regular price if first quality! BULLSHIT! Remember that except in rare instances, where you are buying in an incredibly high volume shop which has the buying and selling power to acquire job lots and closeouts from the manufacturers and importers, you will only get what you pay for. If a small shop in Bugtussle, Oklahoma is paying 75% of the listed retail price for his merchandise, how can he give you 50% OFF?? If you've gone past Sand-box I in school, you know this is impossible. There's got to be a catch somewhere. These cigars are either wormy, old, stale, seconds, or stolen. Hopefully, if they're stolen, the original thief stole fresh cigars. If not, your next best bet is that they are seconds which actually should sell for about 50% off the normal retail price. If the cigars are wormy, old, or stale, they're completely worthless. Would you buy wormy apples for half price?

Everything you don't want to buy

First of all, you want to buy cigars — not atmosphere. Don't expect to get your money's worth in a very elite, carpeted, well fixtured, swanky looking shop. Cigar shops of this type do not cater to the educated consumer. The clientele they attract is the *wife* of the consumer, the friend bringing a gift to the consumer, the tourist, the transient, the egomaniac, or the guy who was born to money. Wealthy people who have earned their own money are amongst the sharpest cigar buyers around. Apparently their wealth hasn't snuffed out their desire to get the most for their money.

The singularly shrewdest cigar buyer has been, and always will be, the New York cab driver. As a group, they are undoubtedly the cheapest bastards that ever stalked the face of the earth. If you see a cab in front of a cigar store, you'll know "This is the place" to buy your cigars. Most cab drivers smoke garbage (don't think I hate cab drivers — I'm just making an observation). If it's on sale they'll buy it, if it's cheap enough they'll smoke it or return it to some other store claiming to have bought it there at full price.

The second cheapest is the accountant. An accountant can quote cigar prices down to the puff. The rag dealers are next (members of the garment industry). you'll never see these people in the Swanky Places. They're too cheap but also they're too smart. They go to the big drab stores that have the good selection and competitive prices.

Second, you don't want private label cigars at inflated prices. There are fewer than 5 stores in the entire country that have the selling power to have a manufacturer create a brand of cigars exclusively for them. Most private labels are just alternative packages of products you are already familiar with under nationally known trademarks. Most retailers get 5 to 10 cents per cigar more than the original selling price for these cigars. Naturally the shopkeeper will tell you "Mr. So and So, I went to Honduras and selected the tobaccos for these fine cigars, then they were hand rolled under my supervision, and are amongst the world's finest cigars." Well, Mr. So and So, if this shop's brand of cigars is not listed in the back of this book, your shopkeeper is probably jerking you off. Private labels for the most part are a method of selling you less cigar for more money. Forget them.

Third, you don't want cigars from the "Legion of Lost Cigars" which appears in the next section of this book, They are a total waste of money.

Fourth, (and I hope I don't get sued for this) you don't want cigars in 3-packs, 4-packs, 5-packs,

6-packs, or any other kind of packs. You want to know why? Well, I'm not exactly sure why — but they never seem to taste the same. You ever taste a hard roll from a bakery? Then compare it with those rubber rolls they sell in plastic bags at the supermarket. When I was a kid I wanted to be an olympic weightlifter. One of the exercises was trying to rip those rolls in half. The packaged cigars seem rubbery to me   it's almost impossible to make a packaged cigar stale, you bite on the tip — it tries to bite you back. By the time you get the outer cellophane off the pack, the pack open, remove and open the inner pack, and get the cellophane of your cigar — you're too tired to smoke anyway. Maybe shopkeepers just don't take care of packaged cigars as well as regular boxes — or maybe those cigars are different. How come the really good brands of cigars don't come in packs? For my own satisfaction I like to select my cigars from an open box. Packaged cigars bring back memories of "C" rations (Ugh!).

Fifth, you don't want stale cigars. When you buy, squeeze the body of the cigar — it'll either be resilient or noisy. Remember one of the Ten Commandments of Cigar Smoking. Fresh cigars don't talk back when you squeeze them. Don't squeeze the damned head of the cigar — it doesn't have to be dry to crack. How'd you like someone to squeeze your head? Squeezing the head of a cigar is an immediate tipoff to all knowledgeable cigarmen around you that you are an idiot.

Sixth, watch out for bleached cigars. Cigar wrappers "bleach" or fade rapidly on exposure to light. If the cigar you intend purchasing is lighter on one side than another, you'll know it's been hanging around the dealer's shop for quite some time.

Seventh, don't buy cigars that are too soft. Some cigar stores use a very crude humidifying device in their cigar cases. It's a light bulb inverted over a tank of water. The bulb makes heat, the water evaporates — Presto! you've got humidity. What you've also got is a steambath. Steamy conditions cause mushy cigars. Mushy cigars are rotten lousy smokes. Phooey!

Eighth, don't buy uncellophaned loose cigars. Most shopkeepers don't know how to store them and therefore your chances of getting bad cigars are greatly increased. Additionally, they get handled by the public — and who knows where their fingers were before they touched the cigars you intend purchasing.

Ninth, don't buy all these crazy European cigars. Smoke one in the dark and you'll know why. Its like smoking a Roman Candle. Sparks flying everywhere. Can you believe there are people over there that paint cigars for a living? Also, they're incredibly expensive due to higher duties on small imported cigars.

The Legion of Cigars You Shouldn't Buy

When you purchase cigars, regardless of price, 100% of your money should go towards the smoking product itself. Therefore, don't buy any of the following   except perhaps as a gift.

A & C Accents	Don Tomas Corona Grande
A & C Camino	Don Marcos Corona Major
Bances Corona Minor	Don Alvaro Marianos
Bering Imperial	Flamenco Corona Major
Bering Corona Royale	Gold Label Royales
Creme de Jamaica Singulares	Hayo de Monterrey Cafe Royales
Cuesta Rey Imperiales	Macanudo Portofino
Don Diego Royal Palms	Macanudo Hampton Court
Don Diego Monarchs	Macanudo Wellington

Montecruz Chicos
Montecruz Tubes
Montecruz Tubulares
Royal Jamaica Florde Jamaica
Royal Jamaica N.Y. Plaza
Royal Jamaica Park Lane
Royal Jamaica Director #3
Royal Jamaica Director #1
La Corona Americans

La Corona Naturales
Rigoletto Londonaire
H. Hupmann Naturales
H. Hupmann Corona Major
Garcia Vega English Corona
Garcia Vega Grand Premios
Garcia Vega Romeros
Shakespeare Romeos
All other tubed or wrapped cigars

All of the above come in either glass or aluminum tubes, or cedar or paper wrappings. They are an absolute waste of money — unless you collect glass and aluminum. Fancy cigar boxes, as a rule, do *not* inflate the cost of your cigar. However, a tube will normally push up the price of a cigar by 15 cents to a quarter each!

What cigar should I buy?

Relax! You don't have to buy the perfect cigar — you're allowed to buy all you want, anytime you want. I've had people ask me a thousand times "What should I smoke?" As if it were a compelling drive or physical need to find a cigar that simultaneously made that person's taste buds explode, had the particular shape and color they wanted, and fit their pocketbook.

This "right cigar" business is an impossible goal. You don't search for a particular food to eat for the rest of your life. I mean, I love Raisin Bran — but I can't see myself eating that slop forever. Therefore, even if you found the "right" cigar it would only be right for a day or two at most, because your taste buds demand variety, change, and excitement.

The shape and wrapper color of the cigar are factors which vary, but not as frequently. Having observed millions of cigar smokers over the years I've noticed a number of broad generalities. Fat people smoke relatively thin, extra long cigars, skinny people smoke fat cigars, black people tend to favor the light green wrapped cigars, white people smoke dark cigars, short people smoke tall cigars, tall people smoke short cigars, young people smoke thin cigars, older people smoke thicker cigars.

I guess this tells you that the selection of a cigar in terms of size & color somewhat mirrors the desire of the image you wish to project. I personally have never noticed whether or not a fat man smoking a thin cigar really looked thin. However, I have noticed that none of my black customers look green, nor white customers black, regardless of what color cigar they smoke.

Next, don't try to find a cigar that fits your pocketbook —this would be absolutely absurd. A cigar is a luxury, but it can vary in degree. Pick a general price range you are comfortable with. Buy cheaper cigars for the times you're smoking a cigar casually during the day, better cigars for the evening, business lunches etc., when you can really get "into" the cigar and enjoy it fully. Buy fine cigars when you find a packet of money in the street, hit 5 horses in a row at the track, or the uncle you hate completely and totally drops dead, leaving you all his money. Buy really cheap cigars when you're down to your last buck.

When the tax collector comes to repossess your house, and the furniture men take away your furniture, your wife and kids spit in your face, and the son of a bitch next store that you hate, and who was always after your wife is watching your misfortune through his window, take out a giant, incredibly expensive cigar and calmly light it with great ceremony, watching the smoke curl slowly and majestically skyward. All those people who were just laughing at you will immediately stop dead in their tracks. You'll still know you're broke, but they'll be thinking "Holy Shit, that rotten bastard's got a fortune stashed away somewhere and after he's rid of us he's going to be living like a King!"

Cigars have power — they create an image for you, and convey a message to the world around you. It's up to you to choose what message you wish to convey at a particular moment.

Thusly, therefore, and henceforth, however, wherever, whatever, and whenever — what I am attempting to explain in this batch of verbiage is that buying a cigar is an adventure in taste sensation, an experience in image projection, and an exercise in conspicuous consumption, all at the same time. I believe one of the greatest pleasures a cigar smoker derives, is the pleasure of shopping for, and selecting his day's supply of cigars. It sets his mood for the day — and the image he thinks he will project.

Now you're probably saying to yourself, Lew Rothman has just given me the runaround and told me nothing about what particular brand and size to buy. You're right.

This is not Dr. Stillman's Diet — 8 glasses of water, fish, lean meat, rocks, clouds, and all the air you want. This is the realization that selecting a cigar is a uniquely individual prerogative that only you have the right to, and one which is entirely dependent on the mood you're in. PERIOD.

Cigar Terminology

Filler The central body of the cigar.

Long filler Long pieces of tobacco comprising the body of the cigar. Long filler leaves less surface area exposed to the flame therefore making the cigar smoke slower, longer, cooler, and milder.

Short filler Short little pieces of tobacco comprising the body of the cigar, producing rapid burning due to greater surface area being exposed to the flame. A hotter, harsher smoking cigar. To understand the consequences of short filler tobacco, look at the example of a drink made with crushed ice as opposed to one made with large cubes. The drink with crushed ice gets colder faster due to the increased contact of your drink with the great surface area of ice which is exposed by crushing. This ice also melts very rapidly. Similarly, in a cigar this "crushed tobacco" burns hot and fast. The other drink doesn't get cold quickly but the ice lasts and lasts. Similarly the long filler cigar burns slower and doesn't get hot, therefore it lasts longer and is milder.

Mild Every cigar manufacturer claims his cigars to be mild, rich, flavorful, elegant, distinctive, robust, aromatic, soothing etc. Therefore the word "mild" on any cigar box means absolutely nothing.

Very mild Means not too strong.

Extra mild Means not too strong.

Flavorful yet mild **AARGH!** A cigar which will bite off your tongue, burn holes in your throat, and send columns of smoke streaming out of your belly button.

H.T.L. Homogenized Tobacco Leaf or Homogenized Tobacco. Wait a minute! Don't run away. Homogenized tobacco is 99.999% tobacco with vegetable tragacanth added as an emulsifier. This transforms tobacco from a leaf to a sheet, for use in a high speed cigar machine. You can't see it, you can't taste it. It's no different than making paper out of wood. Paper is wood, homogenized tobacco is tobacco, homogenized milk is milk. Get it?

Cigar Band	The identifying ring around a cigar, first used by Bock on the panetela.
Made in Bond	Cigar manufactured in a bonded warehouse. As an example, let's use the Creme de Jamaica Brand. Tobacco from world sources is brought to the island of Jamaica to a "bonded" warehouse. No duty is paid on the leaf because legally that merchandise has not entered Jamaica, nor does the factory have to comply with any rules as to content of cigar leaf from any nation their cigar may contain. After manufacture they are shipped to whatever country they are to be sold to, at which point duties are paid to the nation of entry. This system of "in bond" manufacture allows the freedom from importation restrictions and double and triple duty payments, for the manufacturer to procure the best available tobaccos for his blend without being penalized by extra duties in importing and exporting his product. He can therefore make a better cigar at a competitive price.
Panetela	A thin cigar usually about 6 inches x 36 ring
Corona	A medium sized cigar usually about 5½ inches x 42 ring
Petit Corona	A medium sized cigar usually about 5 inches x 42 ring
Lonsdale	A medium sized cigar usually about 6 inches x 42 ring
Palma	A medium sized cigar usually about 6 inches x 42 ring
No. 1	A medium sized cigar usually about 6½ inches x 42 ring
Cetro	A large sized cigar usually about 7 inches x 42 ring
Churchill	A large sized cigar usually about 7 inches x 50 ring
Double Corona	A large sized cigar usually about 6½ inches x 47 ring
Panatela Larga	A long thin sized cigar usually about 7 inches x 36 ring
50th	Box of 20 1/50th of a thousand.
20th	Box of 50 1/20th of a thousand.
40th	Box of 25 1/40th of a thousand.
100th	Box of 10 1/100th of a thousand.
Boite Nature	Finished cedar box.
Wrap	Wood or cardboard box overwrapped with paper.
Boat	Cardboard sleeve in which commercial packages of cigars are packed for display.
Amatista Jar	Glass jar with cork or rubber gasket on lid — usually a bottle of 50 uncellophaned cigars 6" x 41 ring guage.
8-9-8	Style of packing in box of 25 cigars a row of 8 on top and bottom - row of 9 in between.

13 top	Style of packing boxes of 50 cigars four rows of 13 — bottom layer has cardboard spacer eliminating 2 cigars.
10 top	Style of packing boxes of 50 cigars — 5 row of 10 cigars each.
5 top	Style of packing boxes of 25 — 5 row of 5 cigars each.
Sleeve	A boat containing 10 — 5 packs, 10 — 3 packs, etc.
Wrapper	Fine outer layer of elastic tobacco on a cigar.
Binder	Course heavy tobacco used to hold the bunch together — lies directly beneath wrapper.
Bunch	The body of the cigar — the filler.

WRAPPER COLORS

Name	Color	Other Names (Vary from brand to brand)
Double Claro	Lt Green	Claro-Candela-Cambridge-Jade AMS
Claro	Lt. brown	Natural, English Claro, Rare Corojo
Colorado Claro	Brown	E.M.S., Natural, Oxford Cafe, Ems Claro
Colorado	Med. dark brown	E.M.S., Natural, Oxford Cafe, EMS Claro
Colorato Maduro	Dark brown	Maduro, S.M.S.
Maduro	Very dark brown	Maduro, S.M.S.
Oscuro	Black	Double Maduro

Case	Standard packing unit of cigars usually 2500 cigars on domestics, usually 1000 cigars on imports.
Silky	A term used to describe the fine texture of cigar wrapper leaf.
Fire Cured	Method of curing light green claro wrappers by exposure to extreme heat.
Breva Conserva	Bundled cigars tightly pressed together creating odd shaped cigars.
Box Pressure (pressed cigars)	Squared off cigars made by pressing or putting stacks of boxes into a press.
Rounds	Cigars in their natural round shape with no box pressure.
Crooks	Regular cigars put into a mold when moist, then pressed to create crooked shapes.
Culebras	Three cigars twisted together and ribboned top and bottom to create a corkscrew effect.
Bundle	Cellophaned rather than boxed package of cigars, reducing manufacturing costs by 30 to 70 dollars per thousand.
Vintage	Refers to the year of the tobacco crop from which cigars were made. This term has been badly misused by manufacturers over the years, and all credibility in the

31

term has now been lost.

Sweet as a nut	This term means the manufacturer doesn't have the vaguest idea of what his product tastes like.
Pre Castro Havana	Tobacco which everyone likes to say they have, but no one does.
Envuelto a mano	Sounds like hand made, but means put in the box by hand.
Hand packed	Means envuelto a mano.
Hand rolled	Means machine made, but the wrapper is put on by hand.
"These cigars are predominantly tobacco with a substantial amount of non tobacco ingredients"	One of the cruddiest, non-explicit legends ever forced on an industry. When you see this on a box of cigar it means the contents range from a good cigar with a homogenized binder which is 99% tobacco, all the way to a terrible imitation of a cigar with homogenized wrapper, binder, and possibly even a percentage of homogenized filler.
3/63ᶜ	This means the manufacturer is implying his cigar should actually sell for more than 21 cents, and is now justified in raising his wholesale list price to a point greater than a 21 cent cigar should be. However, he still wants the retailer to charge 21 cents for it. The net result is that the retailer makes less money, therefore less retailers are interested in selling cigars, therefore less retailers sell cigars, therefore the manufacturer sells less cigars, therefore the manufacturer is afraid to raise prices for fear his volume will get even smaller, therefore since his costs keep going up he raises his wholesale list price to the retailer again without raising the suggested retail price of the cigar, therefore the retailer makes less money, is less interested etc. etc.

Touring the Partagas Cigar Factory.

The following series of photos was supplied through the courtesy of the General Cigar Company, manufacturers of Van Dyck, Robert Burns, White Owl, WM. Penn, Gold Label, Shakespeare, Macanudo, Ramon Allones, Creme de Jamaica, Partagas, etc.

These photos and accompanying descriptions will take you step by step through the creation of a fine hand made cigar, from the planting of the seed to the moment the final nail seals shut a box of fine hand made cigars.

Tobacco fields

Seed beds create incubation environment for young tobacco plants until mature enough for transplanting.

Curing sheds in which the green primed tobacco leaves are hung to slowly ripen to their natural tobacco flavor and aroma.

Fine quality wrapper tobacco depends on correct blend of soil and climate found in only very limited areas of the world.

Tobacco leaves are sewed to hanging poles to permit proper circulation of air needed to cure the harvest leaves.

Bunch
making

Straight laid filler tobacco leaves are blended by cigar makers for rolling in binder leaf.

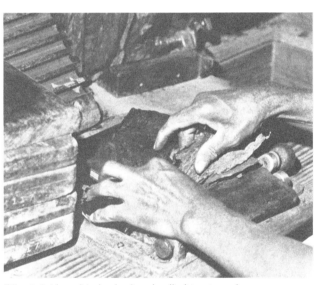

Filler is laid on binder leaf and rolled in cigar shape.

Cigar bunch is carefully finished.

Finished bunch is placed in cigar mold cavity.

Mold is assembled as unit and placed in press to set cigar shape.

Cigar wrapping

Wrapper leaf conditioned for handling and is selected for rolling on molded cigar bunch.

Wrapper leaf is skillfully stretched to assure smooth fit while rolling on cigar bunch.

Unique final cut and meticulous care produces symetrical cigar head.

Cigar is cut to precise finished size.

Finished cigar is gently rolled to assure final refinement of cigar construction.

Cigar packing

Cigar maker tapes finished cigars in bundles of 50 for ease of counting and inspection.

Finished bundled cigars are opened and individually inspected to eliminate less than perfect cigars.

Aged cigars are shaded into compatible color lots for packing.

Shaded cigars are banded, inserted in cellophane tubes, and packed in cedar cigar box.

A finished box of handmade Partagas cigars.

Cigar box making

Cedar lumber is thoroughly air dried before fabricating into box components.

Box sections are pre-cut for assembly.

Boxes are hand-constructed.

Assembled cedar box ready for cleaning and sanding.

Finished cedar cigar boxes ready for packing.

How to read the cigar charts in this section

1. Lew Rothman Rating

At the upper right hand corner of each page is a rating of from one to five stars. One star is the poorest rating, five stars is the best. These ratings are divided into two parts: quality and value.

A.*Quality* — This rating pertains to the construction and consistency of the cigar, as measured against competitive products in its price range. Therefore, a 5 -star rating for quality given, for example, to a 15-cent cigar means that by comparison to other competitive 15-cent products this is a very well made cigar. It does **not** mean that a 5-star 15-cent cigar is better made than a 3-star cigar selling for 90 cents. That would be comparing apples and oranges. These ratings apply only to cigars of similar retail prices.

B.*Value* - This rating equates the retail price of the cigar to competitive products of equal quality. As an example: two different cigars, both hand made, both of equal quality, both of equal size are offered for sale, one at a dollar the other at 75 cents. The cigar selling for 75 cents will get a higher value rating for providing the smoker with an equivalent cigar at a lower price.

2. The Grid chart in the lower left hand corner of the page:

This chart is divided into 8 columns:

Column 1 — Front Mark — This is the name of the cigar size (lonsdale, corona, etc.) and has-been co-ordinated to match the pictures of the cigars shown. Each cigar is shown actual size with the exception of very large cigars which have a wavy cut in them, showing only the top and bottom parts of the cigar.

Column 2 — Length — This is the length of the cigar measured in inches.

Column 3 — Ring Size — This is the diameter of the cigar show in 64ths of an inch.

Column 4 — Retail per each — The manufacturers suggested retail price per cigar, in many instances pre-stamped on the cigar box.

Column 5 — Quantity per box — Number of cigars contained in the most common unit of sale.

Column 6 — Retail per box — The computed full retail price per box of cigars obtained by multiplying the individual price by the number of cigars in a box.

Column 7 — Wholesale per box* — This is the manufacturers, wholesale price to distributors, jobbers, etc.

Column 8 — Wrapper Color** — The stars indicate which wrapper colors are available in each size., C indicating the light green double claro wrapper, N indicating the medium brown natural wrapper, M indicating the very dark brown maduro wrapper.

*Additional discounts from the wholesale list price averaging 13 to 18% are common in the cigar industry. As a general rule these discounts are available to direct, large volume accounts of the manufacturer or importer. These large accounts in turn distribute cigars to local merchants whose discount from the listed wholesale price is determined by their volume and business acumen. This discount is generally from 2 to 10%. A quick glance at the wholesale price list will immediately demonstrate that the cigar business is not a high profit business even at the most favorable discount rates.

**For purposes of clarity I have divided wrapper color into three groups: claro — green, natural — brown, maduro — very dark brown. However, there is an extraordinary number of wrapper shades in between, with no less than 32 shades being offered for sale in Cuba's heyday. Complicating matters even worse each manufacturer has adopted a personal name for wrapper colors. Today a light green cigar may be called by any of the following names by individual manufacturers:

Claro
Double Claro
Candela
A.M.S.
American Market Selection
Cambridge
Jade

Therefore, I have condensed all of these terms into the broad category of claro. Similarly all medium brown cigars are called natural and all dark brown cigars are called maduro.

***While every attempt has been made to picture these cigars accurately, discrepancies exist due to the necessity of photographing pictures of the cigar brands which were supplied by the manufacturers. The correct method, which proved to be an impossible task in the case of many cigar brands, would have been to photograph the actual cigars.

A & C

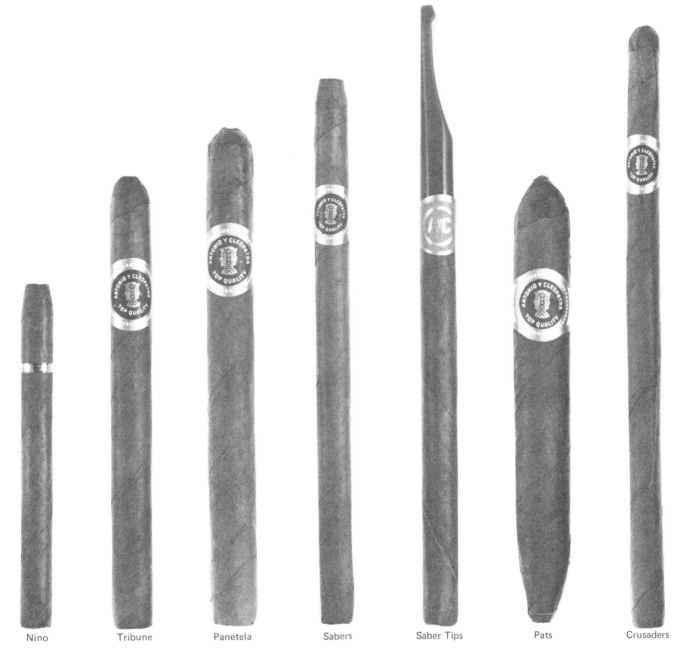

Nino   Tribune   Panetela   Sabers   Saber Tips   Pats   Crusaders

Front Mark	Length	Ring Size	Retail per ea.	Qty. per Box	Retail per Box	Whole sale per Box	Wrapper Color		
							C	N	M
Nino	3-10/16''	24	.12	100	11.50	9.20	*	*	
*Tribune	4-3/4''	32	.16	50	8.00	6.40	*	*	
*Panetela	5-3/16''	35	2/.35	50	8.75	6.95	*	*	
*Sabers	5-11/16''	26	3/.57	50	9.50	7.50	*	*	
*Saber Tips	4-31/32''	26	3/.57	50	9.50	7.50	*	*	
**Pats	4-11/16''	42	3/.57	50	9.50	7.50	*	*	
*Crusaders	6-3/8''	26	.20	50	10.00	7.85	*	*	

* Also available in 5 packs.
** Also available in 7 packs.

- A very well made popular priced cigar.
- A & Cs are available in a wide selection of sizes shapes and colors and are a good value for the consumers dollar. As with all other brands beware of the products in tubes. Incidentally, the A & C Grenadier is probably the largest selling cigar on earth.
- Filler tobaccos from South and Central America and selected domestic tobaccos, wrappers from the Cameroons and South and Central America.
- Distributed by the American Cigar Co. of N.Y., N.Y.

A & C

Pennants   Princess   Classics   Grenadiers   Antonios   Kings   Privateers

Front Mark	Length	Ring Size	Retail per ea.	Qty. per Box	Retail per Box	Whole sale per Box	Wrapper Color		
							C	N	M
*Pennants	5-1/2''	39	.20	50	10.00	7.85	*		
Princess	4-11/16''	42	.20	50	10.00	7.85	*		
*Classics	5-7/16''	44	.21	50	10.50	8.20	*	*	
***Grenadiers	6-1/4''	33	.21	50	10.50	8.20	*	*	
*Antonios	6''	39	.23	50	11.50	8.95	*	*	
*Kings	5-5/16''	42	.23	50	11.50	8.95	*	*	
*Privateers	6''	39	.23	50	11.50	8.95		*	

*Also available in 5 packs.
***Also available in 6 packs.

- A very well made popular priced cigar.
- A & Cs are available in a wide selection of sizes shapes and colors and are a good value for the consumers dollar. As with all other brands beware of the products in tubes. Incidentally, the A & C Grenadier is probably the largest selling cigar on earth.
- Filler tobaccos from South and Central America and selected domestic tobaccos, wrappers from the Cameroons and South and Central America.
- Distributed by the American Cigar Co. of N.Y., N.Y.

A & C

| | Tonys | Conquerors | Deluxe | Accents | Camino |

Front Mark	Length	Ring Size	Retail per ea.	Qty. per Box	Retail per Box	Whole sale per Box	Wrapper Color		
							C	N	M
*Tonys	4-31/32''	43	.23	50	11.50	8.95	*		
****Conquerors	5-15/16''	43	2/.65	50	16.25	12.50	*		
Deluxe	5-2/3''	42	2/.65	50	16.25	12.50	*		
*****Accents (tubed)	6''	39	2/.75	30	11.25	8.64	*		
*****Camino (tubed)	6''	39	2/.75	30	11.25	8.64		*	

*Also available in 5 packs.
****Also available in 4 packs.
*****Also available in 3 packs.

- A very well made popular priced cigar.
- A & Cs are available in a wide selection of sizes shapes and colors and are a good value for the consumers dollar. As with all other brands beware of the products in tubes. Incidentally, the A & C Grenadier is probably the largest selling cigar on earth.
- Filler tobaccos from South and Central America and selected domestic tobaccos, wrappers from the Cameroons and South and Central America.
- Distributed by the American Cigar Co. of N.Y., N.Y.

Bances

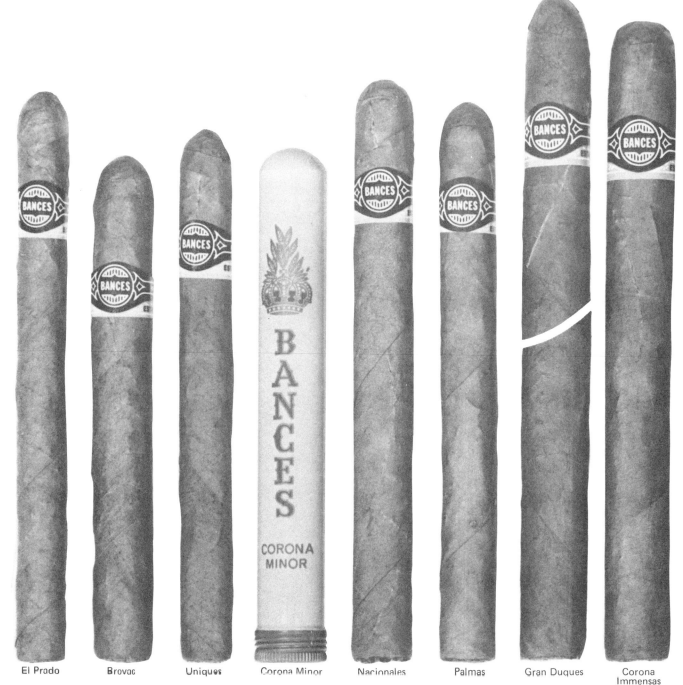

| El Prado | Brevas | Uniques | Corona Minor | Nacionales | Palmas | Gran Duques | Corona Immensas |

Front Mark	Length	Ring Size	Retail per ea.	Qty. per Box	Retail per Box	Whole sale per Box	Wrapper Color		
							C	N	M
*El Prado	6-1/8''	36	.35	25	8.75	6.75	*	*	*
**Brevas (A)	5-1/4''	43	.40	50	20.00	15.40	*	*	*
Uniques (A)	5-1/2''	38	3/1.00	50	16.66	13.13	*	*	*
Corona Minor (tubed)	5-1/4''	42	.60	30	18.00	13.50	*	*	
Nacionales	6-1/8''	43	.55	25	13.75	10.31	*	*	*
**Palmas	6''	42	.40	50	20.00	15.40	*	*	*
Gran Duques (B)	7-1/8''	47	.90	25	22.50	16.88	*	*	*
Corona Immensas (A)(B)	6-3/4''	48	.90	25	22.50	16.88	*	*	*

* Also available in 3 packs.
** Also available in 4 packs.
(A) Also available in Maduro, Maduro.
(B) Hand made sizes.

- A very well constructed, uniformly made cigar.
- Excellent range of sizes, shapes and wrapper colors.
- Very reasonably priced.
- A medium to heavy bodied cigar.
- Made from Honduran and central American tobaccos.
- Distributed by Villazon and Co. of Tampa, Fla.

44

Bances

No. 1   No. 100   Corona Especial   No. 3   Havana Holders   Cazadores   Demi Tasse

Front Mark	Length	Ring Size	Retail per ea.	Qty. per Box	Retail per Box	Whole sale per Box	Wrapper Color		
							C	N	M
No. 1 (B)	6-1/2''	43	.75	25	18.75	14.06	*	*	*
No. 100	7''	39	.60	25	15.00	11.25	*	*	
Corona Especial (B)	5-1/2''	44	.60	25	15.00	11.25	*	*	*
No. 3	5-3/4''	46	.40	25	10.00	7.70	*	*	*
Havana Holders	6-1/2''	30	.30	50	15.00	11.50	*	*	
***Cazadores (A)	6-1/4''	43	.50	50	25.00	18.75	*	*	*
Demi Tasse (C)	3-1/2''	38	.26	50	13.00	10.00	*	*	*

***Also available in 3pack, 30s and 60s.
(A) Also available in Maduro, Maduro.
(B) Hand made sizes.
(C) Not pictured.

- A very well constructed, uniformly made cigar.
- Excellent range of sizes, shapes and wrapper colors.
- Very reasonably priced.
- A medium to heavy bodied cigar.
- Made from Honduran and central American tobaccos.
- Distributed by Villazon and Co. of Tampa, Fla.

45

Bering

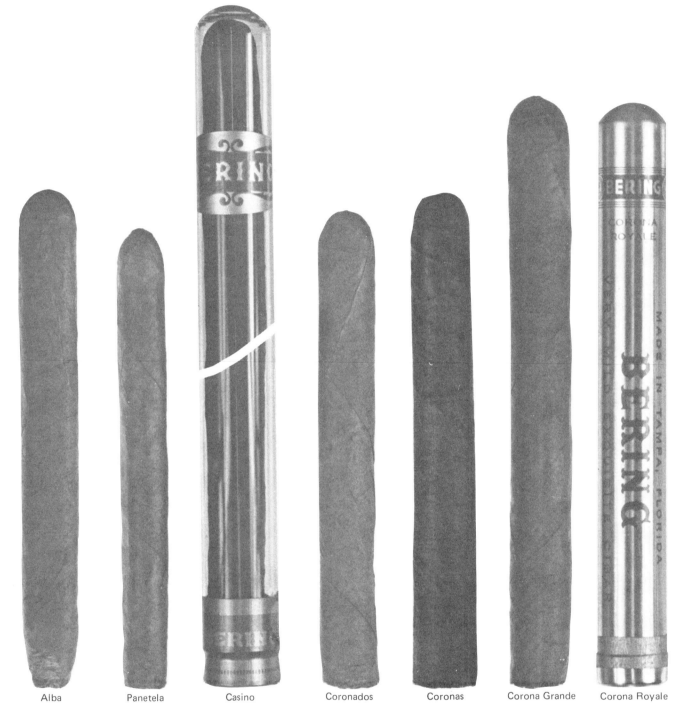

Alba   Panetela   Casino   Coronados   Coronas   Corona Grande   Corona Royale

Front Mark (1st Group)	Length	Ring Size	Retail per ea.	Qty. per Box	Retail per Box	Whole sale per Box	Wrapper Color C	N	M
Alba	5-5/16''	43	.28	50	14.00	10.55	*	*	*
Panetela (5)	5-1/16''	37	.20	50	10.00	7.50	*	*	*
Casino	7-1/8''	42	.70	10	7.00	5.25	*	*	*
Coronados (6)	5-3/16''	44	.28	50	14.00	10.55	*	*	*
Coronas	5-5/8''	44	.60	25	15.00	11.25	*	*	*
Corona Grande (3)	6-1/4''	46	.45	25	11.25	8.44	*	*	*
Corona Royale (3)	6-1/16''	42	.50	25	12.50	9.37		*	*

(3)-Available in 3 packs.
(5)-Available in 5 & 7 packs.
(6)-Available in 4 & 5 packs.

- A uniform, consistant cigar mainly machine made, yet still retaining several handmade sizes.
- This brand has a staggering number of sizes, shapes, and wrapper colors. It is one of the most complete line of domestically made cigars available in this country. A great number of these sizes, shapes and colors are not stocked by the average tobacconist due to the plodding, archaic sales methods of the company.
- Penny for penny this brand in every size offers the consumer an unrivaled value for his purchasing dollar.
- The Table below is separated into three groups. The first being all tobacco, long leaf filler, the second being all tobacco, short filler, and the third being short filler with a homogenized binder.
- An average strength cigar distributed by Corral Wodiska Y C.A. of Tampa, Florida.

Bering

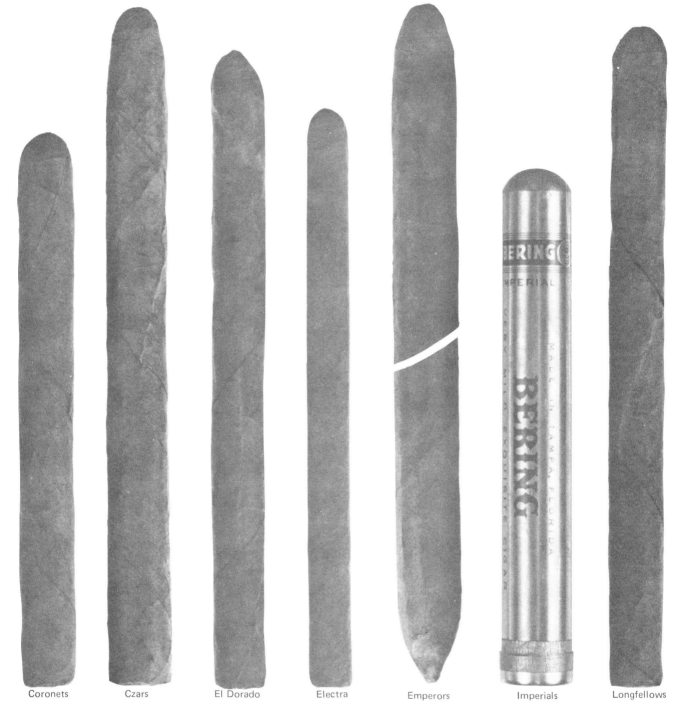

Coronets   Czars   El Dorado   Electra   Emperors   Imperials   Longfellows

Front Mark	Length	Ring Size	Retail per ea.	Qty. per Box	Retail per Box	Whole sale per Box	Wrapper Color		
							C	N	M
Coronets (2)	5-7/8''	40	.28	50	14.00	10.55	*	*	*
Czars	7-1/4''	46	.65	25	16.25	12.20	*	*	*
El Doradors	6-3/16''	40	.40	25	10.00	7.70	*	*	*
Electra (1)	6-1/4''	34	.28	50	14.00	10.55	*	*	*
Emperors	8-1/2''	46	.90	10	9.00	6.75	*	*	*
Imperials (4)	5-5/16''	42	.45	25	11.25	8.44		*	*
Longfellows	7-1/16''	42	.45	25	11.25	8.44	*	*	*

(1)-Available in 5 packs.
(2)-Available in 4 packs.
(4)-Available in 3 & 4 packs.

- A uniform, consistant cigar mainly machine made, yet still retaining several handmade sizes.
- This brand has a staggering number of sizes, shapes, and wrapper colors. It is one of the most complete line of domestically made cigars available in this country. A great number of these sizes, shapes and colors are not stocked by the average tobacconist due to the plodding, archaic sales methods of the company.
- Penny for penny this brand in every size offers the consumer an unrivaled value for his purchasing dollar.
- The Table below is separated into three groups. The first being all tobacco, long leaf filler, the second being all tobacco, short filler, and the third being short filler with a homogenized binder.
- An average strength cigar distributed by Corral Wodiska Y C.A. of Tampa, Florida.

47

Bering

Magnificos   No. 55   Plazas   President   400's   9/09

Front Mark	Length	Ring Size	Retail per ea.	Qty. per Box	Retail per Box	Whole sale per Box	Wrapper Color		
							C	N	M
Magnificos	4''	45	.25	50	12.50	9.50	*	*	*
No. 55	5''	46	.40	50	20.00	15.00	*	*	*
Plazas (2)	6-1/16''	43	.40	50	20.00	15.40	*	*	*
President	7''	44	.70	25	17.50	13.13	*	*	*
400's	5-13/16''	44	.35	25	8.75	6.63	*	*	*
9/09	6-5/16''	42	.50	50	25.00	18.75		*	
(2nd Group)									
Juniors	4-3/16''	39	.14	50	7.00	5.25	*	*	*
Populares	5-1/16''	44	.17	50	8.50	6.75	*	*	*
Champions	4-9/16''	42	.15	50	7.50	5.75	*	*	*
(3rd Group)									
Cigarillos	4-1/2''	28	.10	50	5.00	4.00	*	*	*
Fads	4-1/3''	29	.12	50	6.00	5.00	*	*	*

(2)-Available in 4 packs.

- A uniform, consistant cigar mainly machine made, yet still retaining several handmade sizes.
- This brand has a staggering number of sizes, shapes, and wrapper colors. It is one of the most complete line of domestically made cigars available in this country. A great number of these sizes, shapes and colors are not stocked by the average tobacconist due to the plodding, archaic sales methods of the company.
- Penny for penny this brand in every size offers the consumer an unrivaled value for his purchasing dollar.
- The Table below is separated into three groups. The first being all tobacco, long leaf filler, the second being all tobacco, short filler, and the third being short filler with a homogenized binder.
- An average strength cigar distributed by Corral Wodiska Y C.A. of Tampa, Florida.

48

Bermejo

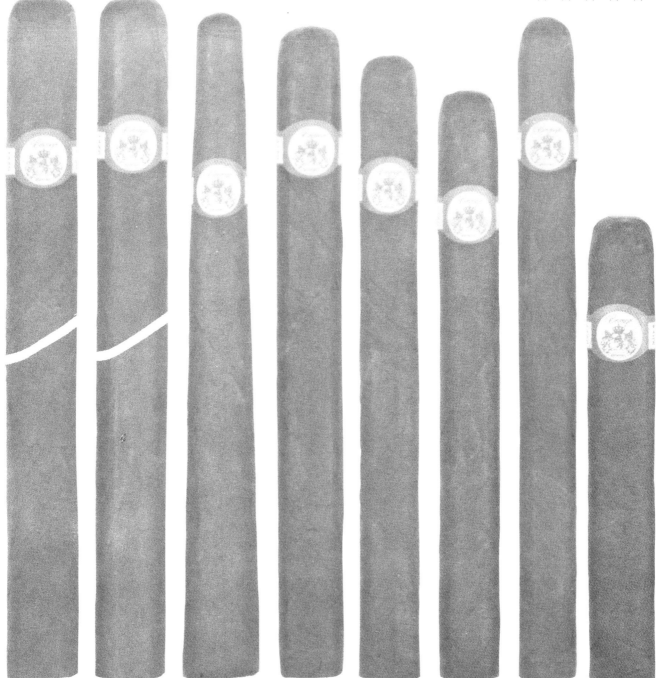

Viajante   Emperador   Pyramide   Churchill   Numero 1   Numero 2   Elegante   Rothchild

Front Mark	Length	Ring Size	Retail per ea.	Qty. per Box	Retail per Box	Whole sale per Box	Wrapper Color		
							C	N	M
Viajante	8-1/2''	52	1.85	10	18.50	10.25		*	*
Emperador	7-3/4''	50	1.75	10	17.50	10.50		*	*
Pyramide	7''	32/50	1.35	24	32.40	18.00		*	*
Churchill	6-7/8''	49	1.35	25	33.75	18.75		*	*
Numero 1	6-5/8''	44	1.15	25	28.75	15.50		*	*
Numero 2	6-1/4''	44	1.00	25	25.00	13.50		*	*
Elegante	7''	42	1.05	25	26.25	14.50		*	*
*Corona	7''	44	1.05	25	26.25	14.25		*	*
Rothchild	5''	50	1.00	25	25.00	13.50		*	*

*Not pictured.

- A fairly well constructed hand made long filler cigar from Nicaragua.
- A good range of sizes and colors.
- The strange value rating above means this cigar can be a good or bad buy for the consumer depending on what price his retailer paid for it. If the store bought it right, hopefully he'll pass on that saving to you.
- Made of long filler tobaccos grown in the Jalapa Valley, located between Honduras and Nicaragua.
- A relatively strong, "bity" cigar.
- Distributed by Bermejo Cigar Co. of Miami, Fla.

Bermejo

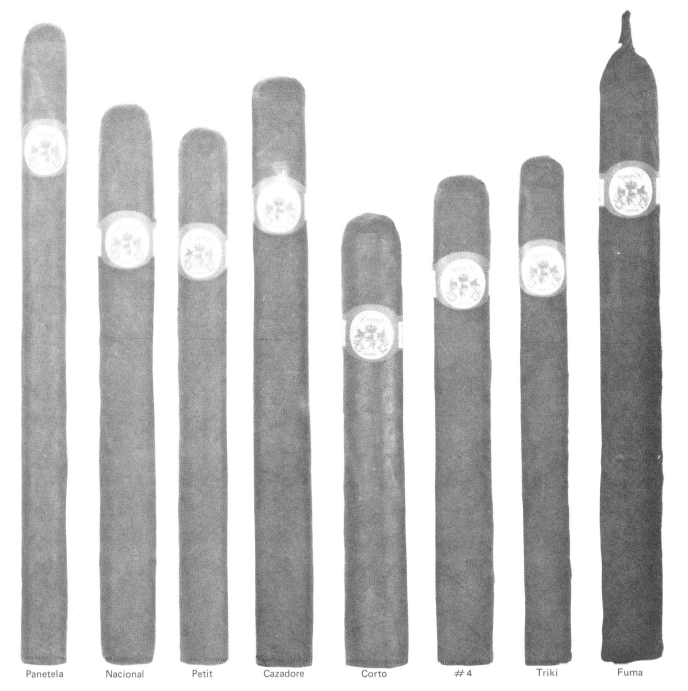

Panetela   Nacional   Petit   Cazadore   Corto   #4   Triki   Fuma

Front Mark	Length	Ring Size	Retail per ea.	Qty. per Box	Retail per Box	Wholesale per Box	Wrapper Color		
							C	N	M
Panetela	6-7/8"	35	.90	25	22.50	12.50		*	*
Nacional	6"	43	.85	25	21.25	11.50		*	*
Petit	5-3/4"	38	.80	25	20.00	11.25		*	*
**Cazadore (Bundle)	6-1/2"	44	.70	25	17.50	10.00			*
Corto	4-7/8"	46	.90	25	22.50	12.50		*	*
#4	5-1/4"	43	.80	25	20.00	11.00		*	*
Triki	5-1/2"	34	.70	25	17.50	10.00		*	*
**Fuma (Bundle)	7"	44	.50	25	12.50	8.25			*

**Short filler.

- A fairly well constructed hand made long filler cigar from Nicaragua.
- A good range of sizes and colors.
- The strange value rating above means this cigar can be a good or bad buy for the consumer depending on what price his retailer paid for it. If the store bought it right, hopefully he'll pass on that saving to you.
- Made of long filler tobaccos grown in the Jalapa Valley, located between Honduras and Nicaragua.
- A relatively strong, "bity" cigar.
- Distributed by Bermejo Cigar Co. of Miami, Fla.

Capitan de Tueros

No.3 No.5 No.7 No.8 No.10

Front Mark	Length	Ring Size	Retail per ea.	Qty. per Box	Retail per Box	Whole sale per Box	Wrapper Color		
							C	N	M
No. 3	4-3/4''	28	5/.47	50	4.70	3.75		*	
No. 5 (1)	6-5/8''	32	5/.92	25	4.60	3.75		*	
No. 7 (2)	6-7/8''	34	5/.99	25	4.95	4.00		*	
No. 8 (3)	5-5/8''	42	5/1.05	25	5.25	4.25		*	
No. 10 (4)	6-7/8''	38	3/.90	25	4.50	3.60		*	

(1)-Also available in 5 pk. 50's.
(2)-Also available in 5 pk. 50's.
(3)-Also available in 5 pk. 50's.
(4)-Also available in 3 pk. 24's.

- A fairly new popular priced cigar in a severely limited range of sizes.
- They're Cameroon wrapped with Asian Latin, and South American filler Tobaccos.
- I like Muriel's girls better than Capitan's John Weitz, and Muriel's prices too.
- Distributed by the Consolidated Cigar Co. of N.Y., N.Y.

Casa Copan

Pinceles   Petit Corona   Numero 2   Palma Extra   Numero Uno

Corona Grande   Churchill   Presidente

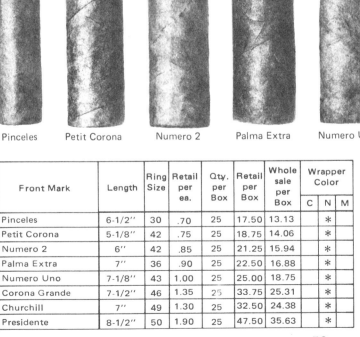

Front Mark	Length	Ring Size	Retail per ea.	Qty. per Box	Retail per Box	Whole sale per Box	Wrapper Color		
							C	N	M
Pinceles	6-1/2''	30	.70	25	17.50	13.13		*	
Petit Corona	5-1/8''	42	.75	25	18.75	14.06		*	
Numero 2	6''	42	.85	25	21.25	15.94		*	
Palma Extra	7''	36	.90	25	22.50	16.88		*	
Numero Uno	7-1/8''	43	1.00	25	25.00	18.75		*	
Corona Grande	7-1/2''	46	1.35	25	33.75	25.31		*	
Churchill	7''	49	1.30	25	32.50	24.38		*	
Presidente	8-1/2''	50	1.90	25	47.50	35.63		*	

- A very well constructed hand made cigar.
- Limited, but well chosen range of sizes.
- Available in natural brown wrappers only.
- A better than average buy for the consumer's dollar.
- Presidente size prone to being ''spongy''.
- Hand made of long filler in Honduras.
- Distributed by Intercontinental Cigars of San Diego.

Connecticut Valley Cigars

Muniemaker Reg.   Muniemaker Strait   Muniemaker Long   Judges Cave   La Moscavita   Knickerbocker   Cueto

Front Mark	Length	Ring Size	Retail per ea.	Qty. per Box	Retail per Box	Whole sale per Box	Wrapper Color		
							C	N	M
Muniemaker Reg.	4-1/2''	47	.20	50	10.00	7.70		*	
*Muniemaker Strait	5-1/8''	48	.25	50	12.50	9.75		*	
Muniemaker Long	6''	46	.30	50	15.00	11.50		*	
Judges Cave	4-1/2''	47	.25	50	12.50	9.75		*	
La Moscavita	5-1/8''	48	.25	50	12.50	9.75		*	
Knickerbocker	4-7/8''	47	.25	50	12.50	9.75		*	
Cueto	4-7/8''	45	2/.45	50	11.25	8.75		*	

* Also available in 6 packs.

- A well constructed all tobacco, short filler cigar, made by machine.
- All tobacco cigars for this kind of money are a thing of the past. Your best values are in the lower end of this line.
- Bear in mind when reading the charts below, that for some reason the ring sizes of all connecticut manufacturers are *always* different from all other manufacturers. I would suggest substracting *at least* 3 ring sizes from everything listed below.
- Good range of sizes and colors.
- Tasty and cheap.
- Distributed by FD Grave & Co. of New Haven, Conn.

Connecticut Valley Cigars

Breva 100   Panetela 100   Palma 100   Perfecto 100   Grave Imperial   Boquet Special

Front Mark	Length	Ring Size	Retail per ea.	Qty. per Box	Retail per Box	Whole sale per Box	Wrapper Color		
							C	N	M
**Breva 100	5-1/8''	48	.30	50	15.00	11.50			*
Panetela 100	6''	33	2/.65	50	16.25	12.30		*	*
Palma 100	6''	46	2/.75	50	18.75	14.40		*	*
Perfecto 100	5-1/4''	53	.55	25	13.75	10.30		*	*
Grave Imperial	5-1/8''	47	.40	50	20.00	15.00		*	
***Boquet Special	5-1/8''	46	.65	25	16.25	12.19		*	*

** Also available in 5 packs
*** Glass tubes.

- A well constructed all tobacco, short filler cigar, made by machine.
- All tobacco cigars for this kind of money are a thing of the past. Your best values are in the lower end of this line.
- Bear in mind when reading the charts below, that for some reason the ring sizes of all connecticut manufacturers are *always* different from all other manufacturers. I would suggest substracting *at least* 3 ring sizes from everything listed below.
- Good range of sizes and colors.
- Tasty and cheap.
- Distributed by FD Grave & Co. of New Haven, Conn.

Corina

Sports Deluxe   Lark   Panatela   Western   Baron

Front Mark	Length	Ring Size	Retail per ea.	Qty. per Box	Retail per Box	Whole sale per Box	Wrapper Color		
							C	N	M
Sports Deluxe	4-19/32''	35	5/.59	50	5.90	4.80		*	
Lark	5-3/8''	41	5/1.05	50	10.50	8.40		*	
Panatela	5-9/16''	37	5/.87	50	8.70	7.05		*	
Western	5-3/8''	41	5/1.05	50	10.50	8.40	*		
Baron	5-11/16''	42½	5/1.05	50	10.50	8.40		*	

- A well constructed machine made cigar.
- Very, very mild (the name Corina even sounds mild).
- A very limited range of sizes.
- A good value.
- Made from Imported and Domestic filler tobaccos.
- Distributed by the General Cigar Co. of N.Y.

Count Christopher

La Nina   La Pinta   La Santa Maria   Ysabel   Cristobal   Fernando   Continente

Front Mark	Length	Ring Size	Retail per ea.	Qty. per Box	Retail per Box	Whole sale per Box	Wrapper Color C	N	M
La Nina	5-1/2''	38	.55	25	13.75	10.31		*	*
La Pinta	6''	41	.65	25	16.25	12.12		*	*
La Santa Maria	6''	43	.70	25	17.50	13.13		*	*
Ysabel	6-7/8''	35	.75	25	18.75	14.06		*	*
Cristobal	6-5/8''	44	.95	25	23.75	17.81		*	*
Fernando	6-7/8''	49	1.00	25	25.00	18.75		*	*
Continente	8-1/2''	52	1.55	10	15.50	11.63		*	*

- A very well constructed, uniform, hand made cigar.
- A limited range of sizes shapes and colors.
- Really original names... The Nina, The Pinta, The Santa Maria.
- All the sizes are round - that means they'll draw easier.
- A good value in all sizes except the Continente.
- Distributed by Comoy's of London, who are really from New Jersey.

56

Creme de Jamaica

LEW ROTHMAN RATING
Quality: ★ ★ ★ ★ ★
Value: ★ ★ ★

No. 1   No. 7   No. 12   No. 49   No. 50   No. 51

Front Mark	Length	Ring Size	Retail per ea.	Qty. per Box	Retail per Box	Whole sale per Box	Wrapper Color		
							C	N	M
No. 1	6-1/4''	42	1.30	25	32.50	24.38		*	
No. 7	6-1/2''	38	1.25	25	31.25	23.44		*	*
No. 12	7-1/2''	31	1.00	25	25.00	18.75		*	
No. 49	7-1/4''	49	1.60	25	40.00	30.00		*	
No. 50	4-3/4''	38	.95	25	23.75	17.82			*
No. 51	5-7/8''	38	1.05	25	26.25	19.69			*

- A very mild, well constructed, high grade, hand made cigar.
- Adequate range of sizes and shapes. Available in natural medium brown wrappers, and Maduro.
- Excellent consistancy and uniformity of construction, blend, taste and appearance.
- Expensive, especially in smaller sizes.
- Be extremely alert for stale cigars. This is a fine cigar, but has mediocre sales volume. In addition, the brand is most commonly found in tobacconists with a small volume of cigar sales. Therefore the turnover of this merchandise is S-L-O-W.
- Made in Bond in Jamaica, West Indies, under the supervision of Ramon Cifuentes. Cifuentes is one of the world's most reknown manufacturers, and works for Monthego Y Ca, a division of the General Cigar Corp.
- It is distributed by Faber, Coe & Gregg of Clifton, N.J.

Creme de Jamaica

No. 52   No. 53   No. 54   Petite Cazadore   Singulare

Front Mark	Length	Ring Size	Retail per ea.	Qty. per Box	Retail per Box	Whole sale per Box	Wrapper Color		
							C	N	M
No. 52	6-3/4''	38	1.10	25	27.50	20.63			*
No. 53	6-1/4''	42	1.30	25	32.50	24.38			*
No. 54	5-3/8''	42	1.20	25	30.00	22.50			*
Petite Cazadore	5-3/8''	42	.95	50	47.50	35.64			*
Singulare	6-3/4''	34	1.30	25	32.50	24.38		*	

- A very mild, well constructed, high grade, hand made cigar.
- Adequate range of sizes and shapes. Available in natural medium brown wrappers, and Maduro.
- Excellent consistancy and uniformity of construction, blend, taste and appearance.
- Expensive, especially in smaller sizes.
- Be extremely alert for stale cigars. This is a fine cigar, but has mediocre sales volume. In addition, the brand is most commonly found in tobacconists with a small volume of cigar sales. Therefore the turnover of this merchandise is S-L-O-W.
- Made in Bond in Jamaica, West Indies, under the supervision of Ramon Cifuentes. Cifuentes is one of the world's most reknown manufacturers, and works for Montego Y Ca, a division of the General Cigar Corp.
- It is distributed by Faber, Coe & Gregg of Clifton, N.J.

Cuesta Rey Cigars

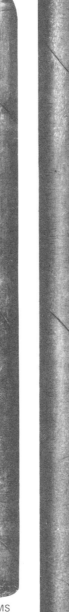
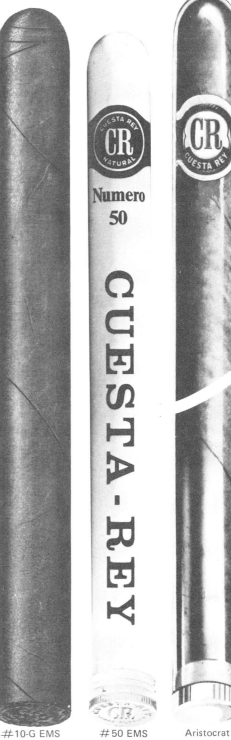

#70 EMS   #1 EMS   #2 EMS   #898 EMS   #95 EMS

#10-G EMS   #50 EMS   Aristocrat

Front Mark (1st Group)	Length	Ring Size	Retail per ea.	Qty. per Box	Retail per Box	Whole sale per Box	Wrapper Color C	N	M
#70 EMS	7-1/4''	39	.95	25	23.75	17.81		*	*
#1 EMS	7-1/4''	44	1.10	20	22.00	16.50		*	*
#2 EMS	7-1/4''	33	.85	25	21.25	15.94		*	*
#898 EMS	6-1/4''	45	.85	25	21.25	15.94		*	*
*#95 EMS	6-1/4''	42	.65	25	16.25	12.38		*	*
#10-G EMS	7-3/8''	50	1.20	25	30.00	22.50		*	
**#50 EMS	7''	36	1.00	25	25.00	18.75		*	
***Aristocrat	7-3/16''	44	1.00	10	10.00	7.50	*	*	*

* Also available in boxes of 50.
** Aluminum tube.
*** Glass tube.
All sizes except Aristocrat, Churchill, Corona Larga, are available in packs.

- An extremely well made domestic cigar, made of imported tobaccos from the Caribbean and Latin America.
- An extensive range of sizes shapes and colors.
- Cuesta Rey Cigars are listed in two groups. The first is long leaf-filler all tobacco cigars. The second is short filler cigars with homogenized binders. Cigars listed as E.M.S. have African Cameroon wrappers.
- An expensive cigar in all cigars of the first category by comparison with any other Tampa Manufacturer.
- All second category cigars are competitively priced.
- Your best bet when buying 3, 4, or 5 packed cigars, as Cuesta Rey Packs contain an inner polly pouch which extends its shelf life far beyond those of other Tampa manufacturers.
- Distributed by M & N Cigar Manufacturers of Tampa, Florida.

Cuesta Rey Cigars

| Churchill | Corona Larga | Palma Supreme | Imperial Corona | ACW Corona | Caravelle | #240 | #120 |

Front Mark	Length	Ring Size	Retail per ea.	Qty. per Box	Retail per Box	Whole sale per Box	Wrapper Color		
							C	N	M
Churchill	7-1/4''	44	1.00	25	25.00	18.75	*	*	*
Corona Larga	6-1/4''	45	.75	25	18.75	14.06	*	*	*
*Palma Supreme	6-1/4''	42	.50	25	12.50	9.56	*	*	*
***Imperial Corona	5-1/4''	42	.65	25	16.25	12.19		*	
(2nd Group)									
ACW Corona	5-1/2''	41	.30	50	15.00	11.50		*	
Caravelle	6-1/4''	34	.21	50	10.50	8.15	*	*	*
#240	5-1/4''	40	.25	50	12.50	9.35		*	
#120	5''	31	.20	70	14.00	12.04		*	

* Also available in boxes of 50.
*** Glass tube.
All sizes except Aristocrat, Churchill, Corona Larga, are available in packs.

- An extremely well made domestic cigar, made of imported tobaccos from the Caribbean and Latin America.
- An extensive range of sizes shapes and colors.
- Cuesta Rey Cigars are listed in two groups. The first is long leaf-filler all tobacco cigars. The second is short filler cigars with homogenized binders. Cigars listed as E.M.S. have African Cameroon wrappers.
- An expensive cigar in all cigars of the first category by comparison with any other Tampa Manufacturer.
- All second category cigars are competitively priced.
- Your best bet when buying 3, 4, or 5 packed cigars, as Cuesta Rey Packs contain an inner polly pouch which extends its shelf life far beyond those of other Tampa manufacturers.
- Distributed by M & N Cigar Manufacturers of Tampa, Florida.

Danlys

| Number 5 | Petit Cetro | Number 4 | Palma Fina | Luchadore | Cetros | Palma Extra |

Front Mark	Length	Ring Size	Retail per ea.	Qty. per Box	Retail per Box	Whole sale per Box	Wrapper Color		
							C	N	M
Number 5	5-5/8''	35	.50	50	25.00	18.75	*	*	
Petit Cetro	5-1/4''	39	2/1.05	25	13.13	9.85	*	*	
Number 4	5-1/2''	42	2/1.15	25	14.38	10.75	*	*	
Palma Fina	7''	32	2/1.25	25	15.63	11.75	*	*	
Luchadore	6''	43	.65	25	16.25	12.06	*	*	
Cetros	6-1/4''	43	.70	25	17.50	13.13	*	*	
Palma Extra	7''	36	.70	25	17.50	13.13	*	*	

- A well constructed hand made cigar of moderate strength.
- Very good selection of sizes, shapes and colors.
- Price range is very reasonable for hand made cigars.
- Made in Honduras of long filler tobaccos.
- Not a real ''firm'' cigar.
- Distributed by Pan American Cigars of Hoboken, N.J.

Danlys

Fancy Tale

Number 1

Churchill

Presidente

Front Mark	Length	Ring Size	Retail per ea.	Qty. per Box	Retail per Box	Whole sale per Box	Wrapper Color		
							C	N	M
Fancy Tale	6-3/4''	43	.75	25	18.75	14.06	*	*	
Number 1	7''	43	.80	25	20.00	15.00	*	*	
Churchill	7''	48	.95	25	23.75	17.81	*	*	
Presidente	8''	46	1.00	25	25.00	18.75	*	*	

- A well constructed hand made cigar of moderate strength.
- Very good selection of sizes, shapes and colors.
- Price range is very reasonable for hand made cigars.
- Made in Honduras of long filler tobaccos.
- Not a real "firm" cigar.
- Distributed by Pan American Cigars of Hoboken, N.J.

62

Dominicana

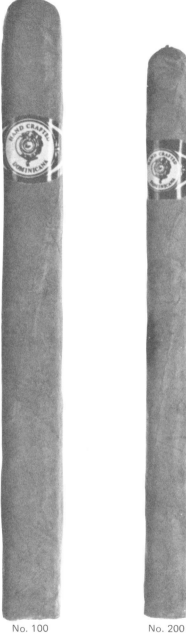

No. 100   No. 200   No. 300   No. 400

Front Mark	Length	Ring Size	Retail per ea.	Qty. per Box	Retail per Box	Whole sale per Box	Wrapper Color		
							C	N	M
No. 100	6-5/8''	44	.90	25	22.50	16.88		*	
No. 200	6-1/4''	34	.60	25	15.00	11.25		*	
No. 300	5-1/2''	43	.70	25	17.50	13.13		*	
No. 400	5-3/4''	49	.90	25	22.50	16.88		*	

- If there were a greater supply of these cigars they could knock the hell out of the whole cigar industry.
- A very, very well constructed, hand made, long filler cigar from the Dominican Republic.
- Sweet, tasty, mild and yummy.
- Unbelievably cheap.
- Rotten selection of sizes, natural only - but how are you gonna argue with success?
- If you can find 'em, buy 'em.
- Distributed by Cigars by Santa Clara Ltd of N.Y., N.Y.

Don Alvaro

Super Star   Elegante   #1   Imperials   Cazadore   Cedro   Don Alvaro   Corona

Front Mark	Length	Ring Size	Retail per ea.	Qty. per Box	Retail per Box	Whole sale per Box	Wrapper Color		
							C	N	M
Super Star	6-11/16''	44	.60	25	15.00	11.25		*	
Elegante	6-11/16''	42	.50	25	12.50	9.38		*	
#1	6-11/16''	39	.50	25	12.50	9.38		*	
Imperiales	6-11/16''	44	.50	25	12.50	9.38		*	
Cazadore	6-11/16''	42	.45	50	22.50	16.88			*
Cedro	5-9/32''	42	.45	25	11.25	8.44		*	
Don Alvaro	5-9/32''	42	.40	25	10.00	7.50		*	
Corona	5-7/16''	42	.40	50	20.00	15.00		*	

- The world's finest machine made, short filler, homogenized binder cigar.
- Super Duper mild.
- Very expensive due to duties arising in importation from Spain.
- Can't compete with U.S. manufacturers of popular priced cigars in terms of retail price.
- Can't compete with Tampa manufacturers in terms of quality. Comparatively priced Tampa cigars are all tobacco.
- Watch those fragile Cameroon wrappers.
- Distributed by Don Alvaro Cigar Distribution Corp. of Ridgefield, N.J.

Don Alvaro

| Breva | Boquet | Senadore | Floretes | Panetelas | Saludos | Marianos | Isleno |

Front Mark	Length	Ring Size	Retail per ea.	Qty. per Box	Retail per Box	Whole sale per Box	Wrapper Color		
							C	N	M
Breva	5-9/32''	42	.35	50	17.50	13.50			*
Boquet	4-13/32''	45	.35	50	17.50	13.50		*	
Senadore	4-27/32''	39	.35	50	17.50	13.50		*	
Floretes	6-11/16''	27	.30	50	15.00	11.50		*	
Panetelas	6-7/64''	32	.30	50	15.00	11.50		*	
Saludos	4-27/32''	39	.30	50	15.00	11.50			*
Marianos	6-11/16''	23	.30	50	15.00	11.50		*	
Isleno	4-21/64''	33	.25	50	12.50	10.00			*

- The world's finest machine made, short filler, homogenized binder cigar.
- Super Duper mild.
- Very expensive due to duties arising in importation from Spain.
- Can't compete with U.S. manufacturers of popular priced cigars in terms of retail price.
- Can't compete with Tampa manufacturers in terms of quality. Comparatively priced Tampa cigars are all tobacco.
- Watch those fragile Cameroon wrappers.
- Distributed by Don Alvaro Cigar Distribution Corp. of Ridgefield, N.J.

Don Diego

| Coronas | Petite Corona | Shorts | Slim Coronas | Monarchs |

Front Mark	Length	Ring Size	Retail per ea.	Qty. per Box	Retail per Box	Whole sale per Box	Wrapper Color		
							C	N	M
Coronas	5-5/8''	42	1.15	25	28.75	21.56	*	*	
Petite Corona	5-1/8''	42	.90	25	22.50	16.88	*	*	
Shorts	4-7/8''	42	.90	25	22.50	16.88	*	*	
Slim Coronas	5-1/2''	38	1.00	25	25.00	18.75			*
*Babies	5-1/2''	32	.40	50	20.00	15.00			*
Monarchs	7''	45	1.85	10	18.50	13.88	*	*	

*Not pictured and machine made, short filler.

- A well constructed, hand made, high grade cigar
- Very mild
- A good range of sizes and shapes, available in English market selection and Double Claro AMS wrappers.
- Very good consistancy and uniformity of construction, blend and taste.
- Expensive, but the public keeps buying them. It's one of America's largest selling imports.
- A nice clean tasting cigar. Stay away from some of the cockamamie sizes like shorts petite grecos, slim coronas etc. As these are usually stale due to very poor sales.
- Made in the Canary Islands, Spain, under the supervision of Menendez and Garcia of H. Upmann and Montecristo Fame in Havana, Cuba.
- Marketed by many Regional Distributors.

Don Diego

| Cesvantes | Lonsdale | Greco | Amatista | Royal Palms | Petite Grecos |

Front Mark	Length	Ring Size	Retail per ea.	Qty. per Box	Retail per Box	Whole sale per Box	Wrapper Color		
							C	N	M
Cesvantes	7"	42	1.35	25	33.75	25.31	*	*	
Lonsdale	6-5/8"	42	1.25	25	31.25	23.41	*	*	
Greco	6-1/2"	38	1.20	25	30.00	22.50	*	*	
Amatista Glass Jars	5-7/8"	41	1.30	50	65.00	48.75		*	
Royal Palms	6-1/8"	35	1.20	25	30.00	22.50		*	
Petite Grecos	5-1/8"	38	.90	25	22.50	16.88	*	*	

- A well constructed, hand made, high grade cigar
- Very mild
- A good range of sizes and shapes, available in English market selection and Double Claro AMS wrappers.
- Very good consistancy and uniformity of construction, blend and taste.
- Expensive, but the public keeps buying them. It's one of America's largest selling imports.
- A nice clean tasting cigar. Stay away from some of the cockamamie sizes like shorts petite grecos, slim coronas etc. As these are usually stale due to very poor sales.
- Made in the Canary Islands, Spain, under the supervision of Menendez and Garcia of H. Upmann and Montecristo Fame in Havana, Cuba.
- Marketed by many Regional Distributors.

Don Marcos

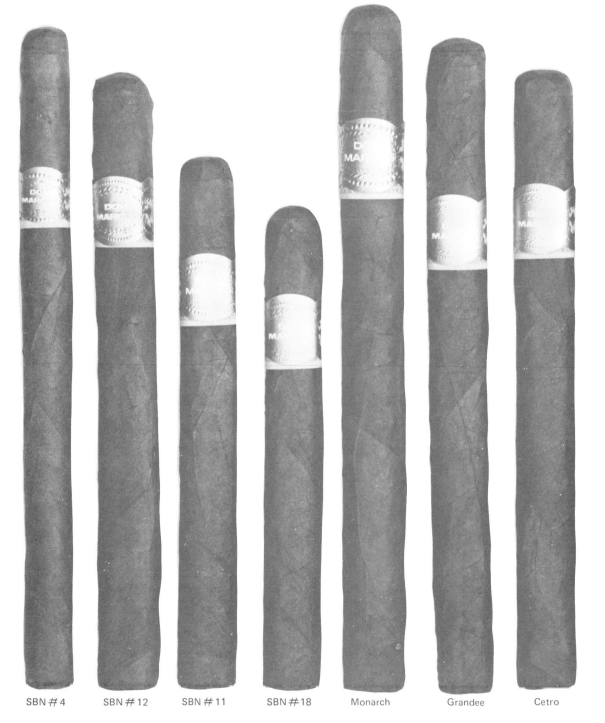

SBN #4   SBN #12   SBN #11   SBN #18   Monarch   Grandee   Cetro

Front Mark (1st Group)	Length	Ring Size	Retail per ea.	Qty. per Box	Retail per Box	Whole sale per Box	Wrapper Color		
							C	N	M
SBN # 4	7″	36	1.35	25	33.75	25.31		*	
SBN # 12	6-5/8″	42	1.40	25	35.00	26.25		*	
SBN # 11	5-3/8″	42	1.30	25	32.50	24.38		*	
SBN # 18	5-1/8″	42	1.15	25	28.75	21.56		*	
Monarch	7-3/8″	46	1.75	10	17.50	13.13		*	
Grandee	7″	42	1.45	25	36.25	27.18		*	
Cetro	6-5/8″	42	1.35	25	33.75	25.31		*	

- A very well made uniform, high grade cigar.
- Excellent range of sizes, poor selection of wrappers.
- Made in Canary Islands Spain by Compania Insular de Tobaccos of Latin American and Caribbean filler tobaccos, with Connecticut shade grown and African Cameroon wrappers.
- A fine but extremely expensive cigar, though not as high priced as its main competitor, the Montecruz, due to more liberal discounts allowed by the importer.
- Watch those Cameroon wrappers - they're easy to damage.
- The first group listed are handmade long filler. The second group listed are machine made. The Demi Tasse and Baby are short fillers.
- Distributed by Peterson's Ltd of Carlstadt, N.J.

Don Marcos

Amatista   Trump   Deliciosa #1   Deliciosa #2   Naturals   Corona Major

Front Mark	Length	Ring Size	Retail per ea.	Qty. per Box	Retail per Box	Whole sale per Box	Wrapper Color		
							C	N	M
Amatista	6''	40	1.25	25	31.25	23.44		*	
Trump	5-1/4''	42	1.00	25	25.00	18.75		*	
Deliciosa #1	7''	36	1.30	25	32.50	24.38		*	
Deliciosa #2	6-1/8''	36	1.20	25	30.00	22.50		*	
Naturals	5-7/8''	36	1.30	25	32.50	24.38		*	
Corona Major	5''	42	1.15	25	28.75	21.56	*		
*Corona	5-3/4''	42	1.20	25	30.00	22.50		*	

*Not pictured

- A very well made uniform, high grade cigar.
- Excellent range of sizes, poor selection of wrappers.
- Made in Canary Islands Spain by Compania Insular de Tobaccos of Latin American and Caribbean filler tobaccos, with Connecticut shade grown and African Cameroon wrappers.
- A fine but extremely expensive cigar, though not as high priced as its main competitor, the Montecruz, due to more liberal discounts allowed by the importer.
- Watch those Cameroon wrappers - they're easy to damage.
- The first group listed are handmade long filler. The second group listed are machine made. The Demi Tasse and Baby are short fillers.
- Distributed by Peterson's Ltd of Carlstadt, N.J.

Don Marcos

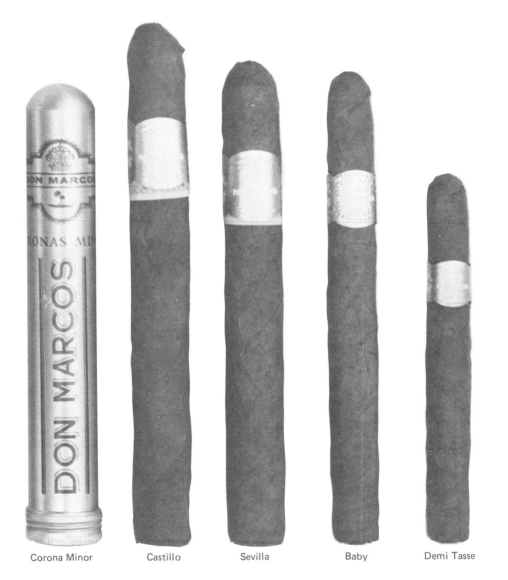

Corona Minor   Castillo   Sevilla   Baby   Demi Tasse

Front Mark (2nd Group)	Length	Ring Size	Retail per ea.	Qty. per Box	Retail per Box	Whole sale per Box	Wrapper Color C	N	M
Corona Minor	4-3/8"	41	.80	25	20.00	15.00	*		
Castillo	5-1/2"	40	.65	25	16.25	12.18		*	
Sevilla	5-1/8"	41	.65	25	16.25	12.18		*	
Baby	4-7/8"	33	.40	50	20.00	15.00		*	
Demi Tasse	3-7/8"	28	.40	50	20.00	15.00		*	

- A very well made uniform, high grade cigar.
- Excellent range of sizes, poor selection of wrappers.
- Made in Canary Islands Spain by Compania Insular de Tobaccos of Latin American and Caribbean filler tobaccos, with Connecticut shade grown and African Cameroon wrappers.
- A fine but extremely expensive cigar, though not as high priced as its main competitor, the Montecruz, due to more liberal discounts allowed by the importer.
- Watch those Cameroon wrappers - they're easy to damage.
- The first group listed are handmade long filler. The second group listed are machine made. The Demi Tasse and Baby are short fillers.
- Distributed by Peterson's Ltd of Carlstadt, N.J.

Don Miguel

| Superbos | Lonsdales | Tubulares | Delicados | Aromas | Amigos |

Front Mark	Length	Ring Size	Retail per ea.	Qty. per Box	Retail per Box	Whole sale per Box	Wrapper Color		
							C	N	M
Superbos	7-1/2''	50	1.30	10	13.00	9.75		*	
Lonsdales	6-7/8''	42	1.05	25	26.25	19.69		*	
Tubulares	6-5/16''	42	1.25	10	12.50	9.38		*	
Delicados	6-7/8''	37	.90	25	22.50	16.88		*	
Aromas	5-1/2''	42	.80	25	20.00	15.00		*	
Amigos	5''	38	.75	25	18.75	14.06		*	
*Domingo	4-1/2''	50	1.00	25	25.00	18.75		*	
*Churchill	8''	51	1.50	25	37.50	28.13		*	
*Exquisito	6''	40	.95	25	23.75	17.82		*	
*Dorado	6-1/2''	34	.85	25	21.25	15.94		*	

*Not pictured.

- A well constructed hand made cigar.
- Good consistancy and uniformity of construction, blend, taste and appearance.
- It's overpriced.
- Since it's a relatively poor seller, be alert for stale cigars.
- Made in La Romana, Dominican Republic of Caribbean fillers and Cameroon and Connecticut shade grown wrappers.
- Distributed by Pan American Cigar Co. of Hoboken, N.J.

Don Tomas

| Corona | Panetal Larga | Toro | Panetela | Blunt |

Front Mark	Length	Ring Size	Retail per ea.	Qty. per Box	Retail per Box	Whole sale per Box	Wrapper Color		
							C	N	M
Corona	5-1/2''	50	.80	25	20.00	15.00	*	*	*
Panetal Larga	7''	36	.75	25	18.75	14.06	*	*	*
Toro	5-1/2''	46	.70	25	17.50	13.13	*	*	*
Panetela	6''	36	.65	25	16.25	12.19	*	*	*
Blunt	5''	42	.55	25	13.75	10.31	*	*	*

- A well made uniform cigar, hand made of long filler tobaccos.
- Imported from Honduras.
- A very good range of sizes and colors, although most tobacconists carry the natural wrappers only.
- A heavy cigar, definitely not for the novice cigar smoker.
- A good value for the consumer's dollar.
- Distributed by Honduran Cigar Imports of Greenwich, Conn.

Don Tomas

| President | Imperiale #1 | Corona Grande | Cetro #2 | Supremo |

Front Mark	Length	Ring Size	Retail per ea.	Qty. per Box	Retail per Box	Whole sale per Box	Wrapper Color		
							C	N	M
President	7-1/2''	50	1.25	25	31.25	23.44	*	*	*
Imperiale #1	8''	44	1.00	25	25.00	18.75	*	*	*
*Corona Grande	6-1/2''	44	1.00	25	25.00	18.75	*	*	*
Cetro #2	6-1/2''	44	.90	25	22.50	16.88	*	*	*
Supremo	6-1/4''	42	.80	25	20.00	15.00	*	*	*

- A well made uniform cigar, hand made of long filler tobaccos.
- Imported from Honduras.
- A very good range of sizes and colors, although most tobacconists carry the natural wrappers only.
- A heavy cigar, definitely not for the novice cigar smoker.
- A good value for the consumer's dollar.
- Distributed by Honduran Cigar Imports of Greenwich, Conn.

*In plastic tubes.

73

Dutch Masters

Cadet Regular Cadet Tipped   Sprint   Racer   Elite   Royal   Panetela   Perfecto

Front Mark	Length	Ring Size	Retail per ea.	Qty. per Box	Retail per Box	Whole sale per Box	Wrapper Color		
							C	N	M
Cadet Regular	4-3/4''	26	5/.47	50	4.70	3.75		*	
Cadet Tipped	5-1/8''	26	5/.41	50	4.10	3.45		*	
Sprint	5-1/8''	36	5/.69	50	6.90	5.70		*	
Racer	4-7/8''	38	5/.69	50	6.90	5.70		*	
Elite	6-1/8''	32	5/.79	50	7.90	6.55		*	
Royal	6-1/8''	32	5/.79	50	7.90	6.55	*		
Panetela	5-1/2''	36	5/.89	50	8.90	7.30		*	
Perfecto	4-3/4''	42	5/.89	50	8.90	7.30		*	

- One of the Kings of the Domestic Cigar Business light, mild, oodles of sizes.
- Dutch Masters are made from filler tobaccos from the Caribbean, South America, and Asia. Wrappers are Connecticut Shade Grown, Florida and African Cameroon.
- Manufactured in Pennsylvania and Puerto Rico.
- Distributed by the Consolidated Cigar Co. of N.Y., N.Y.

74

Dutch Masters

| Blunt | Belevedere | President | Whiffs | Cameroon #140 | Cameroon #150 | Corona Deluxe |

Front Mark	Length	Ring Size	Retail per ea.	Qty. per Box	Retail per Box	Whole sale per Box	Wrapper Color		
							C	N	M
Blunt	5-1/8''	42	5/.89	50	8.90	7.30		*	
Belvedere	4-7/8''	44	5/.99	50	9.90	8.00		*	
President	5-5/8''	42	5/.99	50	9.90	8.00		*	
Whiffs	2-1/2''	30	5/.69	50	6.90	5.70		*	
Cameroon #140	6''	42	5/.99	50	9.90	8.00		*	
Cameroon #150	6-3/8''	36	5/.99	50	9.90	8.00		*	
Corona Deluxe	5-3/4''	44	5/1.15	50	11.50	9.25		*	

- One of the Kings of the Domestic Cigar Business light, mild, oodles of sizes.
- Dutch Masters are made from filler tobaccos from the Caribbean, South America, and Asia. Wrappers are Connecticut Shade Grown, Florida and African Cameroon.
- Manufactured in Pennsylvania and Puerto Rico.
- Distributed by the Consolidated Cigar Co. of N.Y., N.Y.

El Producto

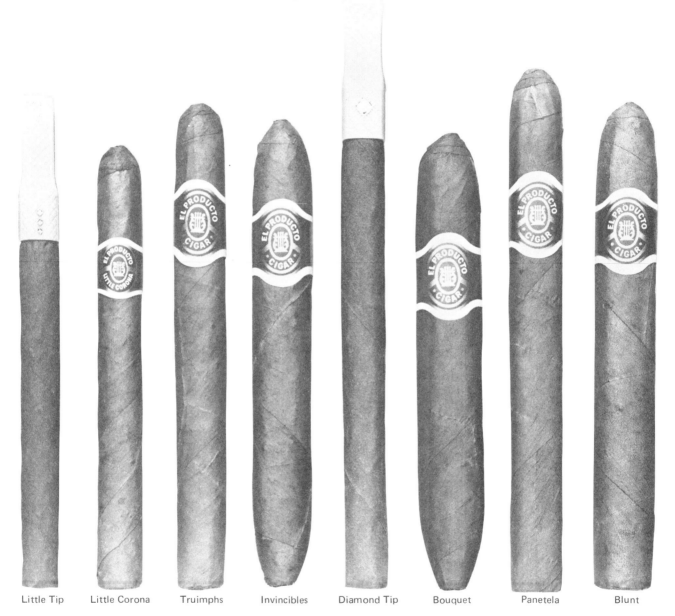

| Little Tip | Little Corona | Truimphs | Invincibles | Diamond Tip | Bouquet | Panetela | Blunt |

Front Mark	Length	Ring Size	Retail per ea.	Qty. per Box	Retail per Box	Whole sale per Box	Wrapper Color		
							C	N	M
Little Tip	5-1/8''	28	5/.41	50	4.10	3.45		*	
Little Corona	4-5/8''	28	5/.47	50	4.70	3.75		*	
Truimphs	5''	34	5/.69	50	6.90	5.70		*	
Invincibles	4-3/16''	40	5/.69	50	6.90	5.70		*	
Diamond Tip	6-1/8''	36	5/.62	50	6.20	5.10		*	
Bouquet	4-3/4''	42	5/.89	50	8.90	7.30		*	
Panetela	5-1/2''	36	5/.89	50	8.90	7.30		*	
Blunt	5-1/8''	42	5/.89	50	8.90	7.30		*	

- A big range of sizes for the popular price field.
- These extra mild cigars, manufactured in Pennsylvania and Puerto Rico are wrapped in Connecticut Shade Grown, Florida, and African Cameroon wrappers.
- The fillers come from tobaccos from Asia, South America and the Caribbean.
- Distributed by the Consolidated Cigar Co. of N.Y., N.Y.

El Producto

Excellents · Puritano Finos · Granadas · Favoritas · Coronas · Excepcionales · Queens

Front Mark	Length	Ring Size	Retail per ea.	Qty. per Box	Retail per Box	Whole sale per Box	Wrapper Color		
							C	N	M
Excellents	5-3/8''	36	5/.89	50	8.90	7.20		*	
Puritano Finos	4-7/8''	44	5/.99	50	9.90	8.00		*	
Granada	5-5/8''	38	5/.99	50	9.90	8.00		*	
Favoritas	5''	46	5/1.15	50	11.50	9.25		*	
Coronas	5-3/4''	42	5/1.15	50	11.50	9.25		*	
Escepcionales (1)	5-1/8''	48	5/1.50	25	7.50	6.00		*	
Queens (2)	5-5/8''	42	3/1.20	25	10.00	8.00		*	

(1) Also available in boxes of 50.
(2) Also available in boxes of 30.

- A big range of sizes for the popular price field.
- These extra mild cigars, manufactured in Pennsylvania and Puerto Rico are wrapped in Connecticut Shade Grown, Florida, and African Cameroon wrappers.
- The fillers come from tobaccos from Asia, South America and the Caribbean.
- Distributed by the Consolidated Cigar Co. of N.Y., N.Y.

Excalibur

| No. I | No. II | No. III | No. IV | No. V |

Front Mark	Length	Ring Size	Retail per ea.	Qty. per Box	Retail per Box	Whole sale per Box	Wrapper Color		
							C	N	M
No. I	7-1/4''	52	1.50	20	30.00	22.50		*	
No. II	7-1/4''	47	1.35	20	27.00	20.25		*	
No. III	6''	50	1.25	20	25.00	18.75		*	
No. IV	5-3/8''	45	1.15	20	23.00	17.25		*	
No. V	6-1/8''	44	1.15	20	23.00	17.25		*	

- A great hand made cigar from Honduras.
- You just can't make better cigars than these.
- Cost a lot - but they are gooood.
- Limited range of sizes and colors.
- Nice light wrapper with very little ''bite''.
- Distributed by Villazon & Co. of Englewood, N.J.

Flamenco

No. 101   Petit Flamenco   Palmitas   Corona Major   Trumps   Breva Conserva

Front Mark	Length	Ring Size	Retail per ea.	Qty. per Box	Retail per Box	Whole sale per Box	Wrapper Color		
							C	N	M
No. 101	7-5/16''	46	1.70	25	42.50	31.88		*	
** Petit Flamenco	3-3/4''	28	.35	50	17.50	13.13		*	
Palmitas	5-1/2''	32	.40	60	24.00	18.00		*	
Corona Major	4-1/2''	42	.95	25	23.75	17.83		*	
Trumps	5''	42	1.10	25	27.50	20.63			*
***Breva Conserva	5-3/8''	42	1.00	50	50.00	37.50			*

** Also available in tins of 10 cigars.
*** No cello.

- A very well constructed hand made cigar from the Dominican Republic. (Some sizes still made in the Canary Islands, Sp.).
- Long leaf fillers from Latin America, Connecticut shade grown and African Cameroon wrappers.
- A handsome array of sizes, shapes, and colors.
- Definitely overpriced compared to competitive merchandise originating from the same manufacturer.
- My favorite cigar name and they taste good.
- Distributed by Faber, Coe & Gregg of Clifton, N.J.

79

Flamenco

No. 1   No. 2   No. 3   No. 4   No. 35

Front Mark	Length	Ring Size	Retail per ea.	Qty. per Box	Retail per Box	Whole sale per Box	Wrapper Color		
							C	N	M
No. 1	6-5/8''	42	1.25	25	31.25	23.44	*	*	
No. 2	6-1/2''	38	1.20	25	30.00	22.50	*	*	
No. 3	5-5/8''	42	1.15	25	28.75	21.57	*	*	
No. 4	5-1/8''	42	.90	25	22.50	16.88	*	*	
*Amigo (Alum. tube)	6-1/8''	35	1.20	25	30.00	22.50		*	
No. 35	5''	38	.75	25	37.50	28.13	*	*	

*Not pictured.

- A very well constructed hand made cigar from the Dominican Republic. (Some sizes still made in the Canary Islands, Sp.).
- Long leaf fillers from Latin America, Connecticut shade grown and African Cameroon wrappers.
- A handsome array of sizes, shapes, and colors.
- Definitely overpriced compared to competitive merchandise originating from the same manufacturer.
- My favorite cigar name and they taste good.
- Distributed by Faber, Coe & Gregg of Clifton, N.J.

Flamenco

Cetro   Corona   Club Corona

Front Mark	Length	Ring Size	Retail per ea.	Qty. per Box	Retail per Box	Whole sale per Box	Wrapper Color		
							C	N	M
Cetro	6-5/8''	42	1.35	25	33.75	25.31			*
Corona	5-5/8''	42	1.25	25	31.25	23.44			*
Club Corona	4-15/16''	42	1.05	25	26.25	19.69			*
*No. 6	5-1/8''	35	.90	25	22.50	16.88			*
*No. 7	5-1/2''	35	1.00	25	25.00	18.75			*
*No. 8	6-1/8''	35	1.10	25	27.50	20.63			*

*Not pictured.

- A very well constructed hand made cigar from the Dominican Republic. (Some sizes still made in the Canary Islands, Sp.).
- Long leaf fillers from Latin America, Connecticut shade grown and African Cameroon wrappers.
- A handsome array of sizes, shapes, and colors.
- Definitely overpriced compared to competitive merchandise originating from the same manufacturer.
- My favorite cigar name and they taste good.
- Distributed by Faber, Coe & Gregg of Clifton, N.J.

Flor Del Caribe

La Perla   Duques   Bravo   Viva   Castillion   Super Cetro   Diamantes   Sovereign

Front Mark	Length	Ring Size	Retail per ea.	Qty. per Box	Retail per Box	Whole sale per Box	Wrapper Color C	N	M
La Perla	4-5/8″	42	.65	25	16.25	12.18		*	*
Duques	5-1/2″	42	.75	25	18.75	14.06		*	*
Bravo	5-3/4″	42	.80	25	20.00	15.00		*	*
Viva	6-1/2″	42	.95	25	23.75	17.81		*	*
Castillion	6-7/8″	36	.95	25	23.75	17.81		*	*
Super Cetro	7-1/4″	46	1.10	25	27.50	20.62		*	*
Diamantes	8″	42	1.30	25	32.50	24.38		*	*
Sovereign	7-1/4″	52	1.55	25	38.75	29.06		*	*

- A very well constructed high grade, hand made cigar.
- All long filler tobaccos and natural leaf wrappers from Honduras.
- Limited range of sizes shapes and colors.
- A quality cigar, but a bit overpriced. (The Super Cetro is a pretty good value.)
- Distributed by Peterson's Ltd of Carlstadt, N.J.

82

Flor De Mexico

LEW ROTHMAN RATING
Quality: ★ ★
Value: ★ ★ ★ ★

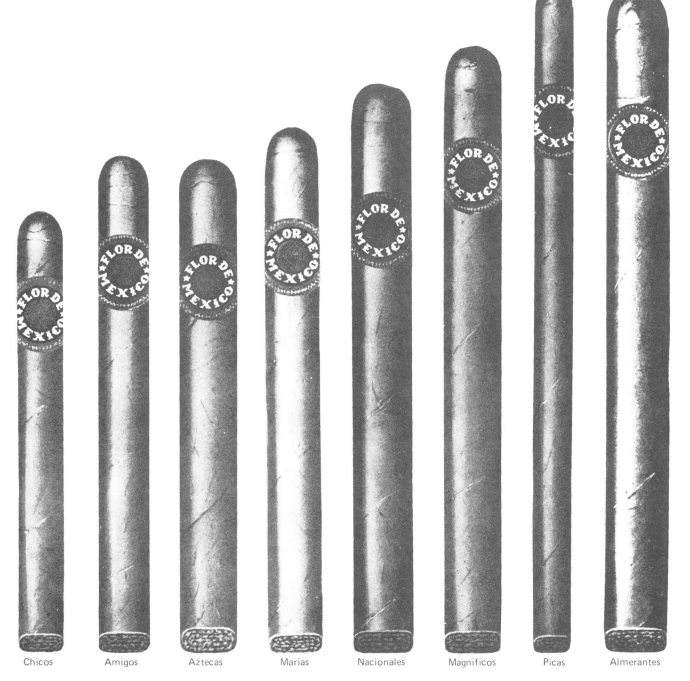

Chicos   Amigos   Aztecas   Marias   Nacionales   Magnificos   Picas   Almerantes

Front Mark	Length	Ring Size	Retail per ea.	Qty. per Box	Retail per Box	Whole sale per Box	Wrapper Color		
							C	N	M
Chicos	4-1/2''	36	2/.75	50	18.75	13.90		*	
Amigos	5-1/4''	38	.40	25	10.00	7.50		*	
Aztecas	5''	42	.55	25	13.75	9.95		*	
Marias	5-1/2''	40	.50	25	12.50	9.13		*	
Nacionales	6''	42	.60	25	15.00	11.00		*	
Magnificos	6-1/2''	42	.65	25	16.25	11.88		*	
Picas	7''	30	.50	25	12.50	9.13		*	
Almirantes	7''	44	.70	25	17.50	12.65		*	

- Historically a shabbily made cigar, however recent production has improved quality substantially. Hand made of long leaf tobaccos in San Andres, Tuxtla, Veracruz, Mexico.
- Very inexpensive for a hand made long filler cigar.
- Limited range of sizes in natural wrapper only.
- Several other sizes are available, however, the importer was ''too busy'' to supply information.
- Distributed by Pan American Cigars in ''Busy'' downtown Hoboken, N.J.

Arturo Fuente

| Palma 26 | Elegante | Conserva | Curly Head | Plaza Deluxe | Brevas-Royale |

Front Mark	Length	Ring Size	Retail per ea.	Qty. per Box	Retail per Box	Whole sale per Box	Wrapper Color		
							C	N	M
Palma 26	6''	42	.40	50	20.00	15.40	*	*	*
Elegante	5-1/4''	38	.35	50	17.50	13.25	*	*	*
Conserva	5-1/2''	43	.35	50	17.50	13.25	*	*	*
*Delight	6''	36	.35	50	17.50	13.25	*	*	*
†Curly Head	6-1/2''	43	2/.55	50	13.75	10.55	*	*	*
†Plaza Deluxe	6''	42	.26	50	13.00	10.00	*	*	*
†Brevas-Royalr	5-1/2''	42	2/.45	50	11.25	8.75	*	*	*

†Short filler.
*Not pictured.

- Excellent machine made cigars from the top of the line to the bottom, that accounts for the 5 stars rating. Their hand made cigars are just O.K. — three stars on bottom.
- Very good value throughout this cigar line, don't let their tasteless packaging turn you off this brand.
- An extremely broad range of sizes shapes and colors.
- Distribution very spotty so you'll have to hunt for them.
- A medium to heavy bodied cigar.
- Sold by Arturo Fuente of Tampa, Florida.

84

Arturo Fuente

Privada #1   Cazadore   #100   Nacionale   Corona Grande

Front Mark	Length	Ring Size	Retail per ea.	Qty. per Box	Retail per Box	Whole sale per Box	Wrapper Color		
							C	N	M
*Fuma	7"	44	.50	25	12.50	9.38	*	*	*
Privada #1	7"	46	.65	25	16.25	12.06	*	*	*
*19-12	6-1/4"	44	.50	50	25.00	18.75	*	*	*
Cazadore	6-1/4"	46	.50	50	25.00	18.75	*	*	*
#100	6-1/4"	43	.45	50	22.50	16.75	*	*	*
Nacionale	5-1/2"	42	.45	25	11.25	8.38	*	*	*
Corona Grande	6-1/4"	44	.40	25	10.00	7.70	*	*	*

*Not pictured.

- Excellent machine made cigars from the top of the line to the bottom, that accounts for the 5 stars rating. Their hand made cigars are just O.K. — three stars on bottom.
- Very good value throughout this cigar line, don't let their tasteless packaging turn you off this brand.
- An extremely broad range of sizes shapes and colors.
- Distribution very spotty so you'll have to hunt for them.
- A medium to heavy bodied cigar.
- Sold by Arturo Fuente of Tampa, Florida.

Arturo Fuente

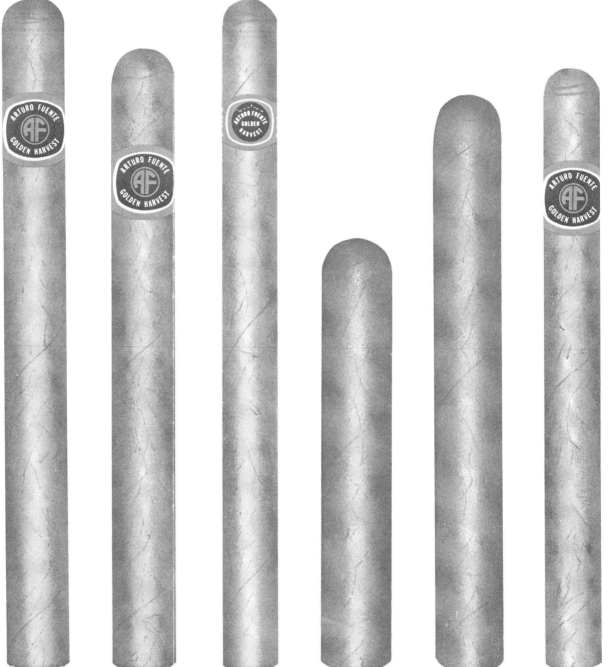

Churchills　　Coronas Imperial　　Panetela Fina　　Rothschild　　8-5-8　　Cetro

Front Mark	Length	Ring Size	Retail per ea.	Qty. per Box	Retail per Box	Whole sale per Box	Wrapper Color		
							C	N	M
*Canones	8-1/2''	52	1.50	10	15.00	11.25	*	*	*
*Dantes	6-7/8''	49	1.00	25	25.00	18.75	*	*	*
**Churchills	7''	45	.85	25	21.25	15.94	*	*	*
**Corona Imperial	6-1/2''	46	.75	25	18.75	14.06	*	*	*
**Panetela Fina	7''	39	.70	25	17.50	13.13	*	*	*
**Rothschild	4-1/2''	50	.70	25	35.00	26.25	*	*	*
**8-5-8	6''	47	.65	25	16.25	12.06	*	*	*
**Cetro	6-1/4''	42	.60	25	15.00	11.25	*	*	*

*Not pictured.
**Hand made.

- Excellent machine made cigars from the top of the line to the bottom, that accounts for the 5 stars rating. Their hand made cigars are just O.K. — three stars on bottom.
- Very good value throughout this cigar line, don't let their tasteless packaging turn you off this brand.
- An extremely broad range of sizes shapes and colors.
- Distribution very spotty so you'll have to hunt for them.
- A medium to heavy bodied cigar.
- Sold by Arturo Fuente of Tampa, Florida.

86

Garcia Vega

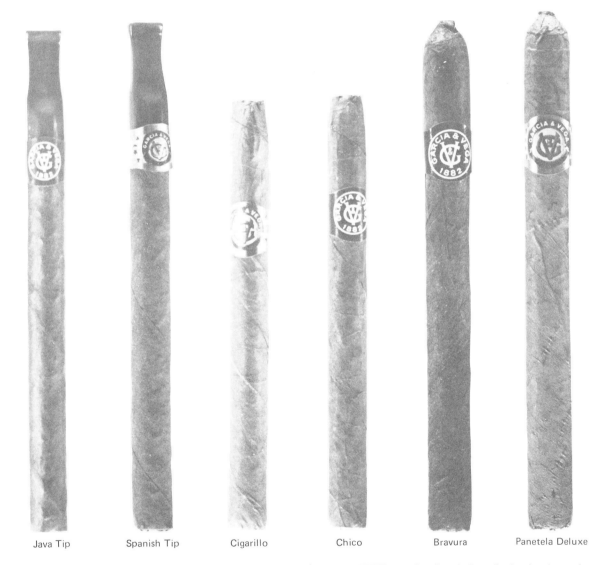

| Java Tip | Spanish Tip | Cigarillo | Chico | Bravura | Panetela Deluxe | Senator |

Front Mark	Length	Ring Size	Retail per ea.	Qty. per Box	Retail per Box	Whole sale per Box	Wrapper Color		
							C	N	M
Java Tip	4-1/4''	26	.08	100	8.00	6.00		*	
Spanish Tip	4-1/4''	26	.08	100	8.00	6.00	*		
Cigarillo	4-1/2''	28	.10	50	5.00	4.08	*		
Chico	4-1/2''	28	.10	50	5.00	4.08		*	
Bravura	5-1/2''	34	.16	50	8.00	6.20		*	
Panetela Deluxe	5-1/2''	34	.16	50	8.00	6.20	*		
Senator	4-5/8''	42	.16	50	8.00	6.20	*	*	*

Most sizes available in packs.

- A well made domestic cigar in a tremendous range of sizes.
- Wrapper selection somewhat limited, stay away from the tubed cigars unless you like to collect tubes. Good value in all other sizes.
- A very, very mild cigar possibly the best packaging in the entire cigar industry.
- Distributed by the Bayuk Cigar Co. of Florida.

Garcia Vega

| Maestro | Elegante | Gallante | Napoleon | Regalos | Fancy Tales | Washingtons |

Front Mark	Length	Ring Size	Retail per ea.	Qty. per Box	Retail per Box	Whole sale per Box	Wrapper Color		
							C	N	M
Maestro	5-3/8''	41	3/.50	50	8.33	7.05	*		
Elegante	6-1/2''	34	.20	50	10.00	7.50	*		
Gallante	6-1/2''	34	.20	50	10.00	7.50		*	
Napoleon	6''	42	.26	50	13.00	10.00	*	*	*
Regalos	5-3/4''	46	.26	50	13.00	10.00		*	
Fancy Tales	5-3/4''	45	2/.55	25	6.88	5.28	*	*	*
Washingtons	5-3/8''	41	3/1.00	30	10.00	7.71	*		

Most sizes available in packs.

- A well made domestic cigar in a tremendous range of sizes.
- Wrapper selection somewhat limited, stay away from the tubed cigars unless you like to collect tubes. Good value in all other sizes.
- A very, very mild cigar possibly the best packaging in the entire cigar industry.
- Distributed by the Bayuk Cigar Co. of Florida.

Garcia Vega

English Corona   Granada   Romero   Gran Corona   Gran Premio   Corona Larga   Churchill

Front Mark	Length	Ring Size	Retail per ea.	Qty. per Box	Retail per Box	Whole sale per Box	Wrapper Color		
							C	N	M
English Corona	5-3/8"	41	.35	30	10.50	8.10		*	
Granada	6-1/2"	34	.35	30	10.50	8.10	*		
Romero	6-1/2"	34	.35	30	10.50	8.10		*	
Gran Corona	6-1/4"	44	.40	30	12.00	9.30		*	
Gran Premio	6-1/4"	44	.40	30	12.00	9.30	*		
Corona Larga	6-3/8"	46	.45	25	11.25	8.63	*	*	*
Churchill	7-1/4"	46	.65	25	16.25	12.25	*	*	*

Most sizes available in packs.

- A well made domestic cigar in a tremendous range of sizes.
- Wrapper selection somewhat limited, stay away from the tubed cigars unless you like to collect tubes. Good value in all other sizes.
- A very, very mild cigar possibly the best packaging in the entire cigar industry.
- Distributed by the Bayuk Cigar Co. of Florida.

89

Gold Label

LEW ROTHMAN RATING
Quality: ★ ★ ★ ★
Value: ★ ★ ★

Swagger   Panatela Grande   Corona   Palma   Royale   Regal   Jaguar

Front Mark	Length	Ring Size	Retail per ea.	Qty. per Box	Retail per Box	Whole sale per Box	Wrapper Color		
							C	N	M
Swagger	4-21/32''	29	5/.65	60	6.50	6.48	*	*	
Panatela Grande	5-5/16''	37½	6/1.15	50	10.00	7.85	*		
Corona	5-11/16''	42½	5/.98	50	10.00	7.85		*	
Palma	6-1/16''	42	4/1.55	50	20.00	15.50	*		
Royale	5-9/16''	37½	4/1.35	30	10.50	8.10		*	
Regal	5-9/16''	37½	4/1.35	30	10.50	8.10	*		
Jaguar	6-1/4''	36	4/1.35	50	17.50	13.50	*		

- Well constructed machine made cigars.
- The nicest wrappers in their field.
- As with all all other brands, the tubed sizes do not represent a good ''cigar value'', but they're handy for keeping nuts and bolts and things in.
- Very mild.
- Presented in a nice selection of shapes and sizes, although wrapper choices are limited.
- Distributed by General Cigar Co. of N.Y.

90

Gold Label

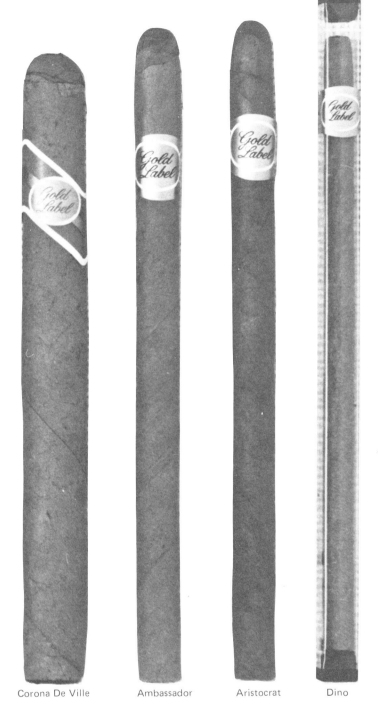

Corona De Ville   Ambassador   Aristocrat   Dino

Front Mark	Length	Ring Size	Retail per ea.	Qty. per Box	Retail per Box	Whole sale per Box	Wrapper Color		
							C	N	M
Corona De Ville	6-9/16''	45	3/1.59	25	13.75	10.31	*		
Ambassador	7''	32	5/.99	50	10.00	7.85		*	
Aristocrat	7''	32	5/.99	50	10.00	7.85	*		
Dino	6-11/16''	23	6/1.10	50		7.50		*	

- Well constructed machine made cigars.
- The nicest wrappers in their field.
- As with all all other brands, the tubed sizes do not represent a good ''cigar value'', but they're handy for keeping nuts and bolts and things in.
- Very mild.
- Presented in a nice selection of shapes and sizes, although wrapper choices are limited.
- Distributed by General Cigar Co. of N.Y.

91

Harrow's

| Esquire | Rothschild | Regent | No. 1 | Camelot | Londonderry |

Front Mark	Length	Ring Size	Retail per ea.	Qty. per Box	Retail per Box	Whole sale per Box	Wrapper Color		
							C	N	M
Esquire	6''	33	.45	10	4.50	3.37		*	
Rothschild	4-1/2''	46	.45	20	9.00	6.75		*	
Regent	5-9/16''	44	.55	20	11.00	8.25		*	
No. 1	6-1/4''	43	.65	20	13.00	9.75		*	
Camelot	7''	43	.75	20	15.00	11.25		*	
Londonderry	8''	48	.85	20	17.00	12.75		*	

- A well constructed hand made, long filler cigar.
- Produced in the Phillipines using a method of hand rolling in which tobacco leaf is twirled "spaghetti style" around two slender sticks, which are then withdrawn when the cigar is wrapped.
- An even burning cigar, nice and mild, but doesn't have the density Americans are used to.
- Value? Where are you gonna get a completely hand made cigar for 45 cents.
- Limited but well selected range of sizes, natural wrappers only.
- Made in the Phillipines and imported by Cigars by Santa Clara Ltd. of N.Y., N.Y.

92

House of Windsor

Palma   Panetela   Sportsman   Imperiale   Breva

Front Mark	Length	Ring Size	Retail per ea.	Qty. per Box	Retail per Box	Whole sale per Box	Wrapper Color		
							C	N	M
*Palma	6-1/2''	43	.25	50	12.50	9.75	*		
**Panetela	6-1/2''	33	3/.55	50	9.17	7.20	*		
**Sportsman	5''	43	3/.55	50	9.17	7.20	*		
*Imperiale	8''	42	.25	50	12.50	9.75	*		
***Breva	4-3/4''	34	.16	50	8.00	6.40	*		

* Also available in 4 packs.
** Also available in 5 packs.
*** 5 packs only.

- Very, very well constructed machine made cigars.
- Very limited range of sizes.
- Very mild
- Very cheap.
- Very nice.
- The Imperiale is one of the ''great'' buys still available to the public ''a giant heater for a quarter''.
- Distributed by House of Windsor, Yoe, Pa.

Hoyo De Monterrey

Demi Tasse   Rothschild   Sabrosa   No. 55   Margaritas   Super Hoyo   Coronas

Front Mark	Length	Ring Size	Retail per ea.	Qty. per Box	Retail per Box	Whole sale per Box	Wrapper Color		
							C	N	M
Demi Tasse	3-7/8''	39	.35	50	17.50	13.50		*	
Rothschild (A)(B)	4-1/2''	50	.70	50	35.00	26.25		*	*
*Sabrosa	5''	40	.35	50	17.50	13.13		*	*
*No. 55 (B)	5-1/4''	43	.40	50	20.00	15.40	*	*	*
Margaritas (B)	5-1/2''	29	.50	60	30.00	15.40	(B)		
Super Hoyo (B)	5-1/2''	44	.65	25	16.25	12.18	*	*	*
Coronas	5-1/2''	46	.75	25	18.75	14.06		*	

*Machine made sizes.
(A) Available in Maduro, Maduro.
(B) Available in rare Corojo.

- Extremely well hand made cigars of Honduran & Central American Tobaccos.
- Incredible range of sizes shapes and wrapper colors.
- A heavy bodied cigar - "This Ain't Kid Stuff".
- Excellent value throughout the line except for the Margarita which is really garbage.
- Distributed by Palicio & Co. of Englewood, N.J.

Hoyo De Monterrey

Cetros   Double Corona   No. 1   Churchill   Ambassador   Governors

Front Mark	Length	Ring Size	Retail per ea.	Qty. per Box	Retail per Box	Whole sale per Box	Wrapper Color		
							C	N	M
Cetro	6-7/8''	43	.90	25	22.50	16.88	*	*	*
Double Corona (A)(B)	6-3/4''	48	1.00	25	25.00	18.75	*	*	*
No. 1	6-1/2''	43	.80	25	20.00	15.00	*	*	*
Churchill (A)(B)	6-1/8''	44	.80	25	20.00	15.00	*	*	*
*Ambassador	6-1/8''	44	.60	25	15.00	11.25	*	*	*
Governors (A)(B)	6-1/8''	48	.90	25	22.50	16.88	*	*	*

*Machine made sizes.
(A) Available in Maduro, Maduro.
(B) Available in rare Corojo.

- Extremely well hand made cigars of Honduran & Central American Tobaccos.
- Incredible range of sizes shapes and wrapper colors.
- A heavy bodied cigar - ''This Ain't Kid Stuff''.
- Excellent value throughout the line except for the Margarita which is really garbage.
- Distributed by Palicio & Co. of Englewood, N.J.

95

Hoyo De Monterrey

LEW ROTHMAN RATING
Quality: ★ ★ ★ ★ ★
Value: ★ ★ ★ ★ ★

| Cafe Royale | Culebras | Delights | Presidentes | Cuban Largos | Sultans | Largo Elegante |

Front Mark	Length	Ring Size	Retail per ea.	Qty. per Box	Retail per Box	Whole sale per Box	Wrapper Color		
							C	N	M
Cafe Royale (tubed)(B)	5-1/4''	44	.90	10	9.00	6.75	(B)		
*Culebras	6''	35	.50	50	25.00	18.13		*	
*Delights (B)	6''	39	.40	50	20.00	15.40	*	*	*
Presidentes (A)(B)	8-1/2''	50	1.50	25	37.50	28.13	*	*	*
*Cuban Largos (B)	7-1/8''	47	.70	25	17.50	13.13	*	*	*
Sultans (A)	7-1/8''	52	1.35	25	33.75	25.31		*	*
*Largo Elegante	7-1/8''	32	.60	50	30.00	22.50	*	*	*

*Machine made sizes.
(A) Available in Maduro, Maduro.
(B) Available in rare Corojo.

- Extremely well hand made cigars of Honduran & Central American Tobaccos.
- Incredible range of sizes shapes and wrapper colors.
- A heavy bodied cigar - ''This Ain't Kid Stuff''.
- Excellent value throughout the line except for the Margarita which is really garbage.
- Distributed by Palicio & Co. of Englewood, N.J.

96

Imported La Coronas

Brevas   Finas   Largas   Reinas

Opulencias

Front Mark	Length	Ring Size	Retail per ea.	Qty. per Box	Retail per Box	Whole sale per Box	Wrapper Color		
							C	N	M
Brevas	5-1/2''	43	.90	25	22.50	16.88		*	
Finas	7''	38	.95	25	23.75	17.82		*	
Largas	6-1/2''	43	1.10	25	27.50	20.63		*	
Reinas	6''	50	1.10	25	27.50	20.63		*	
Opulencias	7-1/2''	50	1.40	25	35.00	26.25		*	

- A well constructed hand made cigar.
- Hand made in the Dominican Republic of long leaf tobaccos.
- A medium bodied cigar.
- Extremely limited range of sizes available in the natural wrapper only.
- An overpriced cigar by comparison to other cigars from the Dominican Republic.
- Distributed by the American Cigar Co. of N.Y., N.Y.

Joya de Nicaragua

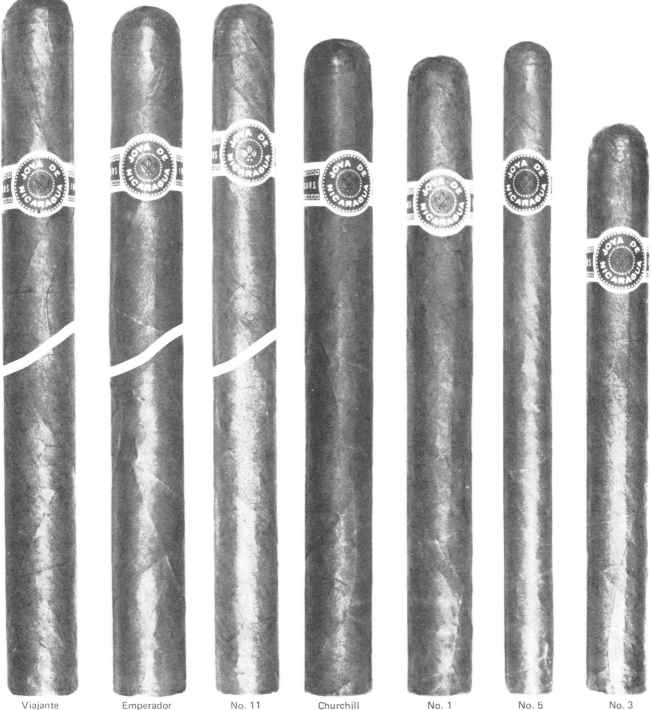

| Viajante | Emperador | No. 11 | Churchill | No. 1 | No. 5 | No. 3 |

Front Mark	Length	Ring Size	Retail per ea.	Qty. per Box	Retail per Box	Whole sale per Box	Wrapper Color		
							C	N	M
Viajante	8-1/8''	52	1.65	10	16.50	12.38		*	*
Emperador	7-3/4''	50	1.40	10	14.00	10.50		*	*
No. 11	7-1/2''	46	1.15	25	28.75	21.56		*	*
Churchill	6-7/8''	49	1.10	25	27.50	20.63	*	*	*
No. 1	6-5/8''	44	1.05	25	26.25	19.69	*	*	*
No. 5	6-7/8''	35	.85	25	21.25	15.94	*	*	*
No. 3	6''	44	.80	25	20.00	15.00	*	*	*

- An extremely well made, uniform high grade cigar.
- Medium to heavy bodied.
- An outstanding range of sizes, shapes, and wrapper selections.
- Excellent consistancy and uniformity of blend, taste, and appearance. You'll rarely encounter any difficulties with this brand.
- An expensive cigar, but well worth the price.
- Made in Nicaragua of Nicaraguan wrappers, fillers and binders.
- Distributed by A. Oppenheimer & Co. of Saddle Brook, N.J.

98

Joya de Nicaragua

No. 7   No. 6   Petit   Senorita   Presidente   Consul   Piccolino

Front Mark	Length	Ring Size	Retail per ea.	Qty. per Box	Retail per Box	Whole sale per Box	Wrapper Color		
							C	N	M
No. 7	7''	30	.75	25	18.75	14.06	*	*	*
No. 6	6''	41	.75	25	18.75	14.06	*	*	*
Petit	5-1/2''	38	.65	25	16.25	12.19	*	*	*
*Senorita	5-1/2''	35	.55	10	5.50	4.13		*	
Presidente	8''	54	2.00	5	10.00	7.50		*	*
Consul	4-1/2''	52	.95	25	23.75	17.81		*	*
Piccolino	4-1/8''	30	.35	10	3.50	2.80		*	

* Also available in boxes of 50.

- An extremely well made, uniform high grade cigar.
- Medium to heavy bodied.
- An outstanding range of sizes, shapes, and wrapper selections.
- Excellent consistancy and uniformity of blend, taste, and appearance. You'll rarely encounter any difficulties with this brand.
- An expensive cigar, but well worth the price.
- Made in Nicaragua of Nicaraguan wrappers, fillers and binders.
- Distributed by A. Oppenheimer & Co. of Saddle Brook, N.J.

La Corona

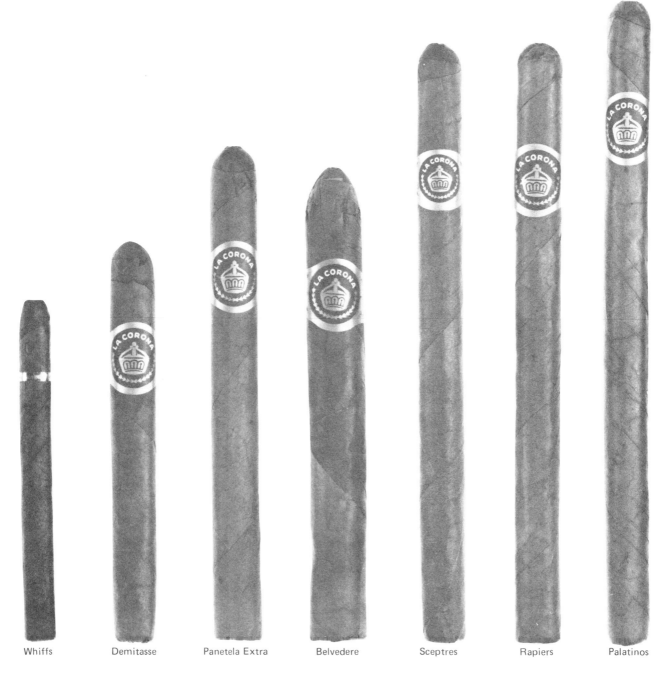

Whiffs   Demitasse   Panetela Extra   Belvedere   Sceptres   Rapiers   Palatinos

Front Mark	Length	Ring Size	Retail per ea.	Qty. per Box	Retail per Box	Whole sale per Box	Wrapper Color C	N	M
Whiffs	3-5/8''	24	10/1.40	100	14.00	11.10		*	
*Demitasse	4-7/32''	35	2/.35	60	11.50	8.34	*		
Panetela Extra	5-3/16''	35	3/.63	50	10.50	8.20	*		
*Belvedere	4-31/32''	41	3/.73	50	12.16	9.45	*	*	
*Sceptres	6-1/4''	32	3/.73	50	12.16	9.45	*	*	
*Rapiers	6-1/4''	33	2/.57	50	14.25	11.00	*		
Palatinos	6-11/16''	34	2/.57	50	14.25	11.00	*		

*Also available in 5 packs.

- La Corona is a mixed up brand with short filler, long filler, all tobacco, and homogenized sizes.
- It is a comparatively well made cigar with an overabundance of sizes shapes and colors.
- A little overpriced, but a good tasting uniform cigar day in and day out.
- Made with filler tobaccos from the West Indies, Central and South America and the Cameroons, wrappers from the Cameroons, South America, and Connecticut.
- Distributed by the American Cigar Co. of N.Y., N.Y.

100

La Corona

| Tapers | Americans | Naturals | Queens | Chicas | Palma Chicas | Corona |

Front Mark	Length	Ring Size	Retail per ea.	Qty. per Box	Retail per Box	Whole sale per Box	Wrapper Color		
							C	N	M
**Tapers	6-11/16''	34	2/.57	50	14.25	11.00	*		
***Americans (tubed)	6-1/4''	33	.40	30	12.00	9.24	*		
***Naturals (tubed)	6-1/4''	33	.40	30	12.00	9.24		*	
**Queens	5-9/16''	43	.45	50	22.50	17.10	*		
Chicas	5-1/4''	43	.45	50	22.50	17.10	*		
**Palma Chicas	5-15/16''	41	.45	50	22.50	17.10	*	*	
***Corona	6''	44	.60	50	30.00	22.50	*	*	

**Also available in 4 packs.
***Also available in 3 packs.

- La Corona is a mixed up brand with short filler, long filler, all tobacco, and homogenized sizes.
- It is a comparatively well made cigar with an overabundance of sizes shapes and colors.
- A little overpriced, but a good tasting uniform cigar day in and day out.
- Made with filler tobaccos from the West Indies, Central and South America and the Cameroons, wrappers from the Cameroons, South America, and Connecticut.
- Distributed by the American Cigar Co. of N.Y., N.Y.

La Corona

#200 Cristales #3 #400 #500 #600 #800

Front Mark	Length	Ring Size	Retail per ea.	Qty. per Box	Retail per Box	Whole sale per Box	Wrapper Color		
							C	N	M
*** #200	6''	44	.60	25	15.00	11.25		*	
Cristales (tubes)	5-5/32''	44	.60	25	15.00	11.25	*		
#3	6-5/16''	44	.65	25	16.25	12.18		*	
#400	6-1/2''	45	.65	25	16.25	12.18		*	
#500	6-2/3''	35	.70	25	17.50	13.13		*	
#600	6-29/32''	44	.75	25	18.75	14.05		*	
#800	6-31/32''	48	.80	25	20.00	15.00		*	

*** Also available in 3 packs.

- La Corona is a mixed up brand with short filler, long filler, all tobacco, and homogenized sizes.
- It is a comparatively well made cigar with an overabundance of sizes shapes and colors.
- A little overpriced, but a good tasting uniform cigar day in and day out.
- Made with filler tobaccos from the West Indies, Central and South America and the Cameroons, wrappers from the Cameroons, South America, and Connecticut.
- Distributed by the American Cigar Co. of N.Y., N.Y.

102

Macanudo

Baron De Rothschild

Earl of Lonsdale

Portofino

Prince Phillip

Somerset

Duke of Wellington

Front Mark	Length	Ring Size	Retail per ea.	Qty. per Box	Retail per Box	Whole sale per Box	Wrapper Color		
							C	N	M
**Baron De Rothschild	6-1/2''	42	1.30	25	32.50	24.38	*	*	*
Earl of Lonsdale	6-3/4''	38	1.25	25	31.25	23.44	*	*	*
Portofino	7''	34	1.30	25	32.50	24.38			*
Prince Phillip	7-1/2''	49	1.60	10	16.00	12.00	*	*	*
Somerset	7-3/4''	31	1.00	25	25.00	18.75	*	*	
Duke of Wellington	8-1/2''	38	2.25	15	33.75	25.31			*

**Also available in cedar cabinet of 50.

- An extremely well constructed hand made cigar.
- Good range of sizes, colors, and shapes.
- Made under the supervision of Ramon Cifuentes of Partagas fame in Havana, Cuba.
- You really can't make a much better cigar than the Macanudo (Macanudo means a really good thing).
- Extremely light in body - very high in price.
- Occasional difficulties with the Lonsdale size in the Maduro wrapper.
- "one of my favorites" distributed by Culbro Corp., N.Y., N.Y.

Macanudo

LEW ROTHMAN RATING
Quality: ★ ★ ★ ★ ★
Value: ★ ★ ★ ½

| Caviar | Petit Corona | Lord Claridge | Claybourne | Duke of Devon | Amatista |

Front Mark	Length	Ring Size	Retail per ea.	Qty. per Box	Retail per Box	Whole sale per Box	Wrapper Color		
							C	N	M
Caviar	4''	36	.60	50	30.00	22.50		*	
*Petit Corona	5''	38	.70	25	17.50	13.13		*	
Lord Claridge	5-1/2''	38	1.00	25	25.00	18.75	*	*	
Claybourne	6''	31	.80	25	20.00	15.00	*	*	
**Duke of Devon	5-1/2''	42	1.20	25	30.00	22.50	*	*	*
Amatista (humidor jar)	6-1/4''	42	1.40	50	70.00	52.50	*	*	

- An extremely well constructed hand made cigar.
- Good range of sizes, colors, and shapes.
- Made under the supervision of Ramon Cifuentes of Partagas fame in Havana, Cuba.
- You really can't make a much better cigar than the Macanudo (Macanudo means a really good thing).
- Extremely light in body - very high in price.
- Occasional difficulties with the Lonsdale size in the Maduro wrapper.
- "one of my favorites" distributed by Culbro Corp., N.Y., N.Y.

*Also available in boxes of 5.
**Also available in cedar cabinet of 50.

104

Madrigal

| Cremas | Corona Extra | Soberano | Churchill | Palma de Mayorca | Presidente |

Front Mark	Length	Ring Size	Retail per ea.	Qty. per Box	Retail per Box	Whole sale per Box	Wrapper Color		
							C	N	M
Cremas	4-1/2''	42	.70	25	17.50	13.13	*	*	*
Corona Extra	5-1/2''	46	.90	25	22.50	16.88	*	*	*
Soberano	7-3/4''	50	1.60	25	40.00	30.00	*	*	*
Churchill	7''	49	1.30	25	32.50	24.38	*	*	*
Palma de Mayorca	8''	38	1.10	25	27.50	20.63	*	*	*
Presidente	8-1/2''	50	1.85	25	46.25	34.69	*	*	*

- A fairly well constructed long filler, hand made cigar, sold by a very nice guy.
- A good cigar in a handsome array of sizes and colors, sold at very competitive prices (stay away from the 2 big sizes).
- Hand made of Honduran Tobaccos and imported by Intercontinental Cigars of San Diego.
- If this brand were marketed by one of the big cigar companies instead of an independant ''little guy'' it would be a big seller. ''Keep pluggin, Nate''.

Madrigal

| Corona Gorda | Panatela Especial | Linda | Nom Plus | Cazadore |

Front Mark	Length	Ring Size	Retail per ea.	Qty. per Box	Retail per Box	Whole sale per Box	Wrapper Color		
							C	N	M
Corona Gorda	6-1/4''	44	.95	25	23.75	17.81	*	*	*
Panatela Especial	6-3/4''	35	.85	25	21.25	15.94	*	*	*
Linda	5-1/2''	38	.75	25	18.75	14.06	*	*	*
Nom Plus	4-1/2''	50	.85	25	21.25	15.94	*	*	*
*Cazadore	6-1/4''	44	.65	25	32.50	24.38		*	*

- A fairly well constructed long filler, hand made cigar, sold by a very nice guy.
- A good cigar in a handsome array of sizes and colors, sold at very competitive prices (stay away from the 2 big sizes).
- Hand made of Honduran Tobaccos and imported by Intercontinental Cigars of San Diego.
- If this brand were marketed by one of the big cigar companies instead of an independant ''little guy'' it would be a big seller. ''Keep pluggin, Nate''.

*Blended with short filler.

Mocha

Panetela   Petite Corona   Corona   Stiletto   DBL Corona

Lonsdale   Ambassador   Churchill

Front Mark	Length	Ring Size	Retail per ea.	Qty. per Box	Retail per Box	Whole sale per Box	Wrapper Color		
							C	N	M
Panetela	6''	36	.60	20	12.00	9.00		*	
Petite Corona	5''	43	.60	20	12.00	9.00		*	
Corona	5-1/2''	45	.70	20	14.00	10.50		*	
Stiletto	7''	36	.70	20	14.00	10.50		*	
DBL Corona	5-5/8''	50	.75	20	15.00	11.25		*	
Lonsdale	6-1/2''	44	.80	20	16.00	12.00		*	
Ambassador	8''	44	.90	20	18.00	13.50		*	
Churchill	7-1/2''	50	1.00	20	20.00	15.00		*	

- A well constructed hand made cigar.
- A heavy bodied rich smoke.
- Made of long filler tobaccos in the Jamastran Valley of Honduras.
- Economy bundle packing.
- A good buy for the price especially the Churchill.
- Distributed by Cigars by Santa Clara of N.Y., N.Y.

Montecruz

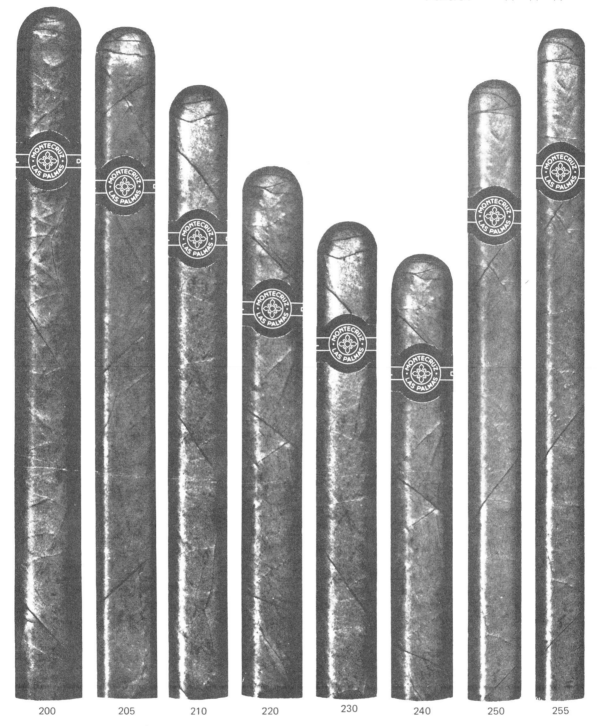

200   205   210   220   230   240   250   255

Front Mark	Length	Ring Size	Retail per ea.	Qty. per Box	Retail per Box	Whole sale per Box	Wrapper Color		
							C	N	M
200	7-1/4''	46	1.65	10	16.50	12.38	*	*	
205	7''	42	1.50	25	37.50	28.13	*	*	
210	6-1/2''	42	1.35	25	33.75	25.31	*	*	
220	5-1/2''	42	1.25	25	31.25	23.44	*	*	
230	5''	42	1.00	25	25.00	18.75	*	*	
240	4-3/4''	44	.95	25	23.75	17.82	*	*	
250	6-1/2''	38	1.30	25	32.50	24.38	*	*	
255	7''	36	1.35	25	33.75	25.31	*	*	

- A very well made, uniform, high grade cigar.
- A truly incredible array of sizes, shapes, and colors to please even the most demanding smoker.
- Made in the Canary Islands, Spain, by Compania Insular de Tobaccos of Latin American filler tobaccos with Connecticut shade grown and African Cameroon wrappers.
- A fine cigar but extremely expensive especially in all its smaller sizes.
- Caution the Montecruz as well as all other cameroon wrapped cigars must be handled with care, as the Cameroon is a thin, brittle wrapper which is easily damaged.
- Steer away from the two short filler sizes, the Junior and Chico as the other sizes are better values and better cigars.
- Distributed by Alfred Dunhill, N.Y., N.Y.

108

Montecruz

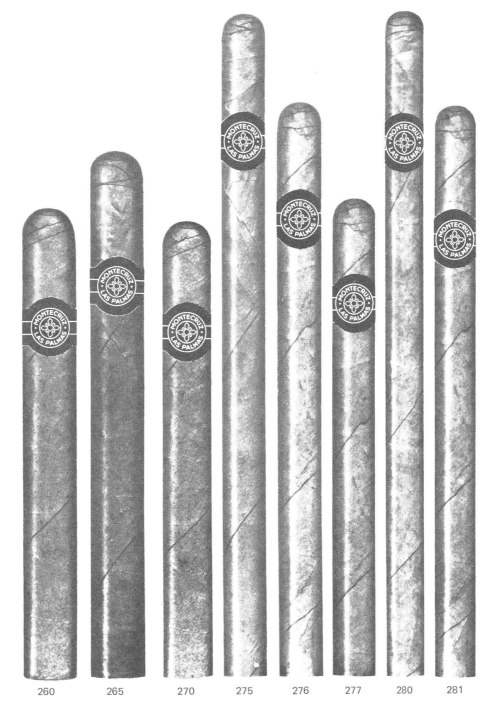

260   265   270   275   276   277   280   281

Front Mark	Length	Ring Size	Retail per ea.	Qty. per Box	Retail per Box	Whole sale per Box	Wrapper Color		
							C	N	M
260	5''	40	1.00	25	25.00	18.75	*	*	
265	5-1/2''	38	1.00	25	25.00	18.75	*	*	
270	4-3/4''	35	.75	50	37.50	28.13	*	*	
275	7''	32	1.05	25	26.25	19.69	*	*	
276	6''	32	.95	25	23.75	17.82	*	*	
277	5''	32	.85	25	21.25	15.94	*	*	
280	7''	33	1.00	25	25.00	18.75	*	*	
281	6''	33	.90	25	22.50	16.88	*	*	

- A very well made, uniform, high grade cigar.
- A truly incredible array of sizes, shapes, and colors to please even the most demanding smoker.
- Made in the Canary Islands, Spain, by Compania Insular de Tobaccos of Latin American filler tobaccos with Connecticut shade grown and African Cameroon wrappers.
- A fine cigar but extremely expensive especially in all its smaller sizes.
- Caution the Montecruz as well as all other cameroon wrapped cigars must be handled with care, as the Cameroon is a thin, brittle wrapper which is easily damaged.
- Steer away from the two short filler sizes, the Junior and Chico as the other sizes are better values and better cigars.
- Distributed by Alfred Dunhill, N.Y., N.Y.

Montecruz

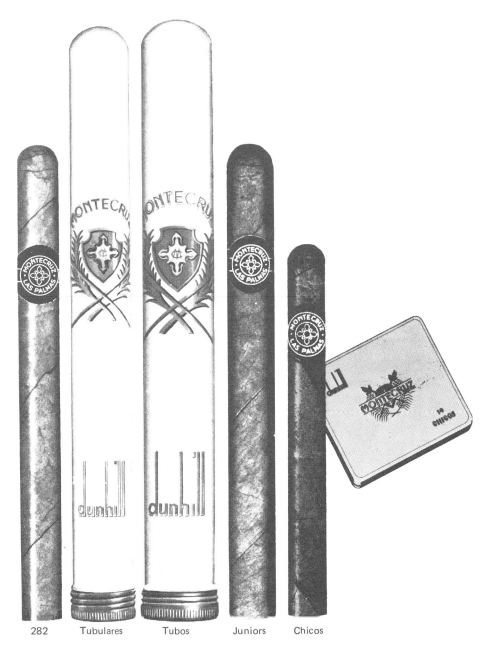

282   Tubulares   Tubos   Juniors   Chicos

Front Mark	Length	Ring Size	Retail per ea.	Qty. per Box	Retail per Box	Whole sale per Box	Wrapper Color		
							C	N	M
282	5''	33	.80	25	20.00	15.00	*	*	
Tubulares	6''	38	1.30	25	32.50	24.38	*	*	
Tubos	6''	42	1.40	25	35.00	26.25	*	*	
*201	6''	46	1.40	25	35.00	26.25	*	*	
*Individuales	7-1/4''	48	4.50	10	45.00	33.75		*	
**Juniors	4-7/8''	33	.40	50	20.00	16.00		*	
**Chicos	3-7/8''	28	.40	100	40.00	32.00		*	

*Not pictured
**Short filler, machine made.

- A very well made, uniform, high grade cigar.
- A truly incredible array of sizes, shapes, and colors to please even the most demanding smoker.
- Made in the Canary Islands, Spain, by Compania Insular de Tobaccos of Latin American filler tobaccos with Connecticut shade grown and African Cameroon wrappers.
- A fine cigar but extremely expensive especially in all its smaller sizes.
- Caution the Montecruz as well as all other cameroon wrapped cigars must be handled with care, as the Cameroon is a thin, brittle wrapper which is easily damaged.
- Steer away from the two short filler sizes, the Junior and Chico as the other sizes are better values and better cigars.
- Distributed by Alfred Dunhill, N.Y., N.Y.

Muriel Cigars

Magnum   Coronas   Senators   Panetela   Coronella King   Blunts

Front Mark	Length	Ring Size	Retail per ea.	Qty. per Box	Retail per Box	Whole sale per Box	Wrapper Color		
							C	N	M
Magnum	5-1/16''	46	5/.69	50	6.90	5.70		*	
*Coronas	5-5/8''	42	5/.65	50	6.50	5.30		*	
*Senators	4-3/16''	42	5/.50	50	5.00	4.08		*	
Panetela	5-1/2''	37	5/.65	50	6.50	5.30		*	
Coronella King	6-1/8''	30	5/.50	50	5.00	4.08		*	
Blunts	4-7/8''	42	5/.50	50	5.00	4.08		*	

* Also available in cannisters of 50.

- One of America's most recognized popular priced cigars, and "procurers" of the most sensational looking women for their ads. The Muriel is a super mild cigar with a tremendous range of sizes and shapes.
- They are wrapped in Connecticut Shade Grown and Florida wrappers. The Filler tobaccos come from South America, the Carribbean and Asia. "Pick one up and give 'em a try."
- Manufactured in Pennsylvania and Puerto Rico.
- Distributed by the Consolidated Cigar Co. of N.Y., N.Y.

Muriel Cigars

Air Tips   Coronella   Tipalet

Front Mark	Length	Ring Size	Retail per ea.	Qty. per Box	Retail per Box	Whole sale per Box	Wrapper Color		
							C	N	M
Air Tips	5-1/32''	30	5/.37	50	3.70	3.10		*	
Coronella	4-5/8''	30	5/.39	50	3.90	3.30		*	
Tipalet	5-1/8''	30	5/.39	50	3.70	3.10		*	

- One of America's most recognized popular priced cigars, and "procurers" of the most sensational looking women for their ads. The Muriel is a super mild cigar with a tremendous range of sizes and shapes.
- They are wrapped in Connecticut Shade Grown and Florida wrappers. The Filler tobaccos come from South America, the Carribbean and Asia. "Pick one up and give 'em a try."
- Manufactured in Pennsylvania and Puerto Rico.
- Distributed by the Consolidated Cigar Co. of N.Y., N.Y.

Partagas

Purito   #4   #6   #3   #2

Front Mark	Length	Ring Size	Retail per ea.	Qty. per Box	Retail per Box	Whole sale per Box	Wrapper Color		
							C	N	M
Purito	4-3/16''	32	.40	100	40.00	30.00		*	
#4	5''	38	1.10	25	27.50	20.63		*	
#6	6''	34	1.10	25	27.50	20.63		*	
#3	5-1/4''	43	1.25	25	31.25	23.44		*	
#2	5-3/4''	43	1.35	25	33.75	25.31		*	

- An unbelievably well constructed hand made cigar.
- Limited, but well chosen range of sizes and shapes.
- Natural wrappers only.
- Very, very, expensive, especially the 8-9-8 size.
- Made under the Supervision of Ramon Cifuentes, a legendary Cuban Master.
- Distributed by Culbro Corp. of N.Y., N.Y.

113

Partagas

| #1 | Sabrosa | #898 | #10 |

Front Mark	Length	Ring Size	Retail per ea.	Qty. per Box	Retail per Box	Whole sale per Box	Wrapper Color		
							C	N	M
#1	6-3/4''	43	1.50	25	37.50	28.13		*	
Sabrosa (tubed)	5-7/8''	44	1.50	20	30.00	22.50		*	
#898	6-7/8''	44	1.75	25	43.75	32.80		*	
#10	7-1/2''	49	1.75	10	17.50	13.12		*	

- An unbelievably well constructed hand made cigar.
- Limited, but well chosen range of sizes and shapes.
- Natural wrappers only.
- Very, very, expensive, especially the 8-9-8 size.
- Made under the Supervision of Ramon Cifuentes, a legendary Cuban Master.
- Distributed by Culbro Corp. of N.Y., N.Y.

114

Perfecto Garcia

London Tower   San Souci   Churchill Corona   Brilliantes   Senator

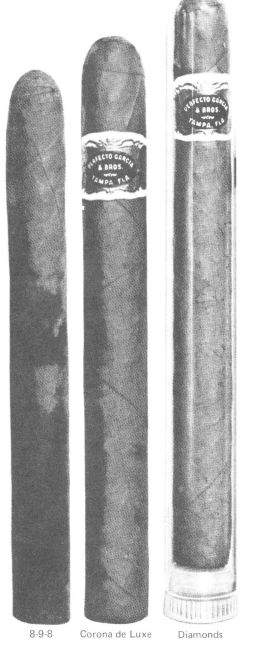

8-9-8   Corona de Luxe   Diamonds

Front Mark	Length	Ring Size	Retail per ea.	Qty. per Box	Retail per Box	Whole sale per Box	Wrapper Color		
							C	N	M
†*Individuales	8-1/2''	50	1.35	10	13.50	10.13	*	*	*
*London Tower	7-1/4''	45	.75	50	37.50	28.00	*	*	*
*San Souci	7-1/4''	45	.70	25	17.50	13.13	*	*	*
*Churchill Corona	6-1/2''	47	.70	25	17.50	13.13	*	*	*
Brilliantes (Glass tube)	6-13/16''	41	.75	10	7.50	5.60	*	*	*
†Weddings (Glass tube)	5-15/16''	41	.75	25	18.75	14.00	*	*	*
†*No. 900	6-3/16''	42	.55	25	13.75	10.58	*	*	*
†*Lords of England	5-1/4''	42	.60	50	30.00	22.75	*	*	*
†*222	5-3/4''	45	.65	25	16.25	12.13	*	*	*
†*Fancy Tales	6-3/4''	38	.65	25	16.25	12.13	*	*	*
Diamonds (Glass tube)	5-15/16''	41	.60	20	12.00	9.10	*	*	*
†Washingtons	6-13/16''	42	.55	25	13.75	10.58	*	*	*
†*Piccadilly	6-1/4''	46	.55	20	11.00	8.46	*	*	*
8-9-8	6''	42	.55	25	13.75	10.58	*	*	*
†Cremas	6-1/4''	42	.45	25	11.25	8.50	*	*	*
†No. 15	6-1/4''	41	.45	50	22.50	17.00	*	*	*
Corona de Luxe	6-1/4''	45	.45	25	11.25	8.50	*	*	*
†Cazadores	6-1/4''	46	.50	50	25.00	19.25	*	*	*
†Hyde Park	5-11/16''	45	.50	50	25.00	19.25	*	*	*
Senator (Alum. tube)	5-1/4''	41	.40	25	10.00	7.70	*	*	*

*Hand made size.
†Not pictured.

- Wow! where do you start with a brand like this. The bulk of this brand is well made long filler, machine made merchandise. In addition there are many hand made sizes.
- An absolutely vast selection of shapes, sizes, and colors. There's no one in the business that comes close to this manufacturer in variety of product.
- Incredibly ugly packaging.
- Distribution of this cigar is very spotty, and most dealers have never heard of 75% of their listed sizes.
- If you can find this brand, buy it. It's an excellent value in almost every size.
- Distributed by Perfecto Garcia & Co., Evanston, Ill.

Perfecto Garcia

Ensigns

Palmas

Waldorfs

Morro Castle

Queens

Commodores   Sublimes   Buccaneers

Front Mark	Length	Ring Size	Retail per ea.	Qty. per Box	Retail per Box	Whole sale per Box	Wrapper Color		
							C	N	M
†Cedros #2	6-3/4''	38	.45	25	11.25	8.50	*	*	*
Ensigns	6-3/4''	38	2/.75	25	9.38	7.20	*	*	*
†No. 72	6-3/4''	38	.40	50	20.00	15.40	*	*	*
Palmas	6''	41	.35	50	17.50	13.25	*	*	*
Waldorfs	5-3/4''	46	3/1.00	25	8.33	6.43	*	*	*
Morro Castle	5-1/4''	46	3/1.00	50	16.66	12.86	*	*	*
Queens	5-1/4''	42	3/1.00	50	16.66	12.86	*	*	*
†Capri	6-1/4''	38	2/.55	50	13.75	10.55	*	*	*
†Corona Chica	5-1/4''	42	.30	50	15.00	11.50	*	*	*
Commodores	5-1/4''	42	2/.55	50	13.75	10.55	*	*	*
Sublimes	4-3/4''	42	.22	50	11.00	8.45	*	*	*
†Diplomats	5-7/8''	39	.22	50	11.00	8.45	*	*	*
†P.G. Panetela	5-1/32''	38	.22	50	11.00	8.45	*	*	*
†Classic Panetela	5-1/32''	35	.20	50	10.00	7.70	*	*	*
†Jefferson's	4-9/16''	43	.20	50	10.00	7.70	*	*	*
Buccaneers	6-1/4''	36	3/.55	50	9.17	7.05	*	*	*
†Ambassadors	4-1/2''	42	.15	50	7.50	5.75	*	*	*
†Babies	4-1/8''	40	2/.25	50	6.25	5.00	*	*	*
†Cigarillos	4-7/16''	29	.08	50	4.00	3.20	*	*	*
†Gems-Tips	4-7/16''	30	2/.25	50	6.25	5.00	*	*	*
†No. 85	6-13/16''	42	.50	50	25.00	19.25	*	*	*

†Not pictured.

- Wow! where do you start with a brand like this. The bulk of this brand is well made long filler, machine made merchandise. In addition there are many hand made sizes.
- An absolutely vast selection of shapes, sizes, and colors. There's no one in the business that comes close to this manufacturer in variety of product.
- Incredibly ugly packaging.
- Distribution of this cigar is very spotty, and most dealers have never heard of 75% of their listed sizes.
- If you can find this brand, buy it. It's an excellent value in almost every size.
- Distributed by Perfecto Garcia & Co., Evanston, Ill.

Perfecto Garcia
(Selection Superior)

Numero 1   Numero 2   Numero 3   Numero 4   Numero 5

Numero 6   Numero 7   Numero 8

Front Mark	Length	Ring Size	Retail per ea.	Qty. per Box	Retail per Box	Whole sale per Box	Wrapper Color		
							C	N	M
*Numero 1	5-1/4''	42	.55	25	13.75	10.58	*	*	*
*Numero 2	5-1/4''	42	.55	25	13.75	10.58	*	*	*
*Numero 3	6-3/16''	42	.60	25	15.00	11.38	*	*	*
*Numero 4	7''	38	.70	25	17.50	13.13	*	*	*
*Numero 5	5-11/16''	45	.60	25	15.00	11.38	*	*	*
*Numero 6	8-1/2''	46	1.35	10	13.50	10.13	*	*	*
*Numero 7	6-3/4''	38	.70	10	7.00	5.25	*	*	*
*Numero 8	7-1/4''	45	.80	25	20.00	15.00	*	*	*
†*Lord Churchill	6-1/4''	46	.80	25	20.00	15.00	*	*	*
†*Double Corona	6-3/4''	50	.90	25	22.50	16.88	*	*	*
†*Sir Lonsdale	6-1/2''	42	.75	25	18.75	14.00	*	*	*
†*Baron de Rothschild	4-1/2''	50	.65	50	33.00	24.25	*	*	*
†*No. 101	6-1/4''	46	.50	25	12.50	19.25	*	*	*
†*Petit Corona	5-1/4''	42	.55	25	13.75	10.58	*	*	*
†*Magnum-10	7-1/4''	48	1.25	10	12.50	9.25	*	*	*
†*Caprichos	6''	46	.75	25	18.75	14.00	*	*	*

*Hand made size.
†Not pictured.

- Wow! where do you start with a brand like this. The bulk of this brand is well made long filler, machine made merchandise. In addition there are many hand made sizes.
- An absolutely vast selection of shapes, sizes, and colors. There's no one in the business that comes close to this manufacturer in variety of product.
- Incredibly ugly packaging.
- Distribution of this cigar is very spotty, and most dealers have never heard of 75% of their listed sizes.
- If you can find this brand, buy it. It's an excellent value in almost every size.
- Distributed by Perfecto Garcia & Co., Evanston, Ill.

117

Phillies

Juniors   Tips   Cheroots   King Cheroots   Blunts   Panatellas

Front Mark	Length	Ring Size	Retail per ea.	Qty. per Box	Retail per Box	Whole sale per Box	Wrapper Color		
							C	N	M
Juniors	4-1/2''	28	.06	50	3.00	2.55		*	
Tips	5-3/8''	28½	.06	50	3.00	2.55		*	
Cheroots	4-11/16''	32	2/.15	50	3.75	3.00		*	
King Cheroots	5-7/16''	32	2/.15	50	3.75	3.00		*	
Blunts	4-5/8''	42	.10	50	5.00	4.08		*	
Panatellas	5-1/2''	34	.10	50	5.00	4.08		*	

- A well constructed machine made cigar.
- A good range of sizes.
- Very mild.
- The cigar of the 80's (most Phillies smokers are about 80 years old).
- The Titan may very well be the greatest value anywhere in "Cigar Land".
- Distributed by Bayuk Cigars of Ft. Lauderdale, Fla.

Phillies

Sports   Coronas   Perfectos   Titan

Front Mark	Length	Ring Size	Retail per ea.	Qty. per Box	Retail per Box	Whole sale per Box	Wrapper Color		
							C	N	M
Sports	4-13/16''	42	.10	50	5.00	4.08		*	
Coronas	5-3/8''	41	2/.23	50	5.75	4.50		*	
Perfectos	5-3/4''	43	2/.25	50	6.25	5.00		*	
Titan	6-1/4''	44	2/.25	50	6.25	5.00		*	

A well constructed machine made cigar.
A good range of sizes.
Very mild.
The cigar of the 80's (most Phillies smokers are about 80 years old).
The Titan may very well be the greatest value anywhere in "Cigar Land".
Distributed by Bayuk Cigars of Ft. Lauderdale, Fla.

119

Por Larranaga

LEW ROTHMAN RATING
Quality: ★ ★ ★ ★
Value: ★ ★

| Petit Cetros | Grandees | Cetros | Cinco Vegas | Nacionales |

Front Mark	Length	Ring Size	Retail per ea.	Qty. per Box	Retail per Box	Whole sale per Box	Wrapper Color		
							C	N	M
Petit Cetros	5''	38	.90	25	22.50	16.88		*	
Grandees	6-7/8''	46	1.30	25	32.50	24.38		*	
Cetros	6-7/8''	42	1.20	25	30.00	22.50		*	
Cinco Vegas	6-5/8''	44	1.15	25	28.75	21.57		*	
Nacionales	5-1/2''	42	1.00	25	25.00	18.75		*	

- A very well constructed, uniform, hand made cigar
- Severely limited range of shapes, sizes and colors.
- A great old time Cuban trademark, but wow! they really want to make you pay for it. The price of this cigar is an insult to the knowledgeable cigar smoker.
- Distributed by Faber Coe & Gregg of Clifton, N.J.

120

Primo Del Rey

#100   #1   #3   #2   #6   Royal   #5

Front Mark	Length	Ring Size	Retail per ea.	Qty. per Box	Retail per Box	Whole sale per Box	Wrapper Color		
							C	N	M
#100	4-1/2''	48	.80	25	20.00	15.00	*	*	*
#1	6-13/16''	42	.85	25	21.25	15.94	*	*	*
#3	6-13/16''	37	.75	25	18.75	14.06	*	*	*
#2	6-1/4''	42	.70	25	17.50	13.13	*	*	*
#6	6''	40	.65	25	16.25	12.19	*	*	*
Royal	5-3/4''	40	.60	25	15.00	11.25	*	*	*
#5	5-3/4''	42	.55	25	13.75	10.31	*	*	*

- A well constructed hand made cigar.
- Very, very mild.
- A truly staggering array of sizes, shapes and colors. Available in Double Claro, Natural, and Maduro.
- Good consistancy and uniformity of construction, blend, taste, and appearance.
- One of the best buys in a hand made cigar today.
- A fast growing brand due to a combination of good quality and very reasonable prices. Watch out for the Cazadore - it's a bummer.
- Made in La Romana, Dominican Republic of Caribbean fillers. Wrapped in African Cameroon & Connecticut shade grown wrappers.
- Distributed by the Moro Cigar Corp. of N.Y.

121

Primo Del Rey

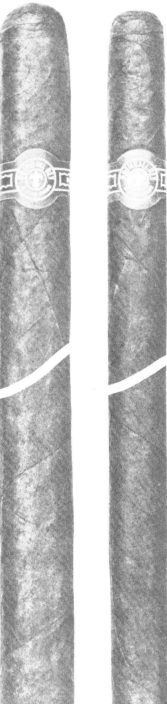
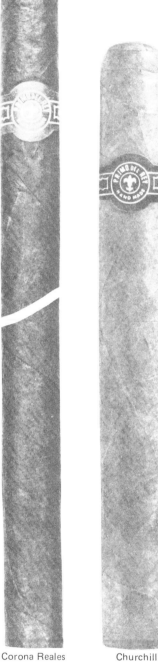

| Soberano | Corona Reales | Churchill | President | Imperiales | Palmas | Monarch |

Front Mark	Length	Ring Size	Retail per ea.	Qty. per Box	Retail per Box	Whole sale per Box	Wrapper Color		
							C	N	M
Soberano	7-1/2''	48	1.35	25	33.75	25.31	*	*	*
Corona Reales	8''	42	1.20	25	30.00	22.50	*	*	*
Churchill	6-1/4''	48	1.00	25	25.00	18.75	*	*	*
President	6-13/16''	44	1.00	25	25.00	18.75	*	*	*
Imperials	6-1/16''	46	.90	25	22.50	16.88	*	*	*
Palmas	8''	38	.95	25	23.75	17.82	*	*	*
Monarch	5-3/4''	46	.85	25	21.25	15.94	*	*	*

- A well constructed hand made cigar.
- Very, very mild.
- A truly staggering array of sizes, shapes and colors. Available in Double Claro, Natural, and Maduro.
- Good consistancy and uniformity of construction, blend, taste, and appearance.
- One of the best buys in a hand made cigar today.
- A fast growing brand due to a combination of good quality and very reasonable prices. Watch out for the Cazadore - it's a bummer.
- Made in La Romana, Dominican Republic of Caribbean fillers. Wrapped in African Cameroon & Connecticut shade grown wrappers.
- Distributed by the Moro Cigar Corp. of N.Y.

122

Primo Del Rey

Panetela Extra   #4   Cazadore   Panetela

Front Mark	Length	Ring Size	Retail per ea.	Qty. per Box	Retail per Box	Whole sale per Box	Wrapper Color		
							C	N	M
Panetela Extra	5-15/16''	36	.55	25	13.75	10.31	*	*	*
#4	5-1/2''	42	.55	25	13.75	10.31	*	*	*
Cazadore	6-1/6''	43	.55	50	27.50	21.00	*	*	*
Panetela	5-3/8''	36	.50	25	12.50	9.38			*

- A well constructed hand made cigar.
- Very, very mild.
- A truly staggering array of sizes, shapes and colors. Available in Double Claro, Natural, and Maduro.
- Good consistancy and uniformity of construction, blend, taste, and appearance.
- One of the best buys in a hand made cigar today.
- A fast growing brand due to a combination of good quality and very reasonable prices. Watch out for the Cazadore - it's a bummer.
- Made in La Romana, Dominican Republic of Caribbean fillers. Wrapped in African Cameroon & Connecticut shade grown wrappers.
- Distributed by the Moro Cigar Corp. of N.Y.

Punch

President   Casa Grande   Super Cetro   Largo Elegantes   Double Coronas   No. 1   Punch   Amatista

Front Mark	Length	Ring Size	Retail per ea.	Qty. per Box	Retail per Box	Whole sale per Box	Wrapper Color		
							C	N	M
President (A)(B)	8-1/2''	50	1.50	25	37.50	28.13	*	*	*
*Casa Grande (B)	7''	46	.70	25	17.50	13.13	*	*	*
Super Cetro	6-7/8''	43	.90	25	22.50	16.88	*	*	*
*Largo Elegantes	7-1/8''	32	.60	50	30.00	22.50	*	*	*
Double Coronas(A)(B)	6-3/4''	48	1.00	25	25.00	18.75	*	*	*
No. 1	6-1/2''	43	.80	25	20.00	15.00	*	*	*
Punch (A)(B)	6-1/8''	44	.80	25	20.00	15.00	*	*	*
*Amatista (B)	6-1/8''	44	.60	25	15.00	11.25	*	*	*

(A) Also available in Maduro, Maduro.
(B) Also available in rare Corojo.
*Machine made size.

- Extremely well constructed hand made cigars.
- Great range of sizes, incredible range of wrappers.
- A heavy cigar for real cigar smokers. Packs a punch.
- Super Cetro is the sleeper size — I've never seen a better cigar in terms of consistency in construction.
- Great value.
- Distributed by Palicio & Co. of Englewood, N.J.

Punch

Pitas   No. 75   Elites   London Club   Rothschild

Front Mark	Length	Ring Size	Retail per ea.	Qty. per Box	Retail per Box	Whole sale per Box	Wrapper Color		
							C	N	M
Pitas (A)(B)	6-1/8"	48	.90	25	22.50	16.88	*	*	*
No. 75 (B)	5-1/2"	44	.65	25	16.25	12.18	*	*	*
*Elites (B)	5-1/4"	44	.40	50	20.00	15.40	*	*	*
*London Club (B)	4-7/8"	40	.35	50	17.50	13.13	*	*	*
Rothschild (A)(B)	4-1/2"	50	.70	50	35.00	26.25		*	*
**Pyramide	5-3/4"	46	.65	25	16.25	12.18	*	*	*
**Napoleon	7-1/8"	47	1.00	25	25.00	18.75	*	*	*

(A) Also available in Maduro, Maduro.
(B) Also available in rare Corojo.
*Machine made size.
**Not pictured.

- Extremely well constructed hand made cigars.
- Great range of sizes, incredible range of wrappers.
- A heavy cigar for real cigar smokers. Packs a punch.
- Super Cetro is the sleeper size — I've never seen a better cigar in terms of consistency in construction.
- Great value.
- Distributed by Palicio & Co. of Englewood, N.J.

125

Ramon Allones

Redondos   A   B   BB   C   D   E   Privado

Front Mark	Length	Ring Size	Retail per ea.	Qty. per Box	Retail per Box	Whole sale per Box	Wrapper Color		
							C	N	M
Redondos	7''	49	1.65	10	16.50	12.38		*	
A	7''	45	1.55	25	38.75	29.06		*	
B	6-1/2''	42	1.40	25	35.00	26.25		*	
BB	6''	45	1.45	25	36.25	27.19		*	
C	5-1/2''	42	1.30	25	32.50	24.38		*	
D	5''	42	1.20	25	30.00	22.50		*	
E	6''	38	1.25	25	31.25	23.44		*	
Privado Tube	7''	34	1.35	25	33.75	25.31		*	

- An unusually well constructed cigar.
- Mild, medium bodied, and flavorful.
- Decent selection of sizes and shapes. Medium brown natural wrappers only.
- Rigid control of construction, blend, taste, and appearance.
- Very, very, very expensive (overpriced).
- Made in Bond in Jamaica West Indies under the supervision of Ramon Cifuentes. Cifuentes is one of the world most reknown manufacturers, and works for Montego Y Ca., a division of the General Cigar Co. Ramon Allones is distributed by Alfred Dunhill of London Inc.
- Ramon Allones bears the name of the original trademark formerly made in Havana, Cuba.
- It is as fine a cigar, as is available today.

Rey Del Mundo

LEW ROTHMAN RATING
Quality: ★ ★ ★ ★ ★
Value: ★ ★ ★

No. 1   No. 2   No. 3   No. 4   Plantation   Prime Minister   Emperor

Front Mark	Length	Ring Size	Retail per ea.	Qty. per Box	Retail per Box	Whole sale per Box	Wrapper Color		
							C	N	M
No. 1	6-3/4''	42	1.05	25	26.25	19.69		*	*
No. 2	6-1/4''	42	.95	25	23.75	17.82		*	*
No. 3	5-3/4''	42	.85	25	21.25	15.94		*	*
No. 4	5-1/8''	44	.75	25	18.75	14.07		*	*
Plantation	6-3/4''	30	.75	25	18.75	14.07		*	*
Prime Minister	6-5/8''	48	1.05	25	26.25	19.69		*	*
*Emperor	8-1/2''	52	1.60	25	40.00	30.00		*	*

* Also available in boxes of 10.

- An extremely well constructed, hand made cigar.
- Tightly packed and heavy bodied.
- A good range of sizes, shapes, and colors.
- Somewhat overpriced for a Honduran cigar.
- Beware of stale cigars, as this brand is most often found in small shops with inadequate humidification and/or sale volume.
- Distributed by Faber, Coe, and Gregg of Clifton, N.J.

Rey Del Mundo

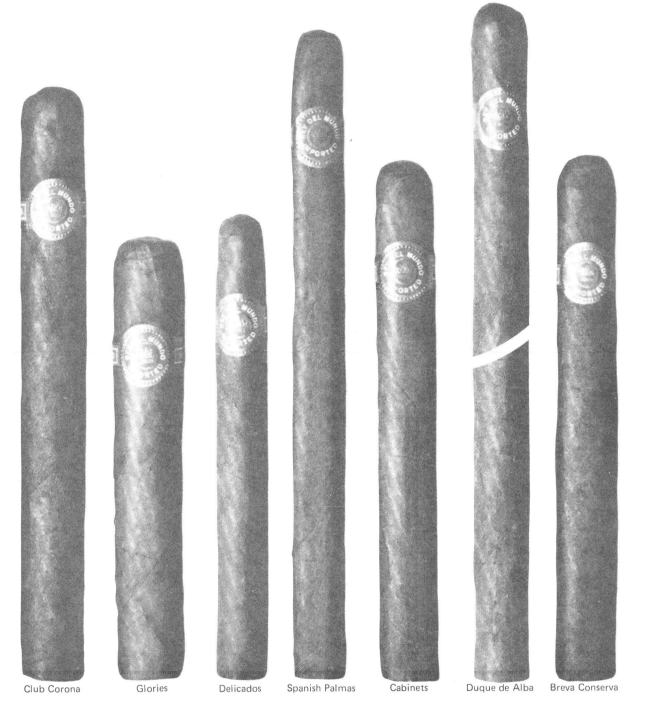

Club Corona   Glories   Delicados   Spanish Palmas   Cabinets   Duque de Alba   Breva Conserva

Front Mark	Length	Ring Size	Retail per ea.	Qty. per Box	Retail per Box	Whole sale per Box	Wrapper Color		
							C	N	M
Club Corona	6-1/8''	44	.85	25	21.25	15.94		*	*
Glorias	4-1/2''	46	.75	50	37.50	28.13		*	*
Delicados	4-3/4''	38	.55	50	27.50	20.64		*	
Spanish Palmas	6-3/4''	36	.80	25	20.00	15.00		*	
Cabinets	5-1/4''	39	.70	25	17.50	26.26		*	
Duque de Alba	7-3/4''	38	1.00	25	25.00	18.75		*	
Breva Conserva	5-3/8''	43	.80	50	40.00	30.00			*

- An extremely well constructed, hand made cigar.
- Tightly packed and heavy bodied.
- A good range of sizes, shapes, and colors.
- Somewhat overpriced for a Honduran cigar.
- Beware of stale cigars, as this brand is most often found in small shops with inadequate humidification and/or sale volume.
- Distributed by Faber, Coe, and Gregg of Clifton, N.J.

Rigoletto Cigars

Londonaire   Black Jack   Palma Cedar   Kings Maduro   Natural Coronas   Palma Grande   Panetela Grande

Front Mark	Length	Ring Size	Retail per ea.	Qty. per Box	Retail per Box	Whole sale per Box	Wrapper Color		
							C	N	M
Londonaire	6-1/4''	42	.40	30	12.00	9.00		*	
Black Jack	5-1/2''	48	.30	50	15.00	11.50			*
Palma Cedar	6-1/4''	42	.30	50	15.00	11.50		*	
Kings Maduro	6-1/4''	42	.23	50	11.50	8.70			*
Natural Coronas	6-1/4''	42	.23	50	11.50	8.70		*	
Palma Grande	6-1/4''	42	.20	60	12.00	9.42	*		
*Panetela Grande	6-1/4''	38	.20	60	12.00	9.42	*		

All sizes except Londonaire available in packs.
*Not pictured

- A well made, uniform, popular priced cigar.
- Rigolettos are made from a blend of Latin American Tobaccos.
- Severely limited range of sizes, shapes, and colors.
- Very competitively priced.
- Steer clear of the Londonaire and Palma Cedar. They're the reason this brand didn't get 5 stars for value.
- Distributed by M & N Cigar Manufacturers of Tampa, Florida.

129

Robt. Burns

| Cigarillo | Panatela | Macduff | Black Watch | Tiparillo |

Front Mark	Length	Ring Size	Retail per ea.	Qty. per Box	Retail per Box	Whole sale per Box	Wrapper Color		
							C	N	M
Cigarillo	4-17/32''	27	5/.35	50	3.50	3.00		*	
Panatela	5-9/16''	37	5/.85	50	8.50	7.05		*	
Macduff	5-9/16''	37½	3/.95	30	9.50	7.80		*	
Black Watch	6''	41½	3/1.15	30	11.50	9.30		*	
Tiparillo	5-1/8''	27	5/.35	50	3.50	3.00		*	

- A well constructed machine made cigar.
- Extremely mild, and immensly popular.
- Blended Domestic and Caribbean Tobaccos.
- Limited range of sizes shapes and colors.
- They ought to make a corona size without a tube.
- Distributed by the General Cigar Corp. of N.Y., N.Y.

130

Roi-Tan

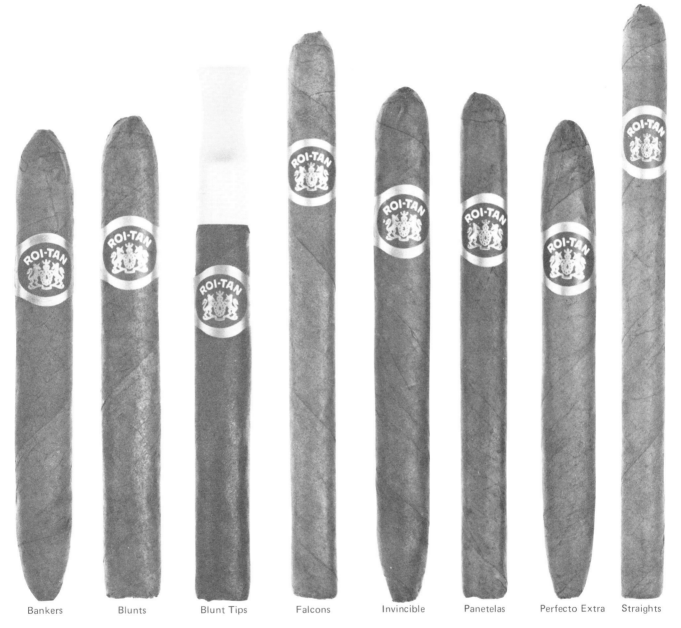

Bankers   Blunts   Blunt Tips   Falcons   Invincible   Panetelas   Perfecto Extra   Straights

Front Mark	Length	Ring Size	Retail per ea.	Qty. per Box	Retail per Box	Whole sale per Box	Wrapper Color		
							C	N	M
Bankers	4-31/32''	41	3/.47	50	7.50	6.20		*	
Blunts	4-31/32''	41	3/.47	50	7.50	6.20		*	
Blunt Tips	4-16/32''	41	3/.47	50	7.50	6.20		*	
Falcons	5-15/16''	33	3/.47	50	7.50	6.20		*	
Invincible	5-13/32''	40	3/.47	50	7.50	6.20		*	
Panetelas	5-3/16''	35	3/.47	50	7.50	6.20		*	
Perfecto Extra	4-31/32''	41	3/.47	50	7.50	6.20		*	
Straights	6-3/16''	31	3/.47	50	7.50	6.20		*	

All Roi-Tans are also available in 5 packs.

- A very well made, uniform popular priced cigar.
- This exceptionally mild cigar is available in a light natural wrapper.
- Lots of nice sizes and the prices won't hurt you. My hat's off to the American Cigar Co. on this brand - 20th century cigars at 19th century prices.
- Made with domestic, South American, and Caribbean fillers with South American and Connecticut wrappers.
- Distributed by the American Cigar Co. of N.Y., N.Y.

131

Roi-Tan

Charger   Dudes   Scout   Trump   Tips   Golfers

Front Mark	Length	Ring Size	Retail per ea.	Qty. per Box	Retail per Box	Whole sale per Box	Wrapper Color		
							C	N	M
Charger	5-7/16''	40	.10	50	5.00	4.00		*	
Dudes	5-15/16''	26	.10	50	5.00	4.00		*	
Scout	5-1/32''	43	.10	50	5.00	4.00		*	
Trump	4-3/8''	31	5/.45	50	4.50	3.70		*	
Tips	4-7/16''	27	5/.39	50	3.90	3.20		*	
Cherry Tips	4-7/16''	27	5/.39	50	3.90	3.20		*	
Golfers	3-7/8''	31	.07	50	3.50	2.80		*	

All Roi-Tans are also available in 5 packs.

- A very well made, uniform popular priced cigar.
- This exceptionally mild cigar is available in a light natural wrapper.
- Lots of nice sizes and the prices won't hurt you. My hat's off to the American Cigar Co. on this brand - 20th century cigars at 19th century prices.
- Made with domestic, South American, and Caribbean fillers with South American and Connecticut wrappers.
- Distributed by the American Cigar Co. of N.Y., N.Y.

Royal Jamaica

| Quatro | Pirate | Coronita | Bucaneer | Petit Corona | Churchill Minor |

Front Mark	Length	Ring Size	Retail per ea.	Qty. per Box	Retail per Box	Whole sale per Box	Wrapper Color		
							C	N	M
Quatro	4''	32	4/1.95	50	24.50	18.50		*	
Pirate	4-1/2''	30	3/1.70	50	28.50	21.25		*	
Coronita	4-1/2''	38	.75	25	18.75	14.06		*	
Bucaneer	5-1/2''	30	.80	25	20.00	15.00		*	
Petit Corona	5''	40	.85	25	21.25	15.95		*	
Churchill Minor	4-1/2''	49	.95	25	23.75	17.63		*	

- A well constructed, high grade, hand made cigar.
- Exceptionally mild, with an almost sweet nutty taste which is unique to this brand alone.
- An incredible range of sizes and shapes. Natural medium brown wrapper only.
- Packaged in heavy locking Spanish cedar chests of highly aromatic Spanish cedar.
- Excellent consistancy of blend, taste, and appearance. Construction not always consistant, and while you will find "soft" spots, or soft cigars from time to time, even these will burn well as the filler tobaccos have been laid in very well.
- Expensive, especially in the smaller sizes.
- Made by Jamaica Tobacco Co. and distributed in the U.S.A. by Pan American Cigar Co.

133

Royal Jamaica

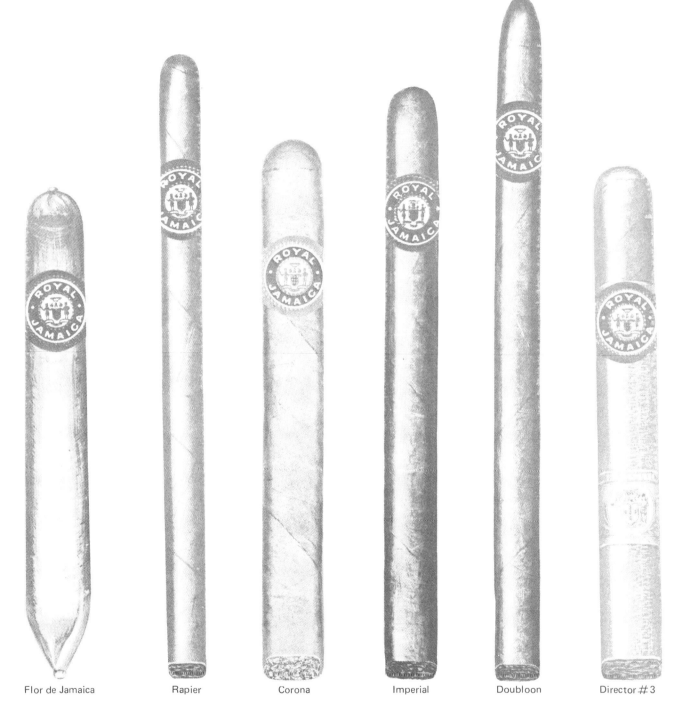

| Flor de Jamaica | Rapier | Corona | Imperial | Doubloon | Director #3 |

Front Mark	Length	Ring Size	Retail per ea.	Qty. per Box	Retail per Box	Whole sale per Box	Wrapper Color		
							C	N	M
Flor de Jamaica	5''	42	.95	25	23.75	17.82		*	
Rapier	6-1/2''	28	1.00	25	15.00	18.50		*	
Corona	5-1/2''	40	1.00	25	25.00	18.75		*	
Imperial	6''	36	1.00	25	25.00	18.75		*	
Doubloon	7''	30	1.05	25	26.25	19.69		*	
Director #3	5-1/4''	40	1.10	25	27.50	20.38		*	

- A well constructed, high grade, hand made cigar.
- Exceptionally mild, with an almost sweet nutty taste which is unique to this brand alone.
- An incredible range of sizes and shapes. Natural medium brown wrapper only.
- Packaged in heavy locking Spanish cedar chests of highly aromatic Spanish cedar.
- Excellent consistancy of blend, taste, and appearance. Construction not always consistant, and while you will find ''soft'' spots, or soft cigars from time to time, even these will burn well as the filler tobaccos have been laid in very well.
- Expensive, especially in the smaller sizes.
- Made by Jamaica Tobacco Co. and distributed in the U.S.A. by Pan American Cigar Co.

Royal Jamaica

Park Drive	Royal Corona	Navarro	Musketeer	N.Y. Plaza	Corona Grande

Front Mark	Length	Ring Size	Retail per ea.	Qty. per Box	Retail per Box	Whole sale per Box	Wrapper Color		
							C	N	M
Park Drive	6''	36	1.10	25	27.50	20.38		*	
Royal Corona	6''	40	1.10	25	27.50	20.63		*	
Navarro	6-3/4''	34	1.10	25	27.50	20.38		*	
Musketeer	7-3/4''	32	1.15	25	28.75	21.08		*	
N.Y. Plaza	6''	40	1.15	25	28.75	21.55		*	
Corona Grande	6-1/2''	42	1.20	25	30.00	22.50		*	

- A well constructed, high grade, hand made cigar.
- Exceptionally mild, with an almost sweet nutty taste which is unique to this brand alone.
- An incredible range of sizes and shapes. Natural medium brown wrapper only.
- Packaged in heavy locking Spanish cedar chests of highly aromatic Spanish cedar.
- Excellent consistancy of blend, taste, and appearance. Construction not always consistant, and while you will find "soft" spots, or soft cigars from time to time, even these will burn well as the filler tobaccos have been laid in very well.
- Expensive, especially in the smaller sizes.
- Made by Jamaica Tobacco Co. and distributed in the U.S.A. by Pan American Cigar Co.

Royal Jamaica

Magnum	Corona Immensa	Ascot	Petit Corona Tube	Fancy Tale	Park Lane

Front Mark	Length	Ring Size	Retail per ea.	Qty. per Box	Retail per Box	Whole sale per Box	Wrapper Color		
							C	N	M
Magnum	6''	45	1.20	25	30.00	22.25		*	
Corona Immensa	6''	47	1.25	25	31.25	23.25		*	
Ascot	71/2''	38	1.25	25	31.25	23.44		*	
Petit Corona Tube	5''	40	1.25	25	31.25	23.45		*	
Fancy Tale	6-1/2''	40	1.30	25	32.50	24.38		*	
Park Lane	6''	47	1.30	25	32.50	24.38		*	

- A well constructed, high grade, hand made cigar.
- Exceptionally mild, with an almost sweet nutty taste which is unique to this brand alone.
- An incredible range of sizes and shapes. Natural medium brown wrapper only.
- Packaged in heavy locking Spanish cedar chests of highly aromatic Spanish cedar.
- Excellent consistancy of blend, taste, and appearance. Construction not always consistant, and while you will find ''soft'' spots, or soft cigars from time to time, even these will burn well as the filler tobaccos have been laid in very well.
- Expensive, especially in the smaller sizes.
- Made by Jamaica Tobacco Co. and distributed in the U.S.A. by Pan American Cigar Co.

Royal Jamaica

LEW ROTHMAN RATING
Quality: ★ ★ ★ ★
Value: ★ ★ ★

Director #1   Double Corona   Giant Corona   Churchill   #10 Downing St.   Goliath

Front Mark	Length	Ring Size	Retail per ea.	Qty. per Box	Retail per Box	Whole sale per Box	Wrapper Color		
							C	N	M
Director #1	6"	45	1.30	25	32.50	24.38		*	
*Double Corona	7"	45	1.45	25	36.25	27.19		*	
Giant Corona	7-1/2"	49	1.55	25	38.75	29.06		*	
*Churchill	8"	51	1.75	25	43.75	32.81		*	
#10 Downing St.	10-1/2"	51	2.50	10	25.00	18.75		*	
Goliath	9"	64	2.95	10	29.50	22.15		*	

* Available in cabinet of 50.
* Available in individuale slide top boxes (Box of 20 cigars retail $2.85 each).

- A well constructed, high grade, hand made cigar.
- Exceptionally mild, with an almost sweet nutty taste which is unique to this brand alone.
- An incredible range of sizes and shapes. Natural medium brown wrapper only.
- Packaged in heavy locking Spanish cedar chests of highly aromatic Spanish cedar.
- Excellent consistancy of blend, taste, and appearance. Construction not always consistant, and while you will find "soft" spots, or soft cigars from time to time, even these will burn well as the filler tobaccos have been laid in very well.
- Expensive, especially in the smaller sizes.
- Made by Jamaica Tobacco Co. and distributed in the U.S.A. by Pan American Cigar Co.

Santa Clara

I   II   III   IV   V   VI

Front Mark	Length	Ring Size	Retail per ea.	Qty. per Box	Retail per Box	Whole sale per Box	Wrapper Color C	N	M
I	7''	51	1.35	20	27.00	20.25		*	*
II	6-1/2''	48	1.20	20	24.00	18.00		*	*
III	6-5/8''	43	1.10	20	22.00	16.50		*	*
IV	5''	44	.85	20	17.00	12.75		*	*
V	6''	44	.95	20	19.00	14.25		*	*
VI	6''	51	1.05	20	21.00	15.75		*	*

All sizes also available in boxes of 10.
All sizes packed is locking, heavy cedar cabinets.

- An unusually well made, uniform, hand made high grade cigar.
- Good range of sizes, shapes, and colors.
- Dynamite packaging.
- Hand made of long filler tobaccos from the San Andres Region of Mexico.
- Several unusual shapes.
    The No. VI is the thickest ring gauge available anywhere in a 6 inch cigar.
    The No. VII is the thinnest hand made cigar anywhere.
    The Quino is the lowest priced completely hand made long filler cigar on the market today.
- A product of Santa Clara S.A., San Andres, Mexico.
- Distributed by Associated Imports, Lynbrook, N.Y.

138

Santa Clara

VII   VIII   Quino

Front Mark	Length	Ring Size	Retail per ea.	Qty. per Box	Retail per Box	Whole sale per Box	Wrapper Color		
							C	N	M
VII	5-1/2''	25	.50	20	10.00	7.50		*	
VIII	6-1/2''	30	.80	20	16.00	12.00		*	
Quino	4-1/4''	30	.35	20	7.00	5.25		*	

- An unusually well made, uniform, hand made high grade cigar.
- Good range of sizes, shapes, and colors.
- Dynamite packaging.
- Hand made of long filler tobaccos from the San Andres Region of Mexico.
- Several unusual shapes.
   The No. VI is the thickest ring gauge available anywhere in a 6 inch cigar.
   The No. VII is the thinnest hand made cigar anywhere.
   The Quino is the lowest priced completely hand made long filler cigar on the market today.
- A product of Santa Clara S.A., San Andres, Mexico.
- Distributed by Associated Imports, Lynbrook, N.Y.

All sizes also available in boxes of 10.
All sizes packed in locking, heavy cedar cabinets.

Siboney

No. 22   No. 33   No. 44   No. 55   No. 66   No. 77

Front Mark	Length	Ring Size	Retail per ea.	Qty. per Box	Retail per Box	Whole sale per Box	Wrapper Color		
							C	N	M
No. 22	5-15/16''	34	.65	25	16.25	12.19		*	
No. 33	5-1/5''	42	.70	25	17.50	13.13		*	
No. 44	6-1/4''	42	.75	25	18.75	14.06		*	
No. 55	6-3/4''	37	.80	25	20.00	15.00		*	
No. 66	6-3/4''	42	.85	25	21.25	15.94		*	
No. 77	6-3/4''	46	.95	25	23.75	17.82		*	

- A well constructed hand made cigar.
- Very mild.
- Severely limited range of sizes. Available in medium brown natural only.
- The singularly ugliest package ever produced, the designer of this package should be flogged.
- A consistantly uniform cigar in terms of taste, blend and construction.
- ''Ho Hum'' best describes this brand. En Garde for stale cigars, as this brand has not exactly enjoyed earth shaking success.
- Made in La Romana. Dominican Republic of Caribbean Fillers and African Cameroon and Connecticut shade grown wrappers.
- Prices are quite reasonable.
- Distributed by the Moro Cigar Corp. of N.Y.

140

Suerdieck

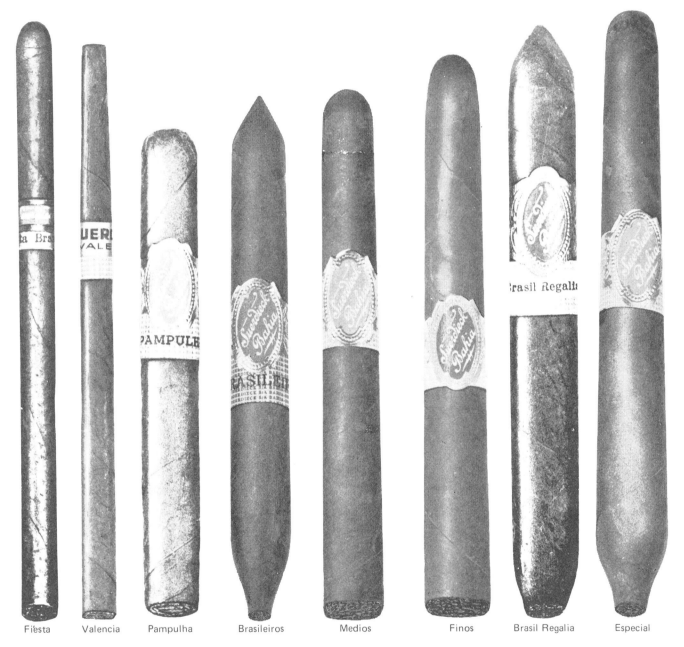

Fiesta   Valencia   Pampulha   Brasileiros   Medios   Finos   Brasil Regalia   Especial

Front Mark	Length	Ring Size	Retail per ea.	Qty. per Box	Retail per Box	Whole sale per Box	Wrapper Color		
							C	N	M
Fiesta	6''	30	.25	50	12.50	9.50		*	*
Valencia	6''	30	.25	50	12.50	9.25		*	
Pampulha	5''	38	.25	50	12.50	9.75		*	
Brasileiros	5-1/2''	38	.40	25	10.00	7.50		*	
Medios	5-1/2''	40	.40	25	10.00	7.50			*
Finos	5-3/4''	42	.45	20	9.00	6.74			*
Brasil Regalia	6''	45	.45	20	9.00	6.74			*
Especial	6-1/2''	42	.60	50	30.00	22.50			*

- A fairly well made cigar from Brazil.
- Nice and mild.
- Good range of sizes and shapes.
- The best buy anywhere, from any country when judged by cost versus quality.
- You can't go wrong buying any size of this brand.
- Distributed by Pan American Cigars of Hoboken, N.J.

141

Suerdieck

LEW ROTHMAN RATING
Quality: ★ ★ ★
Value: ★ ★ ★ ★ ★

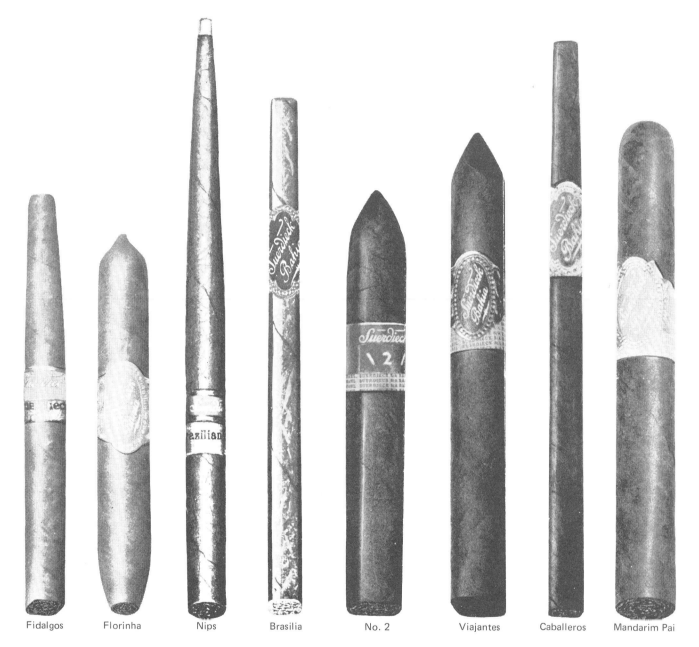

Fidalgos   Florinha   Nips   Brasilia   No. 2   Viajantes   Caballeros   Mandarim Pai

Front Mark	Length	Ring Size	Retail per ea.	Qty. per Box	Retail per Box	Whole sale per Box	Wrapper Color		
							C	N	M
Fidalgos	4-1/2''	28	.15	50	7.50	5.50		*	*
Florinha	4''	32	.20	50	10.00	7.05			*
Brasilia	5-1/4''	30	.20	50	10.00	7.50			*
Nips	6''	30	.20	50	10.00	7.70		*	*
No. 2	4-1/4''	36	.20	50	10.00	7.70			*
Viajantes	4-3/4''	36	.20	50	10.00	7.70			*
Caballeros	6''	30	.25	50	12.50	8.60			*
Mandarim Pai	5''	38	.25	50	12.50	8.90			*

- A fairly well made cigar from Brazil.
- Nice and mild.
- Good range of sizes and shapes.
- The best buy anywhere, from any country when judged by cost versus quality.
- You can't go wrong buying any size of this brand.
- Distributed by Pan American Cigars of Hoboken, N.J.

Tabacalera

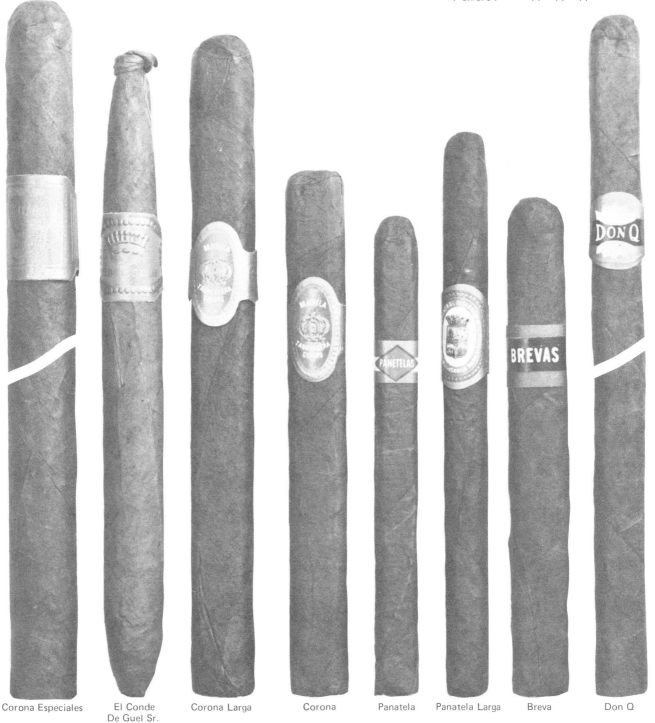

Corona Especiales   El Conde De Guel Sr.   Corona Larga   Corona   Panatela   Panatela Larga   Breva   Don Q

Front Mark	Length	Ring Size	Retail per ea.	Qty. per Box	Retail per Box	Whole sale per Box	Wrapper Color		
							C	N	M
Corona Especiales	7-7/8''	48	.65	25	16.25	12.06		*	
El Conde De Guel Sr.	6-3/4''	Torpedo	.50	25	12.50	9.38		*	
Corona Larga	6-7/8''	42	.55	25	13.75	10.31		*	
Corona	5-1/2''	43	.50	25	12.50	9.38		*	
Panatela	5-1/8''	33	.30	50	15.00	11.25		*	
Panatela Larga	5-7/8''	33	.35	25	8.75	6.56		*	
Breva	5-1/4''	42	.30	50	15.00	11.25		*	
Don Q	7-3/8''	33	.50	25	12.50	9.38		*	

- Tabacalera one of the best of the Phillipine cigars being imported today. It is a uniform "quasi" hand made cigar.
- (The Phillipine method of hand rolling cigars is completely different than any other. Tobaccos are rolled up on two slender sticks which are withdrawn after the cigar is made. The result is a cigar with much less density than the American public is accustomed to, and very rapid burning characteristics.
- Tabacalera is a reasonably priced, milder than average cigar.
- Good range of sizes, natural wrappers only.
- Extremely hard to find due to very poor distribution.
- Distributed by Petersons Ltd of Carlstadt, N.J.

143

Te-Amo

Relaxation   Meditation   Torero   No. 4   Picador

Front Mark	Length	Ring Size	Retail per ea.	Qty. per Box	Retail per Box	Whole sale per Box	Wrapper Color		
							C	N	M
Relaxation	6-5/8''	42	1.10	25	27.50	20.63		*	*
Meditation	6''	42	.95	25	23.75	17.81		*	*
Torero	6-9/16''	39	.90	25	22.50	16.88		*	*
No. 4	5''	42	.85	25	21.25	15.94		*	*
*Picador	7''	30	.80	25	40.00	30.00		*	*
**Pauser	4''	30	2/.85	50	21.25	15.94		*	

* Also available in box of 50.
** Not pictured.

- An extremely well constructed, hand made cigar.
- A fairly heavy bodied cigar made from tobaccos grown in the San Andres Valley of Mexico.
- Good range of shapes, sizes and colors.
- A very good value in every size.
- Distributed by Geryl Co. of Union City, N.J.

144

Te-Amo

LEW ROTHMAN RATING
Quality: ★ ★ ★ ★ ★
Value: ★ ★ ★ ★ ★

| Coronita | Cetro | Imperial | Epicure | Elegante | Amatista |

Front Mark	Length	Ring Size	Retail per ea.	Qty. per Box	Retail per Box	Whole sale per Box	Wrapper Color		
							C	N	M
Coronita	5-1/4''	39	.75	25	18.75	14.06		*	*
Cetro	7''	40	1.05	25	26.25	19.69		*	*
Imperial	8''	50	1.65	10	16.50	12.38		*	*
Epicure	5''	30	2/1.05	50	26.25	19.69		*	
Elegante	5-3/4''	30	2/1.15	50	28.75	21.56		*	
Amatista	6-1/4''	40	.90	25	22.50	16.88		*	*

- An extremely well constructed, hand made cigar.
- A fairly heavy bodied cigar made from tobaccos grown in the San Andres Valley of Mexico.
- Good range of shapes, sizes and colors.
- A very good value in every size.
- Distributed by Geryl Co. of Union City, N.J.

145

Te-Amo

| Churchill | Super Cetro | Ambassador | Presidente | Torito | Toro |

Front Mark	Length	Ring Size	Retail per ea.	Qty. per Box	Retail per Box	Whole sale per Box	Wrapper Color		
							C	N	M
Churchill	7-1/2''	50	1.35	25	33.75	25.30		*	*
Super Cetro	7-1/2''	40	1.10	25	27.50	20.63		*	*
Ambassador	7-1/4''	42	1.15	25	28.75	21.56		*	*
Presidente	7''	49	1.25	25	31.25	23.44		*	*
Torito	4-3/4''	49	.90	50	45.00	33.76		*	*
Toro	6''	49	1.05	25	26.25	19.69		*	*

- An extremely well constructed, hand made cigar.
- A fairly heavy bodied cigar made from tobaccos grown in the San Andres Valley of Mexico.
- Good range of shapes, sizes and colors.
- A very good value in every size.
- Distributed by Geryl Co. of Union City, N.J.

146

H. Upmann

| Naturales | Corona Major | Lonsdale | Corona | Petite Corona |

Front Mark	Length	Ring Size	Retail per ea.	Qty. per Box	Retail per Box	Whole sale per Box	Wrapper Color		
							C	N	M
Naturales	6-1/8''	35	1.30	25	32.50	24.38		*	
Corona Major	5-1/8''	42	1.20	25	30.00	22.50		*	
Lonsdale	6-5/8''	42	1.35	25	33.75	25.31		*	
Corona	5-5/8''	42	1.25	25	31.25	23.44		*	
Petite Corona	5-1/8''	42	1.10	25	27.50	20.63		*	
*Churchill	5-3/4''	46	1.40	25	35.00	26.25		*	

*Not pictured

- A very well made, uniform, high grade, hand made cigar.
- Very mild
- A good range of sizes although lacking both panetela, and heavy ring gauge sizes. Available in brown English market selection wrappers only.
- Good consistancy and uniformity of blend, taste, and appearance. Not as firmly packed as its Jamaican, Mexican and Honduran competition, but you'll never have a problem drawing through this cigar.
- Up and down the line this brand is expensive, especially in deluxe packaging such as the Topacio, Amatista Jar and #2000.
- Made in the Canary Islands, Spain under the supervision of Menendez and Garcia, of H. Upmann and Montecristo Fame.
- Latin American and Caribbean Filler Tobaccos with Connecticut Shade and African Cameroon wrappers.
- Marketed by a number of Regional Franchised Distributors.

H. Upmann

| #2000 | Amatista Glass Jar | Amatista Box | Topacio | Corona Imperials |

Front Mark	Length	Ring Size	Retail per ea.	Qty. per Box	Retail per Box	Whole sale per Box	Wrapper Color		
							C	N	M
*Emperadores	7-1/4''	45	1.65	25	41.25	30.94		*	
#2000	6-11/16''	43	1.60	25	40.00	30.00		*	
Amatista Glass Jar	5-7/8''	42	1.35	50	67.50	50.63		*	
Amatista Box	5-7/8''	41	1.30	25	32.50	24.38		*	
Topacio	5-3/16''	43	1.25	25	31.25	23.44		*	
Corona Imperials	7''	45	1.50	5	37.50	28.13		*	

*Not pictured

- A very well made, uniform, high grade, hand made cigar.
- Very mild
- A good range of sizes although lacking both panetela, and heavy ring gauge sizes. Available in brown English market selection wrappers only.
- Good consistancy and uniformity of blend, taste, and appearance. Not as firmly packed as its Jamaican, Mexican and Honduran competition, but you'll never have a problem drawing through this cigar.
- Up and down the line this brand is expensive, especially in deluxe packaging such as the Topacio, Amatista Jar and #2000.
- Made in the Canary Islands, Spain under the supervision of Menendez and Garcia, of H. Upmann and Montecristo Fame.
- Latin American and Caribbean Filler Tobaccos with Connecticut Shade and African Cameroon wrappers.
- Marketed by a number of Regional Franchised Distributors.

Valdez

Executive Numero 4 Petit Churchill Caballeros Panetelas Corona DeLuxe

Front Mark	Length	Ring Size	Retail per ea.	Qty. per Box	Retail per Box	Whole sale per Box	Wrapper Color		
							C	N	M
Executive	6-3/4''	30	.75	50	37.50	28.12		*	*
Numero 4	5''	44	.85	25	21.25	15.94		*	*
Petit Churchill	4-1/2''	50	.85	25	21.25	15.94		*	*
Caballero	6-1/4''	42	.85	25	21.25	15.94		*	*
Panetelas	6-5/16''	38	.85	25	21.25	15.94		*	*
Corona DeLuxe	6''	44	.95	25	23.75	17.81		*	*

- A very well constructed hand made cigar made from long San Andres filler.
- Good range of sizes and colors.
- A good tasting cigar that holds together well.
- Very competitively priced.
- Distributed by Intercontinental Cigars of San Diego, Cal.

149

Valdez

Double Corona   Palma Elites   Churchill   Presidente

Front Mark	Length	Ring Size	Retail per ea.	Qty. per Box	Retail per Box	Whole sale per Box	Wrapper Color		
							C	N	M
Double Corona	6''	50	1.00	25	25.00	18.75		*	*
Palma Elites	6-5/8''	43	1.05	25	26.25	19.69		*	*
Churchill	7''	50	1.25	25	31.25	23.44		*	*
Presidente	7-1/2''	50	1.35	25	33.75	25.30		*	*

- A very well constructed hand made cigar made from long San Andres filler.
- Good range of sizes and colors.
- A good tasting cigar that holds together well.
- Very competitively priced.
- Distributed by Intercontinental Cigars of San Diego, Cal.

Van Dyck

Perfecto   Sraights

Front Mark	Length	Ring Size	Retail per ea.	Qty. per Box	Retail per Box	Whole sale per Box	Wrapper Color		
							C	N	M
Perfecto	4-15/16''	42½	5/.33	50	3.30	2.75		*	
Straights	5-15/16''	37	5/.33	50	3.30	2.75		*	

- Hmm? What do you say about a brand with two sizes?
- After lengthy research by a team of marketing experts the two sizes shown above were selected as appealing to the greatest segment of seven cent cigar smokers.
- Obviously at 5 for 33 this cigar is a whale of a buy in either size.
- Distributed by General Cigar of N.Y., N.Y.

151

White Owl

| Miniature | Perfecto Special | Demi-Tip | Invincible | Panatela Deluxe | New Yorker | Corona Dark |

Front Mark	Length	Ring Size	Retail per ea.	Qty. per Box	Retail per Box	Whole sale per Box	Wrapper Color		
							C	N	M
Miniature	4-21/32"	29	5/.37	50	3.70	3.10		*	
Perfecto Special	4-3/4"	44	5/.72	50	7.20	6.00		*	
Demi-Tip	5-7/32"	32	5/.35	50	3.50	3.00		*	
Invincible	5-3/8"	41	5/.79	50	7.90	6.56		*	
Panatela Deluxe	5-3/8"	34½	5/.79	50	7.90	6.56		*	
New Yorker	5-11/16"	42½	5/.79	50	7.90	6.56		*	
Corona Dark	5-11/16"	42½	5/.83	50	8.30	6.80		*	

- A very well constructed machine made cigar.
- Extremely mild.
- Made from a blend of domestic & Latin American filler tobaccos.
- A very broad range of sizes and shapes.
- Very, very low prices throughout the line.
- Distributed by the General Cigar Co. of N.Y.

White Owl

| | Tips | Ranger | Swinger | Diplomat |

Front Mark	Length	Ring Size	Retail per ea.	Qty. per Box	Retail per Box	Whole sale per Box	Wrapper Color		
							C	N	M
Tips	5-3/4''	40	5/.72	50	7.20	6.00		*	
Ranger	6''	33	5/.79	50	7.90	6.56		*	
Swinger	6''	23	5/.35	50	3.50	3.00		*	
Diplomat	7''	32	5/.83	50	8.30	6.80		*	

- A very well constructed machine made cigar.
- Extremely mild.
- Made from a blend of domestic & Latin American filler tobaccos.
- A very broad range of sizes and shapes.
- Very, very low prices throughout the line.
- Distributed by the General Cigar Co. of N.Y.

153

Wm. Penn

Willow   Braves   Willow Tip   Willow Wine Tip   Perfecto   Panatela   Planter's Tip   Patriot

Front Mark	Length	Ring Size	Retail per ea.	Qty. per Box	Retail per Box	Whole sale per Box	Wrapper Color		
							C	N	M
Willow	4-17/32''	27	5/.25	50	2.50	2.16		*	
Braves	4-21/32''	29	5/.30	50	3.00	2.55		*	
Willow Tip	4-13/16''	27	5/.25	50	2.50	2.16		*	
Willow Wine Tip	4-13/16''	27	5/.25	50	2.50	2.16		*	
Perfecto	4-15/16''	42½	5/.33	50	3.30	2.75		*	
Panatela	5-5/16''	37	5/.33	50	3.30	2.75		*	
Planter's Tip	5-1/2''	35	5/.33	50	3.30	2.75		*	
Patriot	5-11/16''	42½	5/.39	50	3.90	3.20		*	

- A well constructed machine made short filler cigar.
- A good range of sizes and shapes.
- Value - unbelievable - only 5 to 8 cents each.
- Very mild.
- The best packaging in the industry.
- Distributed by the General Cigar Co. of N.Y., N.Y.

Camera Shy Section

King Edward

LEW ROTHMAN RATING
Quality: ★ ★ ★ ★
Value: ★ ★ ★ ★ ★

Front Mark	Length	Ring Size	Retail per ea.	Qty. per Box	Retail per Box	Whole sale per Box	Wrapper Color		
							C	N	M
King Edward Cigarillo	4-7/16''	28½	5/.37	50	3.70	3.00		*	
Special	4-7/16''	28½	.06	50	3.00	2.40		*	
Tip Cigarillo	5-1/8''	27	.06	50	3.00	2.40		*	
Imperial	5-1/16''	42	.09	50	4.50	3.60		*	
Inbicible	5-1/2''	43	2/.25	50	6.25	5.00		*	
Imperial Plus	5-1/16''	42	2/.23	50	5.75	4.60		*	
Panetela	5-3/8''	36	2/.25	50	6.25	5.00		*	
Swisher Sweet Cigarillo	4-7/16''	28½	.06	50	3.00	2.40		*	
Swisher Sweet Tip Cigarillo	5-1/8''	27	.06	50	3.00	2.40		*	
Swisher Sweet	5-1/16''	42	.08	50	4.00	3.20		*	
Swisher Sweet kings	5-1/2''	43	.10	50	5.00	4.00		*	
Swisher Sweet Slims	5-3/8''	36	.08	50	4.00	3.20		*	
Home Made	5-1/16''	42	.08	50	4.00	3.20		*	

- America's largest selling cigars.
- Mild, cheap, available everywhere.
- All sizes except Imperial Plus have homogenized wrappers, but how do you knock this kind of success.
- Very limited range of sizes in light natural only.
- Distributed by Jno. Swisher & Son, Jacksonville, Fla.

Lord of Jamaica
Jamaica Heritage
Pride of Jamaica

LEW ROTHMAN RATING
Quality: ★ ★ ★ ★
Value: ★ ★ ★ ★ ★

Front Mark	Length	Ring Size	Retail per ea.	Qty. per Box	Retail per Box	Whole sale per Box	Wrapper Color		
							C	N	M
Lonsdale	6-1/2''	42	1.15	25	28.75	21.56		*	*
Royal Corona	5-1/2''	42	1.05	25	26.25	19.69		*	*
Presidents	6-3/4''	38	1.05	25	26.25	19.69		*	*
Petit Corona	5-1/2''	38	.95	25	23.75	17.81		*	*
Elegante	6''	38	1.00	25	25.00	18.75		*	*
Panatella No. 3	6''	31	.80	25	20.00	15.00		*	*
Panatella No. 2	7''	31	.85	25	21.25	15.94		*	*
Panatella No. 1	8''	31	.90	25	22.50	16.87		*	*
Petit Churchill	6''	45	1.20	25	30.00	22.50		*	*
Prince Ferreri	6-3/4''	45	1.25	25	31.25	20.94		*	*
Churchills	7-1/2''	49	1.45	25	36.25	27.19		*	*
Tubulares	6-1/2''	42	1.35	25	33.75	25.31		*	*

- Well constructed, hand made, high grade cigars.
- Exceptionally mild, light bodied cigars.
- Adequate, if not large range of sizes and shapes. Available in medium brown natural and dark maduro wrappers.
- Lord of Jamaica and Jamaica Heritage are packaged in economical cellophane packages and are somewhat less expensibe than other competitive Jamaican cigars. The Pride of Jamaica is essentially the same item packaged in boxes of twenty five cigars at a somewhat higher price.
- Good consistancy of blend, taste, and appearance. These cigars are constructed somewhat lighter in weight than other Jamaicans, burning a little faster. However, they draw very easily and are a pleasant, enjoyable smoke.
- Manufactured by Combine Tobacco Co., and distributed by Primate Cigar, Brooklyn, N.Y.
- A quality cigar, limited in distribution mainly to the Eastern United States.

Mario Palomino

Front Mark	Length	Ring Size	Retail per ea.	Qty. per Box	Retail per Box	Whole sale per Box	Wrapper Color		
							C	N	M
Half Coronas	3-1/2''	40							
Minor Coronas	4''	40							
Coronitas	4-1/2''	40							
Petit Coronas	5''	40							
Buccaneer	5-1/2''	32							
Coronas	5-1/2''	40							
Cedar Coronas	5-1/2''	40							
La Excepcionales	5-1/2''	44							
Corona Major	5-5/8''	46							
Rapier	6''	32							
Palmitas	6''	34							
Imperial	6''	36							
Royal Coronas	6''	40							
Magnums	6''	45							
Corona Inmensas	6''	47							
Corona Grandes	6-1/2''	42							
Navarro	6-3/4''	34							
Flores	7''	32							
Monte Carlos No.2	7''	36							
Lonsdale	7''	42							
Double Coronas	7''	45							
Cedar Principales	7''	45							
Giant Coronas	7-1/2''	49							
Churchill	8''	51							
Monte Carlos No. 1	8-1/2''	36							

LEW ROTHMAN RATING
Quality: ★ ★ ★ ★

CAMERA SHY AND TEMPORARILY UNDERGOING A RE-ORGANIZATION

- This fine brand from Jamaica is temporarily without a major distributor in the United States. Therefore retail prices are somewhat "fuzzy" at the time of this printing.
- Above are the sizes of Palomino Cigars which size for size usually are comparably priced with those of Royal Jamaica.
- A very solidly rolled cigar in an ocean of shapes, good taste, and excellent burning characteristics.

Marsh Wheeling

LEW ROTHMAN RATING
Quality: ★ ★ ★ ★ ★
Value: ★ ★ ★ ★ ★

- The very first cigar I ever smoked was a Marsh Wheeling Stogie.
- Well constructed machine made cigars.
- This company has a strange fascination with 5½ inch by 33 ring size cigars.
- Great, great value.
- Distributed by M. Marsh & Son Wheeling W. Va.

Front Mark	Length	Ring Size	Retail per ea.	Qty. per Box	Retail per Box	Whole sale per Box	Wrapper Color		
							C	N	M
Pioneer	5-1/2''	36	2/.25	50	6.25	5.08		*	
Virginians	5-1/2''	50	2/.25	50	6.25	5.08		*	
Deluxe	7''	35	3/.50	50	8.33	6.73		*	
Old Reliable	5-1/2''	33	2/.25	100	12.50	10.15		*	
Dry Slitz Regular	5-1/2''	33	2/.15	50	3.75	3.08		*	
Dry Slitz Major	5-1/2''	33	2/.25	50	6.25	5.08		*	
Mountaineer	5-1/2''	33	2/.25	50	6.25	5.08		*	
Pollack Drums	5-1/2''	33	2/.25	50	6.25	5.08		*	
Pollack Crowns	5-1/2''	33	2/.25	50	6.25	5.08		*	
Mello Crowns	5-1/2''	33	2/.10	50	5.00	4.08		*	
Gallaghers	5-1/2''	33	2/.15	100	7.50	6.15		*	
Gallaghers Elite	5-1/2''	33	2/.25	50	6.25	5.08		*	
Stogie Special	6-1/2''	35	2/.35	50	8.75	7.08		*	

Solo/Don Melo

Front Mark	Length	Ring Size	Retail per ea.	Qty. per Box	Retail per Box	Whole sale per Box	Wrapper Color		
							C	N	M
Corona Gorda	6-1/4''	44	.75	25	18.75	14.06		*	
Churchill	7''	49	.95	25	23.75	17.81		*	
Corona Extra	5-1/2''	46	.70	25	17.50	13.13		*	
Linda	5-1/2''	38	.60	25	15.00	11.25		*	
Nom Plus	4-3/4''	50	.65	25	16.25	12.19		*	
Palma de Mayorca	8''	38	.80	25	20.00	15.00		*	
Numero Uno	7-1/8''	43	.75	25	18.75	14.06		*	
Numero Duo	6''	42	.65	25	16.25	12.19		*	
Presidents	8-1/2''	50	1.10	25	27.50	20.63		*	
Sobernanos	7-3/4''	50	1.05	25	26.25	19.69		*	
Corona Grande	7-1/2''	46	.95	25	23.75	17.81		*	

- A less than adequately constructed hand made cigar.
- Moderate strength.
- Lots of sizes.
- Reasonably priced.
- A step above the domestics but inferior to other hand made cigars.
- Distributed by Primate Cigars of Brooklyn N.Y.

Frieder Cigars

Front Mark	Length	Ring Size	Retail per ea.	Qty. per Box	Retail per Box	Whole sale per Box	Wrapper Color		
							C	N	M
*Mark IV Magnate	6-1/2''	43	2/.55	50	13.75	10.60			
**Mark IV Midas	7-1/4''	33	.25	50	12.50	9.75			
***Wolf Crooks	5-7/16''	43	.15	50	7.50	5.90			
***Wolf Crookettes	4-1/2''	30	.11	50	5.50	4.40			
***Wolf Stogies	6-1/8''	34	3/.50	50	8.33	6.75			
***Stetson Panetela	5-1/8''	38	2/.25	50	6.25	5.00			
Corona Smoker	5-1/4''	42	.11	50	5.50	4.40			
Marcello Caravette	7-1/4''	42	2/.45	50	11.25	8.70			
Marcello Slims	7-1/4''	32	.20	50	10.00	7.70			
† Private Stock #3	6-1/2''	35	2/.55	50	13.75	10.60			
***Palma Throwout	6-1/2''	42	.15	50	7.50	6.00			
Tudor Arms Knight	6-1/2''	42	3/.55	50	9.13	7.05			
† Private Stock #1	6-1/2''	42	.30	50	15.00	11.50			
*Caribbean Rounds	7-1/4''	45	2/.55	50	13.75	9.75			
***El Toro Perfecto	5''	44	.10	50	5.00	4.00			
†*** #1033 Connecticut	6''	45	2/.55	50	13.75	9.75			
† Don Seville Corona	6-1/2''	42	2/.55	50	13.75	9.75			
† Don Reynaldo Churchill	6-1/2''	52	.45	25	11.25	8.50			

- A mixed bag of products.
- All sizes available for ''private labeling'' by small to moderate sized tobacconists.
- Distributed by the Frieder Division of The House of Windsor, Yoe, PA.

Index To Manufacturers And Their Products

BRAND	MANUFACTURER IMPORTER

A

Admiration	E. Regensburg & Sons
Agio	James B. Russell, Inc.
Airport-Brazil	Gesty Trading & Mfg. Co.
Ammezzati	Continental Cigar Company
Amorita	A. J. Golden Inc.
Antonio y Cleopatra	American Cigar
Avanti	Continental Cigar Company

B

B-H	Brick-Hanauer Co.
Bances	Danby-Palicio
Bankers Choice	R. G. Dun Cigar Corp.
Belinda	Cigars by Santa Clara
JR Tobacco Co.	Belmont
Ben Franklin	Consolidated Cigar Co.
Bering	Corral, Wodiska Y Ca.
Berthold	San Telmo Cigar Co.
Black Gold	H. L. Neff & Co., Inc.
Black Hawk	National Cigar Corp.
Black Jack	M & N Cigar Manufacturers Inc.
Black Pete	R. G. Dun Cigar Corp.
Blackstone	Universal Cigar Corporation
Blue Ribbon	A. J. Golden Inc.
Blue Seal	A. J. Golden Inc.
Blue Tip	Jacobs Cigar Co.
Bock y Ca	American Cigar
Bold	Frieder Division
Bon Gusto	Continental Cigar Company
Brooks	T. E. Brooks & Co.
Budd's	R. G. Dun Cigar Corp.
Burger Sohne	Gesty Trading & Mfg. Corp.

C

Cadillac	G. W. Van Slyke & Horton
	Garcia Y Vega, Inc.
Canadian Clubs	T. E. Brooks & Co.
Capitan de Tueros	Consolidated Cigar Corp.
Caribbean	Frieder Division
Carl Upmann	Carl Upmann International, Inc.
Casa Copan	Intercontinental Cigars Inc.
Cello	Continental Cigar Company
Certified Bond	Reiss-Dabney Cigar Co.
Cherry Blend	John Middleton, Inc.
Chivis	Cigars By Santa Clara Ltd.
Churchill	Yorkana Cigar Co.
Cima	A. Oppenheimer & Co.
City Club	Frieder Division
Chas Denby	R. G. Dun Cigar Corp.
Corina	General Cigar & Tobacco Company
Cornwall Arms	A. J. Golden, Inc.
Count Christopher	A. Oppenheimer & Co.
Creme de Jamaica	Faber, Coe & Gregg, Inc.
Crown	R. G. Dun Cigar Corp.
Cuesta-Rey	M & N Cigar Manufacturers, Inc.
Custom Palmas	Frieder Division

D

Danlys	Pan American Cigar Co.
Deschler's Monogram	Frieder Division
Dexter Londres	Universal Cigar Corporation
Dixie Maid	Jno H. Swisher & Son, Inc.
Dominicana	Cigars By Santa Clara

BRAND	MANUFACTURER IMPORTER

Don Alvaro	Don Alvaro Corp.
Don Diego	C. I. T.
Don Diego	
Don Marcos	Peterson's Ltd.
Don Rey	T. E. Brooks & Co.
Don Reynaldo	Frieder Division
Don Rubio	Intercontinental Cigars, Inc.
Don Pepe	RJ Tobacco
Don Seville	Frieder Division
Don Tomas	Honduran Cigar Imports Ltd.
Dover Crooks	T. E. Brooks & Co.
Dry Slitz	M. Marsh & Son
Duquesne Club	Frieder Division
Dutch Masters	Consolidated Cigar Co.

E

Earl Marshal	Frieder Division
Economy	Continental Cigar Company
Ebony	H. L. Neff & Co., Inc.
1886	Consolidated Cigar Co.
El Beso	Intercontinental Cigars, Inc.
El Caudillo	Cigars by Santa Clara Ltd.
El Cid	Garcia Y Vega, Inc.
El Producto	Consolidated Cigar Co.
El Toro	Frieder Division
El Trelles	Universal Cigar Corporation
El Verso	National Cigar Corp.
Emerson	R. G. Dun Cigar Corp.
Evermore	National Cigar Corp.
Excalibur	Damby-Palicio

F

Fendrich	R. G. Dun Cigar Corp.
Flamenco	Faber, Coe & Gregg, Inc.
Flor De Mexico	Pan American Cigar Co.
Flor Del Caribe	Peterson's Ltd.
Fort Pitt Broadleaf	Frieder Division

G

Gallagher	M. Marsh & Son
Garcia Grande Crowns	Frieder Division
Garcia y Garcia	Perfecto Garcia & Bros. Inc.
Garcia y Vega	Garcia Y Vega, Inc.
Gladstone	House of Windsor, Inc.
Gold Label	General Cigar & Tobacco Company
Golden's Blue Ribbon	H. L. Neff & Co., Inc.
Golden Grit	A. J. Golden Inc.

H

Haddon Hall	Universal Cigar Corporation
Harvester	Consolidated Cigar Co.
Harrows	Cigars by Santa Clara
Have A Crook	T. E. Brooks & Co.
Have A Sweet	T. E. Brooks & Co.
Hav-A-Tampa	Havatampa Cigar Corporation
Hofnar	Gesty Trading & Mfg. Corp.
House of Windsor	House of Windsor, Inc.
Hoyo de Monterrey	Danby-Palicio

I

Ibold	R. G. Dun Cigar Corp.
Intermission Tip	R. G. Dun Cigar Corp.
Irvin S. Cobb	Yorkana Cigar Corp.

BRAND	MANUFACTURER IMPORTER

J

Jamaica Gold	Brick-Hanauer Co.
Jamaica Heritage	Primate Cigar Co.
Jon Piedro	Brick-Hanauer Co.
Joya De Nicaragua	A. Oppenheimer & Co.
J-R Cameroons	JR Tobacco Co.

K

Keep Moving	Universal Cigar Corporation
Kentucky Cheroots	Continental Cigar Company
Kiel Brazil	Gesty Trading & Mfg. Corp.
King Cotton	A. J. Golden Inc.
King Edward	Jno H. Swisher & Sons, Inc.

L

La Corona	American Cigar
La Diligencia	Corral, Wodiska Y Ca.
La Palina	Consolidated Cigar Co.
La Primadora	Universal Cigar Corporation
Lord Baltimore	A. J. Golden Inc.
Lord Beaconsfield	Danby-Palicio
Lord Clinton	R. G. Dun Cigar Corp.
Lord Horatio	Frieder Division
Lord Robert	A. J. Golden Inc.
Lord of Jamaica	Primate Cigar Co.
Lovera	Consolidated Cigar Co.
Lupo	Continental Cigar Company

M

Mac	H. L. Neff & Co., Inc.
Macanudo	General Cigar & Tobacco Company
Madrigal	Intercontinental Cigars, Inc.
Majestic	R. G. Dun Cigar Corp.
Managua	Yorkana Cigar Co.
Manuel	G. W. Van Slyke & Horton
Mark IV	House of Windsor, Inc.
Mello Coronas	Cigars by Santa Clara
Marsh Tips	M. Marsh & Son
Medalist	E. Regensburg & Sons
Maximo Gomez	Villazon
Mexicana	Cigars by Santa Clara Ltd.
Mississippi River Crooks	A. J. Golden Inc.
Mocha	Cigars by Santa Clara Ltd.
Mocambo	Premier Cigars
Mountaineer	M. Marsh & Son
Montecruz	Alfred Dunhill of London, Inc.
Montoya	Upmann International, Inc.
Muriel	Consolidated Cigar Co.

N

Newcomer	A. J. Golden Inc.
No. 77	Universal Cigar Corporation
No. 211	G. W. Van Slyke & Horton
Nobel	James B. Rusell, Inc.

O

Odin	R. G. Dun Cigar Corp.
Old Reliable	M. Marsh & Son
Ornelas	Pan American Cigar Co.
Optimo	Universal Cigar Corporation
Overland	Brick-Hanauer Co.

P

Partagas	General Cigar & Tobacco Company
Pedro Iglesias	Danby-Palicio
Pennsylvania Dutchman	G. W. Van Slyke & Horton
Perfecto Garcia	Perfecto Garcia & Bros., Inc.
Peter Schuyler	G. W. Van Slyke & Horton
Phillies	Bayuk Cigars Inc.

BRAND	MANUFACTURER IMPORTER

Pioneer	M. Marsh & Son
Pollack	M. Marsh & Son
Pom Pom Opera	Jno H. Swisher & Son, Inc.
Por Larranaga	Faber, Coe & Gregg, Inc.
Pride of Jamaica	Primate Cigar Co.
Primo Del Rey	Moro Cigar Company
Punch	Danby-Palicio

R

Ramrod	Continental Cigar Company
Red Dot	R. G. Dun Cigar Corp.
Rey del Mundo	Faber, Coe & Gregg, Inc.
Ricardo Samuel	Finsbury Products, Inc.
Rigoletto	M & N Cigar Manufacturers, Inc.
Robt. Burns	General Cigar & Tobacco Company
Roi-Tan	American Cigar
Rosalones	Comoy's of London
Rough Rough	Continental Cigar Company
Royal Jamaica	Pan American Cigar Co.
Royal Manna	Brick-Hanauer Co.

S

Santa Clara 1830	Associated Imports
San Felice	R. G. Dun Cigar Corp.
San Pedro	Frieder Division
San Fe	Universal Cigar Corporation
Schimmelpenninck	Alfred Dunhill of London, Inc.
Seal of Philadelphia	G.W. Van Slyke & Horton
Seidenberg	Frieder Division
7-20-4 Londres	Universal Cigar Corporation
Shakespeare	General Cigar & Tobacco Company
Solo Aroma	Primate Cigar Co.
Spanish Maid Crooks	T. E. Brooks & Co.
Spanish Palma	Frieder Division
Stetson	Frieder Division
Suerdieck	Pan American Cigar Co.
Stock Market	Cigars by Santa Clara
Swisher Sweet	Jno H. Swisher & Son, Inc.

T

Tabacalera	Peterson's Ltd.
Tampa Clubs	R. G. Dun Cigar Corp.
Tampa Nuggets	Havatampa Cigar Corporation
Te-Amo	Te-Amo Geryl Company, Inc.
Tequila	JR Tobacco
Tiparillo	General Cigar & Tobacco Company
Tobacco Shed	Jacobs Cigar Co.
Toscanelli	Continental Cigar Corp.
Tudor Arms	Frieder Division

U

Uncle Willie	T. E. Brooks & Co.
H. Upmann	C. I. T.
Upmann	Upmann International, Inc.

V

Valdez	Intercontinental Cigar Inc.
Van Dyck	General Cigar & Tobacco Company
Van Slyke & Horton	G. W. Van Slyke & Horton
Villa de Cuba	Danby-Palicio
Villiger	Tampa Products Co.
Viva	Cigars by Santa Clara Ltd.

W

Webster	Bayuk Cigars Inc.
White & Gold	A. J. Golden Inc.
White Owl	General Cigar & Tobacco Company
Willem II	Consolidated Cigar Co.
Wm. Penn	General Cigar & Tobacco Company
Wolf Bros	United States Tobacco Company

Y

| Y-B | R. G. Dun Cigar Corp. |

Manufacturers
And Their Products

AMERICAN CIGAR

Division of American Brands, Inc.
245 Park Avenue, New York, NY 10017
(212) 557-7000

PRODUCT & SIZE	Packup
La Corona Imported Handmade Cigars	
Nicaragua Finas	1/40
Nicaragua Largas	1/40
Nicaragua Brevas	1/40
Nicaragua Opulencias	1/40
Nicaragua Reinas	1/40
La Corona	
Filter Tips	200s
Whiffs	100s
Demi Tasse	60s
Demi Tasse	1/20-5 pk.
Panetelas Extra	1/20
Belvederes*	1/20
Belvederes	1/40
Belvederes*	1/20-5 pk.
Scepters	1/20
Scepters	1/20-5 pk.
Rapiers	1/20
Rapiers	1/20-5 pk.
Palatinos	1/20
Tapers - NCW only	1/20
Tapers - NCW only	1/25 4 pk
Coronas Chicas*	1/20
Coronas Chicas	1/40
Coronas Queens	1/20
Coronas Queens	1/40
Coronas Queens	1/25-4 pk.
Palmas Chicas*	1/20
Palmas Chicas*	1/25-4 pk.
American - Tube	30s
Americans - Tube	30s/3 pk.
Naturals - Tube - NCW Only	30s
Naturals - Tube - NCW only	30s/3 pk.
Coronas	1/20
Coronas	1/40
Coronas*	3/100-3 pk.
#200 - NCW Only	30s/3 pk.
#200 - NCW Only	1/20
#200 - NCW Only	1/40
Cristales - Glass Tube	1/40
#400 - NCW Only	1/40
#400*	1/40
No. 3	1/40
#500 - NCW Only	1/40
#600 - NCW Only	1/40
#800 - NCW Only	1/40
Bock y Ca.	
Panetelas	1/20
Panctelas	49s/7 pk.
Antonio y Cleopatra	
Little Cigars	
Regular (Filter Tipped)	200s
Menthol (Filter Tipped)	200s
Ninos*	100s
Tribunes*	1/20-5 pk.
Tribunes*	1/20

Caminos - NCW Only	30s
Caminos - NCW Only	30s/3 pk.
Classics*	1/20
Classics*	1/20-5 pk.
Crusaders*	1/20
Crusaders*	1/20-5 pk.
Sabers*	1/20
Sabers*	1/20-5 pk.
Saber Tips*	1/20
Saber Tips*	1/20-5 pk.
Panetelas*	1/20
Panetelas*	1/20-5 pk.
Pats	1/20
Pats	49s/7 pk.
Pennants	1/20
Pennants	1/20-5 pk.
Princess	1/20
Grenadiers*	1/20
Grenadiers*	1/20
Grenadiers	
(it's aBoy/it's aGirl)	
Tonys	1/20
Tonys	1/20-5 pk.
Antonios	1/20
Antonios	1/20-5 pk.
Kings	1/20
Kings	1/20-5 pk.
Privateers - NCW Only	1/20
Privateers - NCW Only	1/20-5 pk.
DeLuxe	1/20
Conquerors	1/20
Accents	30s
Accents Upright	30s
Accents	30s/3 pk.
Deringer	
Little Cigars (Filter Tipped)	200s
Roi-Tan Little Cigars	
Regular 85s (Filter Tipped)	200s
Regular 100s (Filter Tipped)	200s
Cherry Flavor 100s	
(Filter Tipped)	200s
Menthol Flavor 100s	
(Filter Tipped)	200s
Roi-Tan	
Golfers	1/20
Golfers	1/10-5 pk.
Tips	1/20
Tips	1/10-5 pk.
Tips Cherry	1/10-5 pk.
Trumps	1/10-5 pk.
Trumps	1/20
Charger	1/20
Charger	1/20-5 pk.
Dudes	1/20
Dudes	1/20-5 pk.
Scout	1/20
Scout	1/20-5 pk.
Blunt Tips	1/20
Blunt Tips	1/20-5 pk.
Falcons	1/20
Falcons	1/20-5 pk.
Falcons	
(it's a Bow/it's a Girl	1/20)
Panetelas	1/20

*Also available with (dark) natural-cured wrapper.

161

PRODUCT & SIZE	Packup
Panetelas	1/20-5 pk.
Perfectos Extra	1/20
Perfectos Extra	1/20-5 pk.
Perfectos Extra	
(it's a Boy/it's a Girl)	1/20
Invincibles	1/20
Invincible	1/20-5 pk.
Straights	1/20
Straights	1/20-5 pk.
Bankers	1/20
Bankers	1/20-5 pk.
Bankers	
(it's a Boy/it's a Girl	1/20
Blunts	1/20
Blunts Canister	1/20
Blunts	1/20-5 pk.

ASSOCIATED IMPORTS

137 Scranton Avenue, Lynbrook, NY 11563
(516) 599-5995

PRODUCT & SIZE	Packup
Santa Clara - Mexico	
No. I	20s
No. II	20s
No. III	20s
No. IV	20s
No. V	20s
No. VI	20s
No. VII	20s
No. VIII	20s
Quinos	20s

BAYUK CIGARS INC.

2150 S. Andrews Ave.
Ft. Lauderdale, FL 33316
(305) 525-8433

PRODUCT & SIZE	Packup
Phillies	
Perfecto	50 box
Perfecto	50 fp
Titan	50 box
Titan	50 fp
Tips	100 fp
Tips	50 box
Corona Twin Pack	50 fp
Panatella	50 box
Panatella	50 fp
Blunts	50 box
Blunts	fp
King Cheroot	50 fp
Sports	50 box
Sports	50 fp
Junior Phillies	50 box
Junior Phillies	50 fp
Cheroot	50 box
Cheroot	50 fp
Cheroot	100 fp
Webster	
Golden Wedding	50 box
Golden Wedding	50 fp
Queens	50 box
Queens	50 fp
Fancy Tales	50 box
Fancy Tales	50 fp

BRICK-HANAUER CO.

190 Feldon St., Waltham, MA 02154
(617) 899-1002

PRODUCT & SIZE	Packup
B-H Golden Corona 5 Pk. & 50	1000
B-H Grande 5 Pk. & 50	1000
B-H Kings 5 Pk. & 50	1000
B-H Special #76 5 Pk. & 50	1000
B-H Boston Blunts 5 Pk. & 50	1000
B-H Esceptionale 5 Pk. & 50	1000
B-H Reject 5 Pk. & 50	1000
Jon Piedro Acapulco Breva	
5 Pk. & 50	1000
Jon Piedro Acapulco Slim	
5 Pk. & 50	1000
Jon Piedro Acapulco azadores	
50 only	1000
Overland Londres 5 Pk. & 50	1000
Overland Perfecto 5 Pk. & 50	1000
Royal Manna #1	
Natural Maduro	25s
Royal Manna #3	
Natural Maduro	25s
Royal Manna #4	
Natural Maduro	25s
Royal Manna #5	
Natural Maduro	25s
Royal Manna Manchego	
Natural Maduro	25s
Royal Manna Churchill	
Natural Maduro	25s
Royal Manna Corona Immensas	
Natural Maduro	25s
Royal Manna Super Palma	
Natural Maduro	25s
Royal Manna Delgado Extra	
Natural Maduro	25s
Royal Manna Delgado Extra	
Natural Maduro	25s
Royal Manna Largo Extra Fina	
Natural Maduro	25s
Royal Manna Extra Largo	
Natural Maduro	25s
Royal Manna Conchita Maduro	50s
Royal Manna Rothchild	
Natural Maduro	50s
Royal Manna Solera Maduro	50s
Royal Manna Petite Maduro	25s
Royal Manna Jabalina Maduro	25s
Royal Manna Toros Natural Maduro	25s
Royal Manna Lapaices	
Natural Maduro	25s
Imported from Canary Islands	

General Importers:
H. Upmann Cigars
Corona Imperiales
Naturales-Tubes
Lonsdales
Amatista-Cello
Corona
Petit Corona
Above Cellophaned Boxes of (25)
Topacio Cello & No Cello
#2000 Cello & No Cello
Amatista Glass Jar (50s) Cello
S.G. Sungrown

General Importer:

Don Diego
Corona
Lonsdales
Grecos

Cervantes	
Royal Palma Tubes	
Monarchs Tubes (10S)	
Club Corona	
Slim Coronas	
Petit Grecos	
Shorts	
Babies (50S)	
Amastista Glass Jar (50S)	

(Petit Corona-Corona-Lonsdale, AMS & EMS; Slim Corona-Babies (SG) Others - EMS)

Jamaica Gold	25s
Churchill	25s
Giant Corona	25s
Cedar Principales	25s
Double Corona	25s
Royal Corona	25s
Lonsdales	25s
Navarro	25s
Petit Churchill	25s
Corona	25s
Buccaneers	25s
Petit Corona	25s
Coronitas	25s
Rapier	25s
Toro	25s
Trio-Contains	
25 Lonsdale	
25 Navarro	
25 Royal Corona	

T. E. BROOKS & CO.
31 S. Pine Street, Red Lion, PA 17356
(717) 244-3045

PRODUCT & SIZE	Packup
Brooks Grande Prima	1/10-5s
Brooks Palmas	1/20-5s
Tip Cigarillos	1/20-5s
Don Rey	1/20-5s
Have A Sweet Perf.	1/20-5s
Blunt Tips	1/20-5s
Tip Cigarillos	5s
Cigarillos	5s
Have A Crook	1/20-5s
Canadian Clubs Blunt Tips	1/20
Perf.	1/20-5s
Cigarillos	5s
El-Rees-So Blunt Tips	1/20-5s
Sweet	1/20-5s
Kings	1/20-5s
Tip Cigarillos	5s
Cigarillos	5s
Uncle Willie Perf. & Blunt Tips	1/20-5s
Spanish Maid Crooks	1/20-5s
Dover Crooks	1/20-5s

COMOY'S OF LONDON
Division of Cadogan Investments, Ltd. of
America
435 N. Midland Avenue
Saddle Brook, NJ 07662

PRODUCT & SIZE	Packup
Rosalones Cigars from Nicaragua	
No. 100	25s
No. 200	25s
No. 300	25s
No. 400	25s
No. 500	25s

No. 600	25s
No. 700	25s
No. 800	10s
Duque	25s
Baron	26s
Pepe	50s
Selecto	26s
Variety Pack	15s

CONSOLIDATED CIGAR COMPANY
A Division of Gulf & Western Corporation
1 Gulf & Western Plaza
New York, NY 10023
(212) 333-4466

PRODUCT & SIZE	Packup
Dutch Masters	
Cadets Regular	5 pk.
Cadets Regular	1/20 bx
Cadets Tipped	5 pk.
Cadets Tipped	1/20 bx
Sprint	1/20 bx
Sprint	5 pk.
Racer	1/20 bx
Racer	5 pk.
Elite	1/20 bx
Elite	5 pk.
Royal	5 pk.
Royal	1/20 bx
Perfecto	1/20 bx
Perfecto	5 pk.
Perfecto	1/40 can
Perfecto Mini Box	1/100 bx
Blunt	1/20 bx
Blunt	1/20 can
Blunt	5 pk.
Panetela	1/20 bx
Panetela	5 pk.
Panetela Boy/Girl	cnstr
Panetela Mini Box	1/100 bx
Belvedere	1/20 bx
Belvedere	5 pk.
President	1/20 bx
President	5 pk.
President	1/20 can
President Mini Box	1/100 bx
Cameroon 140	1/20 can
Cameroon 140	5 pk.
Cameroon 150	1/20 bx
Cameroon 150	5 pk.
Whiffs	5 pk.
Corona De Luxe	1/20 bx
Corona De Luxe	5 pk.
Little Cigars	
Dutch Treats	
100mm Reg.	20 pk.
100mm Menthol	
El Producto	
Little Corona	5 pk.
Little Corona	1/20 bx
Little Tips	1/20 bx
Little Tips	5 pk.
Diamond Tip	1/20 bx
Diamond Tip	5 pk
Triumphs	1/20 bx
Triumphs	5 pk.
Invincibles	1/20 bx
Invincibles	5 pk.
Bouquet	1/20 bx
Bouquet	1/40 mc
Bouquet	5 pk.

Bouquet Boy/Girl	1/20 bx
Panetela	1/20 bx
Panetela	5 pk
Panetela Boy/Girl	1/40 can
Blunt	1/20 bx
Blunt	5 pk.
Excellentes	1/20 bx
Excellentes	5 pk.
Senadores Dark	1/20 bx
Senadores Dark	5 pk.
Senadores Light	1/20 bx
Senadores Light	5 pk.
Granadas	1/20 bx
Granadas	5 pk.
Puritanos Finos	1/20 bx
Puritanos Finos	5 pk.
Favorita	1/20 bx
Favorita	5 pk.
Corona	1/20 bx
Corona	5 pk.
Escepcionales	1/20 bx
Escepcionales	1/40 bx
Escepcionales	1/40 5 pk.
Queens	1/40 caddy
Queens	1/40 bx
Queens	3 pk.

Muriel

Magnum	1/20 bx
Magnum	5 pk.
Coronas	1/20 bx
Coronas	5 pk.
Coronas	1/20 can
Senators	1/20 bx
Senators	5 pk.
Senators	1/20 can
Senators	1/40 vac can
Senators	
(It's A Girl)	1/40 vac can
(It's A Boy)	1/40 vac can
Panetela	1/20 bx
Panetela	5 pk.
Coronella King	1/20 bx
Coronella King	5 pk.
Blunts	1/20 bx
Blunts	5 pk.
Air-Tips Regular	1/20 bx
Air-Tips Regular	1/20 5 pk.
Air-Tips Regular	1/10 5 pk.
Air-Tips Menthol	1/20 5 pk.
Air-Tips Pipe Aroma	1/20 5 pk.
Air-Tips Pipe Aroma	1/10 5 pk.
Coronella	1/20 bx
Coronella	1/20 5 pk.
Coronella	1/10 5 pk.
Tipalet Natural	1/20 5 pk.
Tipalet Natural	1/10 5 pk.
Tipalet Cherry	1/20 5 pk.
Tipalet Cherry	1/10 5 pk.
Tipalet Apple	1/20 5 pk.
Tipalet Apple	1/10 5 pk.
Tipalet Wild Blueberry	1/20 5 pk.
Tipalet Wild Blueberry	1/10 5 pk.

Capitan de Tueros

No. 3	5 pk.
No. 5	1/40 bx
No. 5	5 pk.
No. 7	1/40 bx
No. 7	5 pk.
No. 8	1/40 bx
No. 8	5 pk.
No. 10	3 pk.
No. 10	1/40 caddy

Ben Franklin

Perfectos	1/20 bx
Perfectos	5 pk.
Blunts	1/20 bx
Blunts	5 pk.

Willem II

Wee Willem	10 pk.
Holland Mini Tips	tin of 10
Willem Tell	bx of 10
No. 30	tin of 10
Extra Senoritas	5 pk.
Holland Panatellas	5 pk.
Holland Corona	bx of 5

Harvester

Perfecto	1/20 bx
Perfecto	5 pk.
Record Breaker	1/20 bx
Record Breaker	5 pk.
Panetela	1/20 bx
Panetela	5 pk.

La Palina
La Palina

Ideals	1/20 bx
Ideals	5 pk.
Ideals	
Boy-Girl Imprint	1/20 bx
Major Tip	1/20 bx
Major Tip	5 pk.
King Size Panetela	1/20 bx
King Size Panetela	5 pk

Lovera

Perfecto De Luxe	1/20 bx
Perfecto De Luxe	5 pk.
Tips	1/20 bx
Tips	5 pk.
Long Star	1/20 bx
Long Star	5 pk.

1886

Queen	1/20 bx
Queen	5 pk.
King	1/20 bx
King	5 pk.

CONTINENTAL CIGAR COMPANY

PRODUCT & SIZE	Packup
Toscani Celio 2 s 1/20	1M
Rough Rough 5s 1/10	3M
Popular Cello 2s 2/10	3M
Popular Ammezzati 5s 2/10	3M
Economy Pack 5s 1/10	2M
King 10/5	2M
Cello 2s 1/10 & 1/20	3M
Ammezzati 5s 1/10	3M
Economy 5 pk. 1/10	2M
Bon Gusto 2s 1/10	3M
Lupo Kings 5 pk. 1/10	2M
Avanti 10/5 pks	2M
Ramrod 1/20	1M
Ramrod 3 pk.	900
Ramrod Deputy 10/5 pks	1M
Tiparodi 1/20 & 1/10	3M
Kentucky Cheroots 1/20	1M
Kentucky Cheroots 10/4 pks	1M
Avanti Continental 10/4 pks	1M
Petri	
Toscani 25/2 pks	1M
AA Cello 50/2 pks	3M
Sigaretto Kings 20/5 pks	2M
Sigaretto Regular 20/5 pks	3M
Toscanelli 20/5 pks	3M

CORRAL, WODISKA Y CA.

P.O. Box 376, Tampa, FL 33601
(813) 248-3125

PRODUCT & SIZE	Packup
Bering	
Admirals-Treasure Chest 40	1/40
Albas .28	1/20
Baron HHS Nat. Wpr. 55	1/40
Balboa HHS Nat. Wpr. 55	1/40
Berring Panetelas .19	†††††1/20
Casinos-Glass Tubes .65	1/100
Cazadores .40	1/20
Cigarillos .09	†1/20
Coronados .26	†††††††1/20
Coronas .55	1/40
Corona Clasica .35	1/40
Coronas Grandes .40	†††1/40
Corona Royale .45*	†††1/40
Coronets .26	††1/20
Czars .65	1/40
El Dorado .35	1/40
Electra .26	†1/20
Emperors .85	1/100
Fads .11	Packs Only
Fairfields .35	1/40
Galleons-Jade Chest .55	1/40
Generals-2 Bdls. .45	1/20
Hispanos .75	1/40
Imperials .40*	†††††1/40
Inmensa .60	1/40
Individuals 1.50	1/1000
Juniors .13	†1/20
Longfellows .45	1/20, 1/40
Magnificos .20	1/20
Bering Matador-Blk Chest .35**	1/42
Number 55 .35	1/20
Plazas .35	††1/20
Presidentes .65	1/40
Rosa Perfectos .35	1/40
Rothchild HHS Nat. Wpr. 60	1/20
400's .35	1/40
9/09 HHS Nat. Wpr. 45	†††1/20, 1/40
Bering Red Label	
Fantasias .35	1/40
Lanceros .40	1/40
Supremos .35	1/40
Bering Straits	
Champions .14	†1/20
Populares .15	†1/20
La Diligencia	
Sublimes .14	1/20

Humidor packed in individual aluminum containers with natural wrappers only.
**24 Cigars.

†Available in 5 Packs.
††Available in 4 Packs.
†††Available in 3 Packs.
††††Available in 3-4 Packs.
†††††Available in 5 and 7 Packs.
††††††Available in 4 and 5 Packs.

DANBY-PALICIO

Division of Villazo & Co.
180 South Van Brunt Street
Englewood, NJ 07631

PRODUCT & SIZE	Packup
Punch	
Presidentes	1/40 & 1/100
Double Coronas	1/40
Pitas	1/40
Punch	1/40 Bundle
No. 1	1/40
Rothschilds	1/20 Bundle
Casa Grande	1/40
Amatistas	1/40
No. 75	1/40
Largo Elegantes	1/20 Bundle
Elites	1/20 Bundle
London Club	1/20
Hoyo de Monterrey de Jose Gener	
Presidents	1/40 & 1/100
Double Coronas	1/40
Governors	1/40
Cetros	1/40
Churchills	1/40 Bundle
No. 1	1/40
Rothschilds	1/20 Bundle
Cuban Largos	1/40
Ambassadors	1/40
Super Hoyos	1/40
Largo Elegantes	1/20 Bundle
Culebras	1/20
Margaritas	60s
Margaritas	1/100 cedar bx
No. 55	1/20 Bundle
Delights	1/20 Bundle
Demi Tasse	1/10 (2 Bdls.)
Sabrosos	1/20
Coronas	1/40
Sultans	1/40
Excalibur By Hoyo de Monterrey	
#1 Cedar Box	1/50
#2 Cedar Box	1/50
#3 Cedar Box	1/50
#4 Cedar Box	1/50
#5 Cedar Box	1/50
Bances	
Bancettes	20-6 pks
Bancettes	1/20
Variety	Assortment
Demi Tasse	1/20
Uniques	1/20 Bdl.
Londres	1/20
*Brevas	1/20 Bdl.
Brevas	12-4 pks
Brevas	1/40
Havana Holders	1/20-4 pks
*Palmas	1/20
**El Prado	1/40
No. 2	1/20
No. 3	1/20
Corona Minors (Alum. Tube)	30s
**Cazadores	1/20 Bdl.
Cazadores	20-3 pks
Nacionales	1/40
Corona Especial	1/40
No. 100	1/40
No. 1	1/40
Aristocrats	1/40
Corona Inmensas	1/40
Gran Duques	1/40
Presidents	1/100
No. 8 Crystals	1/100

*Available in 4 Pks. (40s)
**Available in 3 Pks. (30s)

Pedro Iglesias
  Crowns 1/20
  Regents 1/20
  Lonsdales 1/20
Lord Beaconsfield
  Rounds 1/20
  Lords 1/20
  Corona Superbas 1/20
  Lindas 1/20
  Cremas 1/20
  Cubanolas 1/20
Belinda
  Havana Tripia Largas 1/100
  Tuxedo Park 1/100
Villa De Cuba
  Brevas 1/20
  Majestics 1/20
  Corona Grande 1/40

DON ALVARO DISTRIBUTION CORP.

1000 River Street, Ridgefield, NJ 07657
(201) 945-2800   (212) 947-9165

PRODUCT & SIZE	Packup
Super Star	1/40
Elegantes	1/40
No. 1	1/40
Imperiales	1/20
Cazadores	1/20
Cazadores (Pak)	1/20 pk.
Cedros	1/40
Don Alvaro	1/40
Don Alvaro	1/100
Coronas	1/20
Brevas	1/20
Brevas (Pak)	1/20 pk.
Bouquets	1/20
Senadores	1/20
Floretes	1/20
Floretes	1/20 5 pk.
Panetelas	1/20
Panetelas	1/20 5 pk.
Saludos	1/20
Saludos	1/20 5 pk.
Marianos	1/20
Marianos	1/20 5 pk.
Islenos	1/20
Monic	1/20 5 pk.
Alvaritos	1/20 5 pk.
Mini-Tip	1/20 5 pk.
Mini	1/20 5 pk.

R. G. DUN CIGAR CORP.

435 North Main, Lima, OH 45802
(419) 227-2436

PRODUCT & SIZE	Packup
R.G.Dun	
Palma De Luxe	50s wood
Perfecto Fino	50s wood
	50s pp(10-5 pks) disp cont
Bouquet	50s wood
Boy, Girl, Just Married	50s wood
	50s pp(10-5 pks) disp cont
Panetela	50s wood
	50s pp(10-5 pks) disp cont
Admiral	50s
Boy, Girl, Just Married	50s wood
	50s pp(10-5 pks) disp cont

Youngfellow	50s wood
	50s pp(10-5 pks) disp cont
Babies	50s wood
	50s pp(10-5 pks) disp cont
Regal Blunt	50s wood
	50s pp(10-5 pks) disp cont
Crown	50s wood
	50s pp(10-5 pks) disp cont
Cigarillo	50s wood
	50s pp(10-5 pks) disp cont
	100s pp(10-5 pks) disp cont
Intermission Tip	
	50s pp(10-5 pks) disp cont
	100s pp(10-5 pks) disp cont
San Felice	
King	50s wood
	50s pp(10-5 pks) disp cont
Panetela	50s wood
	50s pp(10-5 pks) disp cont
Original	
Boy, Girl, Just Married	50s wood
	50s pp(10-5 pks) disp cont
Original A or Sweet	50s wood
	50s pp(10-5 pks) disp cont
Ben Bey	
Cystal	6-25s in upright cedar bxs
Emerson	50s wood
Diplomat	50s wood
Boy, Girl	50s wood
	50s pp(10-5 pks) disp cont
Odin	
Viking	50s pp(10-5 pks) disp cont
	50 wood
Ibold	50
Ibold Light Blunt	5-pk
Ibold Light Blunt	50
Ibold Dark Blunt	5-pk
Ibold Dark Blunt	50
Black Pete Perf.	5-pk
Black Pete Perf.	50
Ibold Brevas Blunt Light	5-pk
Ibold Brevas Blunt Light	50
Ibold Brevas Blunt Dark	5-pk
Ibold Cigarillo Light	5-pk
Ibold Cigarillo Dark	5-pk
Ibold Ideal Panatela Light	50
Ibold Ideal Panatela Light	5-pk
Ibold Ideal Panatela Dark	50
Ibold Ideal Panatela Dark	5-pk
Ibold Ideal Panatela Dark	5-pk
Ibold Slims Light	50
Ibold Slims Light	5-pk
Ibold Slims Dark	50
Ibold Slims Dark	5-pk
Majestic Perf.	50
Florida Queen	50s wood
	50s pp(10-5pk) disp cont
Lord Clinton	
Perfectos	50s wood
	50s pp(10-5pks) disp cont.
Panatelas	50s wood
	50s pp(10-5pks) disp cont
Budd Sweets	
Perfectos	50s wood
	50s pp(10-5pks) disp cont
Panetelas	50s wood
	50s pp(10-5pks) disp cont
Red Dot	
Perfectos	50s wood
	50s pp(10-5pks)
Panetelas	50s wood
	50s pp(10-5pks)

166

Cigarillos	50s wood
	50s (10-5pks)
Tippettes	50s (10-5pks)
YB Squires	50s (10-5pks)
	50s (10-5pks)
Tampa Cub	
Gem	50s wood
	50s pp(10-5pks)
Straight	50s wood
	50s pp(10-5pks)
Bankers Choice	50s wood
	50s pp(10-5pks)
La Fendrich	
Favoritas	50s wood
	50s pp(10-5pks)
Rangers	50s wood
	50s pp(10-5pks)
Buds	50s wood
	50s pp(10-5pks)
Little La Fendrich Panetela	50s wood
	50s (10-5pks)
"63"	50s wood
	50s pp(10-5pks)
Chas. Denby	
Inv.	50s wood
	50s (10-5pks)
Blunt	50s wood
	50s (10-5pks)

Net/Net billings include 2% cash discount

ALFRED DUNHILL OF LONDON, INC.
11 East 26 Street, New York, NY 10010
(212) 684-7600

PRODUCT & SIZE	Packup
Montecruz*	
#200	1/100 bx
#201**	1/40 bx
#205	1/40 bx
#210	1/40 bx
#220	1/40 bx
#230	1/40 bx
#240	1/40 bx
#250	1/40 bx
#255	1/40 bx
#260	1/40 bx
#265	1/40 bx
#270	1/40 bx
#275	1/40 bx
#276	1/40 bx
#277	1/40 bx
#280	1/40 bx
#281	1/40 bx
#282	1/40 bx
Tubos	1/40 bx
Tubulares	1/40 bx
Chicos**	1/20 bx
Chicos**	1/100 bx
Juniors**	1/20 bx
Individuales**	1/100 bx
Schimmelpenninck Cigars	
#638 Mini Tips	Box of 10
#640 Calendula	Box of 25
#643 Mulata	Box of 10
#645 Half Corona	Tin of 10
#642 Duet	Pkg of 5

#646 Duet	Tin of 10
#647 Duet	Drum of 25
#648 Vada	Tin of 10
#649 Florina	Tin of 50
#653 Mono	Tin of 20
#654 Media	Tin of 20
#655 Media	Tin of 50
#684 Nostra	Tin of 10
#692 Mini Brazil	Tin of 20
#691 Media Brazil	Tin of 20
#690 Duet Brazil	Tin of 10
#697 Mulata	Box of 25
#698 Simpatia	Box of 10
#699 Cigarillos	Tin of 10
Little Cigars	
Miniatures Oval Regulars	20s pk.
Miniatures Filtertip Rounds	20s pk.

*Available in Sun Grown, Double Claro.
**Available in Sun Grown only

Ramon Allones***	
A	1/40
B	1/40
C	1/40
D	1/40
Privado Tube	1/40

***Available in Natural only.

FABER, COE & GREGG, INC.
National Products Division
9 Entin Rd., Clifton, NJ 07014

PRODUCT & SIZE	Packup
Imported Cigars	
Flamenco	
Selecion Privada Cetros	1/40
Selecion Privada Corona SMS	1/40
Selecion Privada Club Corona SMS	1/40
Selection Privada #8 SMS	1/40
Selecion Privada #7 SMS	1/40
Selecion Privada #6 SMS	1/40
#1 AMS & EMS	1/40
#2 AMS & EMS	1/40
#3 AMS & EMS	1/40
#4 AMS & EMS	1/40
#27 EMS	1/40
Amigo Tubes - EMS	1/40
#35 AMS & EMS	1/20
#80 EMS	1/40
#101 AMS	10s
#101 EMS	1/40
Petit Flamenco EMS (Wood)	1/20
Petit Flamenco EMS (Tins)	1/20
Trumps SMS	140
Palmitas EMS	60s
Brevas a la Conserva SMS	1/20
Corona Majors (Aluminum Tube)	1/40
Don Diego	1/20
Babies SMS	1/20
Corona AMS & EMS	1/40
Grecos AMS & EMS	1/40
Lonsdales AMS & EMS	1/40
Monarch AMS & EMS	
(Aluminum Tubes)	
Petit Corona AMS & EMS	1/40

Royal Palms EMS (Aluminum Tube)	1/40
Shorts EMS	1/40
Slim Corona SMS	1/40
Por Larranaga	
Cetros	1/40
Cinco Vega	1/40
Grandee	1/40
Nacionales	1/40
Petit Cetros	1/40
Creme de Jamaica	
#1 AMS & EMS	1/40
#7 AMS & EMS	1/40
#12 EMS	1/40
#49 EMS	1/40
#50 SMS	1/40
#51 SMS	1/40
#52 SMS	1/40
#53 SMS	1/40
#54 SMS	1/40
Petit Cazadores	1/20
Singulares #1 EMS	1/40
Rey del Mundo	
#1 EMS & SMS	1/40
#2 EMS & SMS	1/40
#3 EMS & SMS	1/40
#4 EMS & SMS	1/40
Plantations EMS	1/40
Prime Ministers EMS & SMS	1/40
Emperor EMS & SMS	1/40
Emperor EMS & SMS	10s
*Club Corona EMS & SMS	1/40
*Glorias EMS & SMS	1/20
*Delicado EMS	1/20
Spanish Palmas EMS	1/40
Cabinets EMS	1/20
Duque de Alba EMS	1/40
Brevas a la Conserva	1/20
Premiers EMS	20s
Royales EMS	30s
*Bundle Packing	
H. Upmann	
#2000	1/40
Amatista	1/20
Amatista	1/40
Topacio	1/40
Churchills	1/40
Corona	1/40
Corona Imperiale	1/40
Corona Major	1/40
Lonsdale	1/40
Naturale Tube	1/40
Petit Corona	1/40
Dannemen Brazil	
Carioca	50s-25s-10s
Flores (Tipped)	50s
Jets	50s-25s
Valenca	50s-25s
Senadores	50s-25s-10s
Toureio	50s-25s-10s
Fancy Tables #3	25s-10s
Breves Populares	40s-10s
Cetros #3	25s-10s
Palmas #1	20s
Reynitas	100s
Bahianos	100s
Juanitas	100s
Speciale Tins 20	200s
Imperiale Tins 20	200s
Lonja Tins 10	100s
Pierrott Tins 10	100s
Menor Tins 10	100s
Speciale (In Glass)	50s
Colifino	5 pack

Indios	5 pack
Panatella	5 pack
Puros	5 pack
Epoca	
Petit Cetros EMS	50s
Cazadores EMS	50s
Private Stock #5 EMS	25s
Churchill EMS	25s

FINSBURY PRODUCTS, INC.
11 Clearbrook Rd., Elmsford, NY 10523
(914) 592-4222

Ricardo Samuel Cigars	bx 25

FRIEDER DIVISION
House of Windsor, Incorporated, A Subs. of
United States Tobacco Company
Windsor, PA 17366
(717) 244-4501

PRODUCT & SIZE	Packup
Crowns	6s
Deschler's Monogram	50s/5s
Tudor Arms	
Knights	50s
Lancers	50s
El Toro	50s/5s
Stetson	50s/5s
Palma Throwout	50s/5s
Spanish Palma	50s/5s
Lord Horatio Seafarer	50s
Don Seville Corona	50s
Don Reynaldo	25s
Kaloma Cedars	50s
Marcello	
Caravettes	50s
Slims	50s
Caribbean Rounds	50s/4s
Caribbean Royales	50s
Caribbean Petites	50s
San Pedro Bouquet	50s
#1033 Connecticut	50s/5s
#864 Maduro	50s/5s

GARCIA Y VEGA, INC.
Div. Bayuk Cigars Inc.
2150 S. Andrews Ave.
Ft. Lauderdale, FL 33316
(305) 525-8433   UPC #70235

PRODUCT & SIZE	Packup
Garcia y Vega	
Cigarillos	50 bx
Cigarillos	50fp
Cigarillos	100fp
Spanish Tips	50 bx
Spanish Tips	100 fp
Java Tips	100 fp
Chicos	100 fp
Panatella Deluxe	50 bx
Panatella Deluxe	50 fp
Bravura	50 bx
Bravura	50 fp
Senators	50 bx
Senators	50 fp
Maestro	50 bx
Maestro	50 fp

168

Epicures	50 bx
Epicures	50 fp
Fiestas	50 bx
Fiestas	50 fp
Mexican Blunts	50 bx
Mexican Blunts	50 fp
Commodores	50 bx
Commodores	50 fp
Elegantes	50 bx
Elegantes	60 fp
Gallantes	50 bx
Vallantes	60 fp
Regalo	50 bx
Regalo	40 fp
English Corona (tubes)	30 bx
English Corona (tubes)	40 fp
Romero (tubes)	30 bx
Romero (tubes)	40 fp
Granadas (tubes)	30 bx
Granadas (tubes)	40 fp
Three Tube Variety	56 bx
Caesars	50 bx
Caesars	50 fp
Napoleons	50 bx
Napoleons	40 fp
Napoleons	25 bx
Fancy Tales	25 bx
Washingtons	25 plastic
Washingtons	30 bx
Washingtons	30 fp
Del Rios	25 bx
Gran Premio	30 bx
Gran Premio	30 fp
Gran Corona	30 bx
Gran Corona	30 fp
Banquets	25 bx
Corona Largas	25 bx
Corona Largas	30 fp
Cordials	25 bx
Cordials	25 plastic
Nacionales	25 bx
EMS No. 3	50 bx
B/n No. 100	25 bx
Coronas	25 bx
EMS No. 1	50 bx
B/n No. 200	25 bx
Churchills	25 bx
Presidents	5 bx
El Cid	
Corona Minors	1/40 box
Monarchs	1/40 box
Supremas	1/40 box
Corona Majors	1/40 box
Conquistadores	1/40 box

GENERAL CIGAR & TOBACCO COMPANY

Division of Culbro Corporation
605 Third Avenue, New York, NY 10016

PRODUCT & SIZE	Packup
Gold Label	
Crystal (Glass Tube)	15s-10s
Casanova (Aluminum Tube)	20s
Cedaroma	50s-25s-3s
Corona De Ville	25s-3s
Romano	50s-25s
Palma	50s-25s-4s
Jaguar 70	50s-25s-4s
Panetela Grande	50s-6s
Royale	30s-4s

Corona	50s-5s
Dino	50s-6s
Marquis	50s-5s
Swagger	60s-5s
Shakespeare	
Romeo (Aluminum Tube)	25s
Diplomat	25s
Savoy	50s-25s
Corona	25s-3s
Breva	50s
Belvedere	50s-25s-3s
Command Performance	50s-6s
Macanudo	
Duke of Wellington	15s
Prince Philip	10s
Amatista (Glass Jar)	50s
Portofino (Aluminum Tube(	25s
Baron de Rothschild	25s
Earl of Lonsdale	25s
Duke of Devon	25s
Somerset	25s
Lord Claridge	25s
Petit Corona	25s-5s
Claybourne	25s
Caviar	50s
Hampton Court (Aluminum Tube)	25s
Partagas	
#10	10s
8-9-8	25s
Sabroso (Aluminum Tube)	20s
#1	25s
#2	25s
#3	25s
#4	25s
#6	25s
White Owl	
Diplomat	50s-5s
Corona Dark	50s-5s
Invincible	50s-5s
Perfecto Special	50s-5s
Tips	50-5s
Ranger	50s-5s
Panatela De Luxe	50s-5s
New Yorker	50s-5s
Swinger	50s-5s
Miniature	50s-5s
Demi-tip	50s-5s
Tiparillo	
Tiparillo (Regular)	50s-5s
Tiparillo M (Menthol)	50s-5s
Tiparillo A (Aromatic)	50s-5s
Robert Burns	
Black Watch	30s-3s
Panatela	50s-5s
Cigarillos	50s-5s
Wm. Penn	
Perfecto	50s-5s
Panatela	50s-5s
Planters Tips	50s-5s
Willows (Cigarillos)	50s-5s
Willow Wine Tips	50s-5s
Willow Tips	50s-5s
Braves	50s-5s
Van Dyck	
Perfecto	50s-5s
On Straights	50s-5s
Tijuana Smalls	
Regular	10s
Aromatic	10s
Menthol	10s
Corina	
Western	50s-5s
Baron	50s-5s

Larks	50s-10s-5s
Panatela	50s-5s
Sports deLuxe	50s-5s

A. J. GOLDEN INC.
P.O. Box 1423, York, PA 17405

PRODUCT & SIZE	Packup
Blue Ribbon	
Monarchs	50s bn
Sabers	50s bn
Sabers	50s
Perfecto Extra	50s, 5 pk.
Corona	50s, 5 pk.
Lord Baltimore	
Cigarillo	10s, 5 pk.
Tips	100s, 5 pk.
Special Perfecto	wd, cn
Mississippi River Crooks	50s, 5 pk.
Newcomer Perfecto Special	50s, 5 pk.
Golden Grit Invincible	50s, 5 pk.
King Cotton Invincible	50s, 5 pk.
Amorita Perfecto	50s, 5 pk.
White Orchid Perfecto	50s, 5 pk.
Lord Robert Perfecto	50s, 5 pk.
White & Gold Perfecto	50s, 5 pk.
Royal Circle	50s
Royal Poet	50s
Blue Seal	50s
Covered Wagon, Jumbo	8s, 4s
La Decema Jumbo	8s
El Tolna Jumbo	8s
Cornwall Arms	
Gold	
B.N. Box	50s
Neff's Coronas	
B.N. Box	50s
Palmas	50s bn
Perfecto	50s bn
John Jrs	50s, 5 pk.
Tennessee River Crooks	50s, 5 pk.
Mississippi Sound Crooks	50s, 5 pk.
Flor de Moss Crooks	50s, 5 pk.
King of Crooks	50s, 5 pk.
Amorita Juniors	100s

HAVATAMPA CORPORATION, MANUFACTURING DIVISION
P.O. Box 1261, Tampa, FL 33601
(813) 685-2911

PRODUCT & SIZE	Packup
Tampa Nugget	
Sublime	50s, 5 pk.
Blunt	50s, 5 pk.
Panetela	50s, 5 pk.
Tampa Nugget "Junior"	50s, 5 pk.
Tip	50s, 5 pk.
Tip Menthol	50s, 5 pk.
Tampa Straights	
King	50s, 5 pk.
Tampa Sweet	50s, 5 pk.
Modern Perfecto	
Hav-A-Tampa	
Debonair	50s, 5 pk.
Sport	50s, 5 pk.
Jewel	50s, 5 pk.
Perfecto	50s, 5 pk.
Blunt	50s, 5 pk.
Panetela	50s, 5 pk.

Companion	50s, 5 pk.
Cool Smoke	50s, 5 pk.
Palma	50s
Don Ce Sar	
Palma	50s
Prince	50s 10/6 pk.
Little Ce Sar	48s 10/5

HONDURAN CIGAR IMPORTS LTD.
100 West Putname Avenue
Greenwich, CT 06830
(203) 661-1100

DON TOMAS

PRODUCT & SIZE	Packup
Presidentes	25s
Imperials No. 1	25s
Cetros No. 2	25s
Coronas	25s
Panatelas Largas	25s
Toros	25s
Panatelas	25s
Blunts	25s
Corona Grandes (Tube)	25s
Supremos	25s

HOUSE OF WINDSOR, INC.
Subsidiary United States Tobacco Co.
Windsor, PA 17366
(717) 244-4501   UPC # 70047

PRODUCT & SIZE	Packup
House of Windsor	
Palmas**	50s-4s
Javelins Panatela**	50s-5s
Sportsman*	50s-5s
Corona	50s-5s
Imperiales*	50s-4s
Mark VI	
Magnates**	50s-4s
Midas**	50s-6s
Gladstone	5s
Tipped Cigarillos	

*Available in imported Candela Wrappers Only
**Available in both imported Natural and Candela Wrappers

INTERCONTINENTAL CIGARS, INC.
San Diego, CAL.
(203) 348-1111

PRODUCT & SIZE	Packup
All Cigars are handmade.	
Madrigal - From Central America	
Presidente	25s
Soberanos	25s
Churchills	25s
Palmas de Mayorca	25s
Corona Gorda	25s
Panatela Especial	25s
Corona Extra	25s
Nom Plus	25s
Lindas	25s
Cremas	25s
Cazadores	50s only

All sizes are available in natural claro claro and maduro. All sizes contain 100% long filler except cazadores. All Cuban seed tobaccos sun grown.

Casa Copan - From Honduras

Presidente	25s
Corona Grande	25s
Churchills	25s
Numero Uno	25s
Palma Extra	25s
Petit Corona	25s
Pinceles	25s

Handmade from long filler tobaccos.

Available in Natural only. All Cuban seed with shade grown wrappers.

Valdez - From Mexico

#1 Churchill	25s
#2 Double Corona	25s
#3 Presidente	25s
#4 Numero 4	25s
#5 Petite Churchill	25s
#6 Corona Delux	25s
#7 Palma Elites	25s
#9 Caballeros	25s
#13 Panateles	25s
#15 Executive	50s

All hand made long filler tobaccos.

Available in Maduro & Natural. Made from Sumatra seed tobaccos grown in San Andres, Mexico.

El Beso - From Mexico Packed in Bundles

#11 Churchill	25s
#12 Double Corona	25s
#13 Presidente	25s
#14 Numero 4	25s
#15 Petit Churchill	25s
#16 Corona Deluxe	25s
#17 Palma Elites	25s
#18 Caballeros	25s
#26 Panatelas	25s
#30 Executive	25s

All hand made - long filler tobacco   s

Available in Natural & Maduro. Made from Sumatra seed tobaccos grown in San Andres, Mexico.

Don Rubio - From Honduras Packed in Bundles

Cremas	25s
Lindas	25s
Nom Plus	25s
Panatela Especial	25s
Corona Extra	25s
Corona Gorda	25s
Palmas De Mayorca	25s
Churchills	25s
Soberanos	25s
Presidente	25s
Pinceles	25s
Petit Corona	25s
Palma Extra	25s
Numero 2	25s
Numero Uno	25s
Corona Grande	25s

All hand made - long filler tobaccos

Available in Natural only. All Cuban seed cigars. Packed in Bundles.

JACOBS CIGAR CO.
Red Lion, PA 17356
(717) 244-5020

PRODUCT & SIZE	Packup
Tobacco Shed (All Tobacco)	1/20-5s
Blue Tip	
inv	1/20-5s

J.R. TOBACCO
108 W. 45th Street, NY, NY 10036
(212) 869-8777

Belmont	
Casadores	1/40
Fumas	1/40
Casa de Cuba	1/40
Don Pepe - Mexico	
#1	1/40
#2	1/40
#3	1/40
#4	1/40
#5	1/40
#6	1/40
JR Cameroons	
#1	1/20
#2	1/20
#3	1/20
#4	1/20
Tequila - Mexico	
Poquitos	1/20

LOU JACK CIGAR
Marion, Ks. 66861
(800) 431-2380

Don Diego	
Babies	1/20
Petit Corona	1/40
Corona	1/40
Lonsdale	1/40
Greco	1/40
Royal Palm	1/40
Monarch	1/100

M & N CIGAR MANUFACTURERS, INC.
2701 Sixteenth St., Tampa, FL 33601
(813) 248-2124

PRODUCT & SIZE	Packup
Cuesta-Rey	
#1 English Market Selection (ACW)	1/50
#1 English Market Selection (ACW)	3 pk.
#50 English Market Selection (ACW)	1/40
#50 English Market Selection (ACW)	30s
#70 English Market Selection (ACW)	1/40
#70 English Market Selection (ACW)	3 pk.
#2 English Market Selection (ACW)	1/40
#2 English Market Selection (ACW)	3 pk.
#8-9-8 English Market Selection (ACW)	1/40
#8-9-8 English Market Selection (ACW)	3 pk.
#95 English Market Selection (ACW)	1/20
#95 English Market Selection (ACW)	1/40
#95 English Market Selection (ACW)	3 pk-30
#10-G (ACW)	1/40

PRODUCT & SIZE	Packup
#10-G (ACW)	cbnt of 5
#10-G (ACW)	3 pk.
ACW Corona (ACW)	1/20
ACW Corona (ACW)	4 pk.
#240 English Market Selection (ACW)	50 in pk.
#120 English Market Selection (ACW)	70 in pk.
Individuals	1/200
Aristocrats (Glass Tubes)	1/100
Churchills	1/40
Sabre VII (ACW)	1/40
Culebras	1/40
Starlites (Glass Tubes)	1/40
Starlites (Glass Tubes)	1/50
Starlites (Glass Tubes)	1/100
Corona Larga	1/40
Monte-Rey	1/40
Imperial Coronas (ACW) (Alum. Tubes)	1/40
Imperial Coronas (ACW) (Alum. Tubes)	3 pk.
Palma Supremes (ACW)	1/20
Palma Supremes (ACW)	1/40
Palma Supremes (ACW)	4 pk-40
Palma Supremes Ex. Cl.	1/20
Palma Supremes Ex. Cl.	1/40
Palma Supremes Ex. Cl.	4 pk-40
London Tip	1/20
Astorias	1/20
Brevas	1/20
Brevas	5 pk.
Petit Palmas (ACW)	1/20
Caravelles (ACW)	1/20
Caravelles (ACW)	6 pk-60
Caravelles Ex. Cl.	1/20
Caravelles Ex. Cl	6pk-60
Aces	1/20
Aces	5 pk.
Jacks	1/20
Jacks	5 pk.
Panetelas Specials	1/20
Dolls	5 pk.
Rigoletto	
Londonaire	Box of 30
Londonaire	3 pk.
Palma Grande	Box of 60
Palma Grande	6 pk.
Panetela Grande	6 pk.
Kings Maduro	box of 50
Kings Maduro	5 pk.
Natural Coronas	box of 50
Natural Coronas	5pk.
Black Jack Maduro	box of 50
Black Jack Maduro	4 pk.
Palma Cedar	Box of 50
Palma Cedar	5 pk.

M. MARSH & SON

915 Market Street, Wheeling, WV 26003
(304) 232-0770

PRODUCT & SIZE	Packup
Pioneer	1/20-5 pk.
Virginians	1/20-5 pk.
Deluxe	1/20-5 pk.
Old Reliable (Kentucky Tobacco)	1/10
Dry Slitz Regular	1/10/10-5 pk.
Dry Slitz Major	1/20
Mountaineer	1/10/20-5 pk.
Pollack Drums	1/10

Pollack Crown	5 pk.
Melo Crown	1/20-5 pk.
Gallaghers	1/10
Gallagher Elite	1/20-50 pk
Marsh Tips	5 pk.
Stogie Special Deluxe	1/20-5 pk.

JOHN MIDDLETON, INC.

King of Prussia, PA 19406
70137

PRODUCT & SIZE	Packup
Cherry Blend Cigars	5 pk.

MORO CIGAR COMPANY

Div. Consolidated Cigar Corporation, A Gulf & Western Company
15 Columbus Circle, 17th Floor
New York, NY 10023
(212) 333-3500

PRODUCT & SIZE	Packup
Primo Del Rey	
Soberanos	1/40 cedar bx
Coronas Reales	1/40 cedar bx
Palmas	1/40
Sublimes	1/40
#100	1/40 cedar bx
Presidentes	1/40
Selection #1	1/40
Selection #2	1/40
Selection #3	1/40
Selection #4	1/40
Selection #5	1/40
Panetela Extras	1/40
Selection	#1/40
Royal	1/20
Panetelas	1/40
Cazadores	1/40 bundle
Cazadores	1/20 bx
Fumas	1/40 bundle
Monarch	1/40
Imperiales	1/40
Churchill	1/40

NATIONAL CIGAR CORPORATION

P.O. Box 97, Frankfort, IN 46041
(317) 659-3326

PRODUCT & SIZE	Packup
El Verso	
Bouquet	50s wood
	50s pp(10-5pk.) disp cont
Bouquet Lt. Leaf	
Girl, Boy, Just Married	50s wood
	50s pp(10-5pk) disp cont
Commodore	50s wood
	50s pp(10-5pk) disp cont
Corona Extra	50s wood
	50s pp(10-5pk) disp cont
Adjutant	50s wood
	50s pp(10-5pk) disp cont
Mellow	50s pp(10-5pk) disp cont
	100s pp(20-5pk) disp cont
El Macco Puritano	50s wood
	50s pp(10-5pk) disp cont
Hauptmann	50s wood
Broadleaf	50s pp(10-5pk) disp cont
Corona	50s wood
	50s pp(10-5pk) disp cont

Natural Maduro	50s wood
	50s pp(10-5pk) disp cont
Palma	50s wood
	50s pp(10-5pk) disp cont
Panetela	50s wood
	50s pp(10-5pk) disp cont
Panetela Maduro	50s wood
	50s pp(10-5pk) disp cont
Perfecto	50s wood
	50s pp(10-5pk) disp cont
	25s tin can
Perfecto Maduro	50s wood
	50s pp(10-5pk) disp cont
	25s tin can
Evermore Original	
Lt. - Med. - Dk.	50s wood
Lt. - Dk.	50s pp(10-5pk) disp cont
Farnam Drive	
Lt. - Med. - Dk.	50s wood
Lt. - Dk.	50s pp(10-5pk) disp cont
Evermore Corona Grande	
Lt. - Med. - Dk.	50s wood
Lt. - Dk.	50s pp(10-5pk) disp cont
Evermore Palma	
Lt. - Med. - Dk.	50s wood
Lt. - Dk.	50s pp(10-5pk) disp cont
Black Hawk Chiefs	50s wood
	50s pp(10-5pk) disp cont

H. L. NEFF & CO.
Mason and Charles Streets
Red Lion, PA 17356
(717) 244-7351

PRODUCT & SIZE	Packup
Golden's Blue Ribbon Perf. Ex.	1/20th
Rasola Perf.	1/20th
Rasola Blunts	1/20th
White Orchid Perf.	1/20th
Golden's Blue Ribbon	
Cigarillos 5-Pack	1/10th
Black Gold, Perf. Ex.	1/20th
Mac Perfecto	1/20th
Mac Tips	1/10th
Golden's Blue Ribbon Tips	1/10th
Ebony Perf. & Blunts	1/20
Ebony Jrs. & Tips	1/10th

OLOGY DISTRIBUTION CO.
420 Plum St., Cincinnati, OH 45202
(513) 721-3135 & 3136

PRODUCT & SIZE	Packup
Ology Dark Blunt	50
Ology Dark Blunt	5 pk.

A. OPPENHEIMER & COMPANY
Division of Cadogan Investments, Ltd. of America
435 North Midland Avenue
Saddle Brook, NJ 07662
(201) 791-8480-1

PRODUCT & SIZE	Packup

Joya de Nicaragua Handmade-
Imported Cigars
Sole Distributors
A. Oppenheimer & Co.

Joya One Hundred**	100s
Presidente*	5s

Viajante*	10s
Emperador*	10s
#11*	25s
Churchill	25s
#1	25s
Consul	25s
#5	25s
#3	25s
#7	25s
#6	25s
Petit	25s
Senoritas*	10s
Senoritas*	50s
Piccolino**	100 Cigars--10 pkgs

Available in Natural, Maduro and Claro Claro except**Natural only *Not in Claro Claro.

**Available in Natural only.

Count Christopher Handmade-
Imported Cigars
Sole Distributors
A. Oppenheimer & Co.

Continente	10s
Fernando	25s
Cristobal	25s
Ysabel	25s
Santa Maria	25s
La Pinta	25s
La Nina	25s

(Available in Natural and Maduro)

CIMA
Sole Distributors
A. Oppenheimer & Co.

Embajadores	50s
*Swinger	50s
Breva	50s

Available in Natural. Maduro, and Claro-Claro *Not available in Claro-Claro.

PAN AMERICAN CIGAR COMPANY
300 Observer Highway
Hoboken, NJ 07030
(201) 792-3838

PRODUCT & SIZE	Packup
Royal Jamaica	
Quatros	1/20
Pirates	1/20
Buccaneer	1/40
Coronita	1/40
Petit Corona	1/40
Rapier	1/40
Flor De Jamaica	
(Tissue Wrapped)	1/40
Corona	1/40
Imperial	1/40
Doubloon	1/40
Director #3 (Cedar Wrapped)	1/40
Royal Corona	1/40
Park Drive	1/40
Navarro	1/40
Petit Corona Tubes (Aluminum)	1/40
New York Plaza	1/40
Musketeer	1/40

Magnum	1/40
Corona Grande	1/40
Park Lane (Tissue Wrapped)	1/40
Ascot	1/40
Director #1 (Cedar Wrapped	1/40
Double Corona	1/40
Double Corona Cabinet Selection	
(No Cello)	1/20
Giant Corona	1/40
Churchill	1/40
No. 10 Downing St.	1/100
Churchill Individual	
(Slide-Top Chest)	1/50
Goliath (9 inch-64 ring)	1/100
Suerdieck (Brazil)	
Fidalgos(10 Pk)	1/20
Florinha	1/20
Nips	1/20
Brasilia	1/20
Suerdieck#2	1/20
Viajantes	1/20
Mandarim Pai	1/20 & 1/50
Caballeros	1/20 & 1/50
Fiesta	1/20 & 1/50
Pampulha	1/20
Valencia	1/20 & 1/50
Brasileiros	1/20
Medios	1/20 & 1/50
Finos	1/20 & 1/50
Brasil Regalia	1/50
Especial	1/20
Suerdieck (W. Germany)	
Reynita	tin of 20
Petela	tin of 20
Mandarim	tin of 10
Reynita Mini-Chest	1/20
D. Pedro	5 pk.
Florinha	1/20
Bella Flor	1/40
Prima Donna	1/40
Danlys (Honduras)	
Number 5	1/20
Petit Cetros	1/40
Number 4	1/40
Palma Fina	1/40
Luchadore	1/40
Cetros	1/40
Palma Extra	1/40
Fancy Tale Extra	1/40
Number 1	1/40
Churchill	140
Presidente	1/40
Flor de Mexico	
Premio Grande	1/40
Gigante	1/40
Hidalgo	1/40
Don Luis	1/40
Almirantes	1/40
Magnificos	1/40
Nacionales	1/40
Aztecas	1/40
Marias	1/40
Picas	1/40
Amigos	1/20
Chicos	1/20
Ornelas (Mexico)	
Ornelas No. 1 (Cedar Wrapped)	1/40
Ornelas No. 2 (Cedar Wrapped)	1/40
Ornelas No. 3 (Cedar Wrapped)	1/40
Ornelas No. 4 (Cedar Wrapped)	1/40
Ornelas No. 5 (Cedar Wrapped)	1/40
Ornelas No. 2 Extra (Alum. Tube)	1/40
Ornelas No. 4 Extra (Alum. Tube)	1/40

Ornelas ABC (Cedar Wrapped)	1/20

PERFECTO GARCIA & BROS., INC.

818 Lake St., Evanston, IL 60201
(312) 864-0300

President	Manuel Garcia, Jr.
**Vice President	Charles Garcia

PRODUCT & SIZE	Packup
Perfecto Garcia	
Churchill Coronas	1/40
San Souci	1/40
London Tower B/N	1/20
Prime Minister B/N	1/20
Brillantes (Glass)	1/100
Admirals 10 Top	1/40
222	1/40
8-9-8 B/N 1 bdle	1/40
Piccadilly B/N	1/20
Corona Grande	1/40
Fancy Tales	1/40
Corona de Luxe	1/40
Hyde Park B/N	1/20
Lord of England	1/20
Diamonds	1/40
Coronas No. 2	1/40
Aristocrats (tips)	1/40
Cedros No. 2 (cedar)	1/40
Ensigns	1/40
Gloria	1/20
Waldorfs	1/40-1/20
Morro Castle	1/20
Palmas	1/20
Palmas 4 pk.	1/16
Queens-Dukes	1/20
Queens 4 pk	1/16
Corona Chica (bundle)	1/20
Diplomat	1/20
Commodores	1/20
Sublimes	1/20
Buccaneer	1/20
Buccaneer	6 pk.
P. G. Panetelas	1/20
Jeffersons	1/20
Classic Panetelas	1/20
Classic Panetelas	5 pk.
Babies	1/20
Babies (5 pk)	1/200
Gems (tips)	1/20
Gems (tips)5 pk.	1/200
Cigarillos	1/20
Cigarillos 5 pk.	1/200
Crown Royal	
Princess	1/20
Princess 5 pk.	1/200
Garcia y Garcia	
Londres 5 pk.	1/200
Londres	1/20
Numero	
1	1/40
2	1/40
3	1/40
4	1/40
5	1/40
6	1/40
7	1/40
8	1/40
Individuales	1/100
Lord Churchills	1/40
Sir Lonsdale	1/40

Baron de Rothschild	1/20
Caprichos	1/40
No. 85	1/20
No. 101	1/40
Petit Corona	1/40
Magnum-10	1/100
Cetros	1/20

PETERSON'S LTD.
75 Triangle Boulevard, Carlstadt, NJ 07072
(201) 939-5400

PRODUCT & SIZE	Packup
Cigars	
Willem II (Made in Holland)	
Sigrettos	20s
Whiffs #30	10s
Long Panatellas	10s
Long Delights	5s
Corona	10s
Bravo	10s
Fantastica	5s
Tabacalera (Philippines)	
Coronas Largas Especiales	25s
Coronas Largas	25s
Panetelas Largas	25s
Don Q	25s
Conde de Guell Sr.	25s
Coronas	25s
Panetelas	50s
Brevas	50s
Don Marcos Cigars (Canary Islands, Spain)	
Amatista	25s
Baby	50s
Castillo	25s
Cetros	25s
Corona	25s
Corona Major	25s
Deliciosos #1	25s
Deliciosos #2	25s
Deliciosos #3	25s
Grandee	25s
Monarch	10s
Natural Tube	25s
Sevilla	25s
Trump	25s
Demi-Tasse 10s	50s
Stubby	25s
SBN 4	25s
SBN 11	25s
SBN 12	25s
SBN 18	25s
Flor Del Caribe (Honduras)	
Sovereign	25s
Diamantes	25s
Super Cetros	25s
Viva	25s
Bravo	25s
Duques	25s
La Perla	25s
Castillions	25s
H. Upmann Cigars	
Topicos SBN	25s
No. 2000 SBN	25s
Amatistas Jar	50s
Imperiales	25s
Naturales Tubes	25s
Corona Major Tubes	25s
Lonsdales	25s
Coronas	25s
Royal Palms Tubes	25s

Babies	50s
Petit Corona	25s
Grecos	25s

PREMIER CIGARS
502 Tyson Avenue, Glenside, PA. 19038
(215) CA 4-1965

Mocambo - Mexico
    Royal Corona
    Dbl. Corona
    S/L
    Premiers
    Churchills

PRIMATE CIGAR CO.
2142 Stuart St., Brooklyn, NY 11229
(212) 332-9103

PRODUCT & SIZE	Packup
Pride of Jamaica	
Lonsdales	25s
Royal Corona	25s
Presidents	25s
Petit Corona	25s
Elegante	25s
Panatella No. 3	25s
Panatella No. 2	25s
Panatella No. 1	25s
Petit Churchill	25s
Churchills	25s

All sizes available in Colorado Clara (Natural), or Madura.

Jamaica Heritage	
No. 100	
No. 200	
No. 300	
No. 500	
No. 700	
No. 900	
No. 1000	

Packed in Square Cello Bundles of 25. Natural Wrappers Only.

Lord of Jamaica	
Lonsdales	25
Royal Coronas	25
Majestic	25
Elagante	25
Lancers	25
Brigante	25
Churchill	25

All sizes packed in cello packages of 25 available in natural madura

Solo Aroma	
Corona Gorda	25
Churchills	25
Coronas Extra	25
Palma Extra	25
Cazadores	25
Lindas	25
Nom Plus	25
Palmas De Mayorca	25
Numero Uno	25
Numero Duo	25
Presidents	25
Soberanos	25
Corona Grande	25

All sizes packed in cello packages of 25 Natural wrapper only.

175

E. REGENSBURG & SONS

Division of Bayuk Cigars
2150 S. Andrews Avenue
Ft. Lauderdale, FL 33316
(305) 525-8433

PRODUCT & SIZE	Packup
Medalist	
Naturales #3	50 box
Naturales #3	50 fp
Naturales #7	50 box
Naturales #7	60 fp
Naturales #66	50 box
Naturales #66	50 fp
Admiration	
Smiles	50 box
Smiles	50 fp
Royals	50 box
Royals	50 fp
Nelson	50 box
Nelson	50 fp
Mayfair	25 box
Mayfair	40 fp
Mayfair	50 box

REISS-DABNEY CIGAR CO.

420 Plum St., Cincinnati, OH 45202
(513) 721-3135 & 3136

PRODUCT & SIZE	Packup
Certified Bond Frontmarks	
Certified Bond Dark	50
Certified Bond Dark	5-pk.
Certified Bond Light	50
Certified Bond Light	5-pk
Certified Bond Panatela Dark	50
Certified Bond Panatela Dark	5-pk.
Certified Bond Palma Dark	5-pk.
Certified Bond Palma Dark	5-pk.
Certified Bond Palma Light	5-pk.
Certified Bond Slims Dark	50
Certified Bond Slims Dark	5-pk.

JAMES B. RUSSELL, INC.

180 So. Van Brunt St.
Englewood, NJ 07631
N.J. (201) 568-1412   N.Y. (212) 586-4276

PRODUCT & SIZE	Packup
Imported from Denmark	
Nobel	
Delicados	10 pk.
Marietta Maxi	10 pk.
Petit Cigarillos	10s
Petit Cigarillos	20s
Petit Cigarillos	50s
Imported from Holland	
Agio	
Wilde Cigarros	5 pk.
Wilde Cigarros Brasil	5 pk.
Wilde Cigarillos	10 pk.
Wilde Cigarillos Brasil	10 pk.
Wilde Cigarillos	20 pk.
Wilde Cigarillos Brasil	20 pk.
Meharis	10 pk.
Meharis Brasil	10 pk.
Biddies Brasil	20 pk.
Filter Tips	10 pk.
Slenderellas	5 pk.
Slenderellas	25 Tin

CIGARS BY SANTA CLARA LTD.

P.O. Box 755
Tuxedo Park, NY 10987
(914) 351-4716

Chivis - Hand made - Honduras	
#100	1/40
#200	1/40
#300	1/40
#400	1/40
#500	1/40
#600	1/40
#700	1/40
#800	1/40
Churchill	1/40
Mexicana - Mexico	
Brevas	
Delgados	
Conchas Finas	
Domingo	
Don Luis	
Augies	
J.Z. (Glass Tube)	
Mocha - Hand made - Honduras	
Panetela	1/50
Petit Corona	1/50
Corona	1/50
Dbl. Corona	1/50
Stiletto	1/50
Lonsdale	1/50
Ambassador	1/50
Churchill	1/50
Stock Market	
Plazas	1/20
Dandy Andy	1/20
Viva - Mexico	
Cazadores	1/20
Silent Jim	1/40
Don Bernardo	1/40
Rosalindas	1/40
M.S. Americans	
Dominicana - Hand made - Dominican Republic	
No. 100	1/40
No. 200	1/40
No. 300	1/40
No. 400	1/40
El Caudillo	
No. 1	1/40
No. 2	1/40
No. 3	1/40
No. 4	1/40
No. 5	1/40
No. 5	1/100
Harrows - Phillipines	
Esquire	1/100
Rothschild	1/50
Regent	1/50
No. 1	1/50
Camolot	1/50
Londonderry	1/50
Nawarait	1/50
Mello Coronas	
Panetela	1/20
Corona	1/20
Dark Slims	1/20

SAN TELMO CIGAR CO.

723 S. Madison Ave., Bay City, MI 48706

PRODUCT & SIZE	Packup
Berthold Brevas DeLuxe .25	50s
Berthold Cedars .30	50s

THE STRAUS-KEILSON CO.
9345 Princeton-Glendale Rd. P.O. Box
Cincinnati, OH 45246
(513) 874-5200

PRODUCT & SIZE	Packup
Rosola	
Blunts 10/5 pk .72	1000
Blunts 1/20 2/.29	1000
Perfectos 10/5 pk .72	1000
Perfectos 1/20 2/.29	1000
Henry Straus	
Broadleaf Blunt 10/5 pk .85	2500
Broadleaf Blunt 1/20 2/.33	2500
Broadleaf Executive 10/5 pk .85	2500
Broadleaf Executive 1/20 2/.33	2500
Broadleaf Perfecto 10/5 pk .85	2500
Broadleaf Perfecto 1/20 2/.33	2500
Custom Made Corona 10/5 pk .85	2500
Custom Made Corona 1/20 2/.33	2500
Custom Made Natural Maduro	
10/5 pk. 1.00	2500
Custom Made Natural Maduro	
1/20 2/.39	2500
Custom Made Palma 10/5 pk 1.00	2500
Custom Made Palma 1/20 2/.39	2500
Number 9 10/5 pk .57	1500
Number 9 1/20 .23	1500

JNO H. SWISHER & SON, INC.
P.O. Box 2230, Jacksonville, FL 32203

PRODUCT & SIZE	Packup
King Edward (Deluxe)	
KE Invincible	50s-5s
KE Panetela	50s-5s
KE Cigarillo	5s
KE It's a Boy	50s
KE It's a Girl	50s
King Edward (Regular)	
KE Imperial	50s-5s
KE Specials	50s-5s
KE Tip Cigarillo	50s-5s
Swisher Sweets by King Edward	
SS Cigars	50s-5s
SS Slims	50s-5s
SS Cigarillo	50s-5s
SS Tips	5s
Home Made	50s-5s
Home Made Tip Cigarillo	5s
Dixie Maid	50s
Dixie Maid Tip Cigarillo	50s
Pom Pom Operas	50s

TAMPA PRODUCTS COMPANY
P.O. Box 2030, Tampa, FL 33601
(813) 248-2124

PRODUCT & SIZE	Packup
Villiger-Kiel	
Villiger-Kiel Mild	5 pkt pk
Villiger-Kiel Mild	10 pkt pk
Villiger-Kiel Mild	
(plastic canister drums)	20 pk cnstr
Villiger-Kiel Brasil	10 pkt pk
Villiger-Kiel Brasil	
(plastic canister drums)	20 pk cnstr
Villiger-Kiel Junior Mild	10 pkt pk
Villiger-Kiel Junior Mild	
(plastic canister drums)	25 pk cnstr
Villiger-Kiel Junior Brasil	10 pkt pk
Villiger-Kiel Junior Brasil	

(plastic canister drums)	25 pk cnstr
Villiger Export	5 pkt pk
Villiger Export	Box of 25
Villiger Braniff #2	10 pkt pk
Villiger Braniff #2	Box of 50
Villiger Paméla Brasil	10 pkt pk

TE-AMO GERYL COMPANY, INC.
34 Exchange Place, Jersey City, NJ 07302
(201) 333-3710 (212)

PCODUCT & SIZE	Packup
No. 1 Relaxations 1.00	1/40
No. 2 Meditations .85	1/40
No. 3 Torero .80	1/40
No. 4 .75	1/40
No. 5 Picador .70	1/20-1/40
No. 6 *Pauser 2/.75	1/20
No. 7 Coronita .65	1/40
No. 8 Cetro .95	1/40
No. 9 Imperial 1.50	1/40-1/100
No. 10 *Epicure 2/.95	1/20
No. 11 Elegante 2/1.05	1/20
No. 12 Amatista .80	1/40
No. 14 Churchill 1.25	1/40-1/100
No. 15 Super Cetro 1.00	1/40
No. 16 Ambassador 1.05	1/40
No. 17 Presidente 1.15	1/40
No. 18 Torito .80	1/20
No. 19 Ioro .95	1/40

UNITED STATES TOBACCO COMPANY
100 West Putnam Ave.
Greenwich, CT 06830
(203) 661-1100

UNIVERSAL CIGAR CORPORATION
660 Madison Avenue
New York, NY 10021
(212) 753-5700

PRODUCT & SIZE	Packup
La Primadora	
Panetelas	1/20-5 pk.
Brevas (XX and Natural)	1/20
Diplomats	
(XX and Natural)	1/20-5 pk.
Coronation (XX and Natural)	1/20-5 pk.
#200 (Maduro)	1/20-4 pk.
Criterion	
(XX and Natural)	1/20-4 pk.
Americana	1/40
Corona No. 1	1/40
Solitaire (Tube)	3/100
Starbrite (Tube)	1/50
Corona Grande	1/40
Cetros Boite Nature (Natural)	1/20
Imperiale	1/40
#400 Boite Nature	
(Natural)	1/20
Palmero Boite Nature	
(Natural)	1/20
#500 Boite Nature (Natural)	1/20
Blackstone	1/20-5 pk.
King	1/20-5 pk.
Golden Corona	1/20-5 pk.
Seville	1/20-5 pk.
Dexter Londres	1/20-5 pk.
7-20-4 Londres	1/20-5 pk.
Haddon Hall	
Imperiale Nat.	1/40-3 pk.

Palma Cameroon	1/20-5 pk.
No. 77	
Corona Deluxe	1/20-5 pk.
Quality Palma	1/20-5 pk.
Optimo	
Sports	1/20-5 pk.
Panetelas	1/20-5 pk.
Corona	1/20-5 pk.
Futuras (XX and Natural)	1/20-5 pk.
Blunt Extra	1/20
Admirals	1/20-5 pk.
Palmas (Maduro)	1/20-5 pk.
Lords	1/20-5 pk.
Longfellow (XX and Natural)	1/20-6 pk.
Riviera (cedar wrap)	1/20
King	
(XX and Cameroon Wrapper)	1/20-4 pk.
Modernos (Tube)	
XX and Natural)	/100-3 pk.
Admiral (Boy or Girl)	1/20
Corona (Boy or Girl)	1/20

EL TRELLES DIVISION

El Trelles	
Panetelas	1/20-5 pk.
Leader	1/20-5 pk.
Grandee	1/20-5 pk.
Blunt Extra	1/20-5 pk.
Kings	1/20-5 pk.
Club House	1/20-5 pk.
Tryangle	1/20-5 pk.
Wonder	1/20
Banker	1/20-1/40
Palmas Deluxe (Tube)	3/100
Keep Moving	
Goodies	1/20-5 pk.
Palmas	1/20
Great Southern Dixies	1/20-5 pk.

SANTA FE DIVISION

Santa Fe	
Panetela	1/20-5 pk.
Laguna	1/20-5 pk.
Pattie	1/20-5 pk.
Mayfair	1/20-5 pk.
Palma (Maduro)	1/20-5 pk.
Flamingo	1/20-6 pk.
Fairway	1/20-5 pk.
Biltmore	1/20-5 pk.
Fairmont	1/20-5 pk.
Imperial (Tube)	3/100
Corona Grande BN (Tube)	1/50
Pattie (Boy or Girl)	1/20-1/40

VILLAZON · SEE DANBY

UPMANN INTERNATIONAL, INC.
326 Lincoln Rd., Miami Beach, FL 33139
(305) 538-1544   (800) 327-3146

PRODUCT & SIZE	Packup
Carl Upmann (Baccarat)	1/40
Colossais	1/100
Churchil	1/40
Palma Larga	1/40
Fancy Tales	1/40
#1	1/40
#2	1/40
#4	1/40
Extiletes	1/40
Luchadores	1/40

Palma Fina	1/40
Petite Corona	1/40
Princesas	1/20
Upmanns Repeaters	1/20
Montoya	
Lonsdales	1/40
Celros	1/40
Royal Corona	1/40
Petit Corona	1/40
Delicados	1/40
Greco	1/40
Managua	
Grand Master	1/100
Grand Master	1/40
Churchill	1/40
Londres	1/40
La Fontana	Bx 26
Gran Premier	1/40
Cordial	1/40
Rothchild	1/40
Demi-tasse	1/40
Aristocrats	1/40
Dominican Specials	Burlap
#1	1/40 Bndl
#2	1/40 Bndl
#3	1/40 Bndl
#4	1/40 Bndl

G. W. VAN SLYKE & HORTON
Drawer 111, Red Lion, PA 17356
(717) 244-1295

PRODUCT & SIZE	Packup
Don Pastillo Finos (All Tobacco)	1/20
Flor de Villar (All Tobacco)	1/20
Pennsylvania Dutchman	1/20-5 pk.
Manuel	
Kings	1/20-5 pk.
Peter Schuyler	
Generals	1/20-5 pk.
Kings	1/20-5 pk.
Panatelas	1/20
It's a Beautiful Girl	1/20-1/40
It's a Handsome Boy	1/20-1/40
Vega Del Rey	
Cedars	1/20-5 pk.
Palmas	1/20-5 pk.
Seal of Philadelphia Cedros	1/20-5 pk.
Madison Avenue Petit Palmas	1/20-5 pk.
Factory #217 Palmas	1/20-5 pk.
Van Slyke & Horton Petit Coronas	1/20-5 pk.
No. 211 Favoritas	1/20-5 pk.
Cadillac Coronas	1/20-5 pk.
Cadillac Perfectos	1/20-5 pk.
Windsor Corona Smokers	1/20-5 pk.
Counsellor	1/20
Rey West Crooks	1/20-5 pk.
Factory Favorites	Bags of 20s

YORKANA CIGAR CO.
131-35 N. Penn Street, York, PA 17404

PRODUCT & SIZE

Churchill
    7 Jupiter
    7 International
    6 Debonair, Corona
    Corona Grande 6
    5 Perfecto
Irvin S. Cobb
    Kings 6 Corona
    Palmas 6
    Perfecto 5

The Cigars of Cuba

No book on cigars would truly be worthy of the term "Almanac" without an in depth section on Cuban cigars.

While it is true that the thrust of this book is aimed at cigars which you can legally purchase in this country, I feel it is only just to give you a little taste of what we used to have. Truthfully, today's manufacturers have created new brands equal in quality to those you are about to see, but they can never equal the romance and magnetism of the Havana cigar.

Due to requirements of space, not all Cuban brands are shown in this section. There are actually twenty one major fine brands:

Partagas	El Rey del Mondo
Bolivar	Davidoff
Belinda	H. Upmann
Ramon Allones	Monte Cristo
LaGloria Cubana	Romeo y Julieta
Gispert	Jose Piedra
Punch	Juan Lopez
Hoyo de Monterrey	Rafael Gonzalez
Por Larranaga	Saint Luis Rey
Sancho Panza	Quintero
La Escepcion	

Of the twenty one major brands, only Belinda (the fifth largest selling line) is missing. This material was out on loan to Palicio and Co. for use in designing packaging for a reintroduction of this brand in early 1980.

Historically, the world's finest cigar leaf and cigar craftsmen were Cuban, and the seal, a reproduction of which is on the cover of this book, assured the connoisseur of the finest product money could buy.

Cuba's very finest tobacco was and remains the world reknown tobaccos of the vuelta abajo. Other major tobacco growing regions are the semi vuelta, partido, remedios and camaguey y oriente. The cigar factories are located in the following cities:

Guana	Camaguey
Pinar del Rio	Bayamo
Habana	Manzanillo
Matanzas	Holguin
Cienfuegos	Palma Soriano
Santa Clara	Baracoa
Caibarien	Moron
Ciego de Avila	

In total, about 70,000 hectares of prime land are devoted to tobacco cultivation, and, while sugar cane is the major crop of Cuba, tobacco leaf and Habana cigars are the most prestigious.

In the ensuing brand lines you will note the many unusual shapes presented in Cuban brands, and the magical, romantic, nostalgic packaging so long absent in the American marketplace.

Now relax, and wander back to 1961, or perhaps ahead to the eighties, when you may in fact be able to once again enjoy these beautiful, beautiful cigars.

On July 16, 1912, the Cuban Government issued a law which established the compulsory use of a seal as a certificate of origin on all hand-rolled cigars, cigarettes and cut tobacco. From that moment on, said seal was to be considered a part of the "habilitación" of the product. This seal includes a reproduction of the Cuban emblem and a partial view of a tobacco field as a guarantee to the legitimacy of the product, with texts in Spanish, English, French and German.

CUBAN GOVERNMENT'S WARRANTY FOR CIGARS EXPORTED FROM HAVANA

REPUBLICA DE CUBA

Sello de garantia nacional de procedencia

SERIE A
N01

Para Tabacos
torcidos y picadura

LEY DE
JULIO 16/1912

GARANTIE DU GOUVERNEMENT CUBAIN POUR DES CIGARES
EXPORTÉS DE LA HAVANE

GARANTIE DER REGIERUNG VON KUBA FUER AUS HAVANA
EXPORTIERTE ZIGARREN

Bolivar

CORONAS GIGANTES

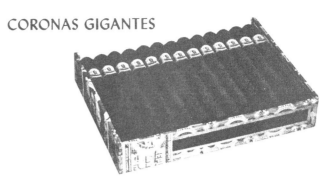

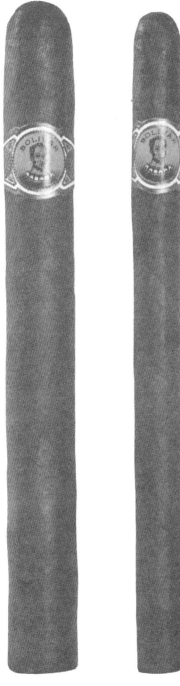   

CORONAS
GIGANTES

25 puros (1/40)
18.65 (47) x 178
14.08 kg. millar

PALMAS

25 puros (1/40)
13.10 (33) x 178
6.97 kg. millar

GOLD MEDAL

10 puros (1/100)
16.67 (42) x 165
10.47 kg. millar

CORONAS
GRANDES

50 puros (1/20)
18.26 (46) x 162
12.33 kg. millar

CORONAS
LARGAS

25 puros (1/40)*
15.48 (39) x 160
8.33 kg. millar

181

Bolivar

PETIT CORONA

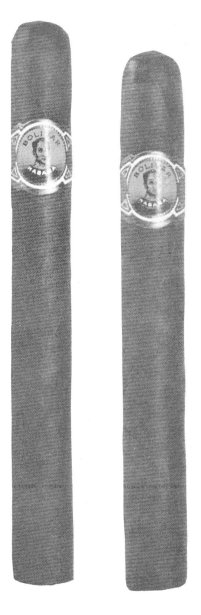

ROYAL DUKES
25 puros (1/40)
16.67 (42) x 152
9.66 kg. millar

CORONAS EXTRA
25 puros (1/40)
17.46 (44) x 143
9.94 kg. millar

BELICOSOS FINOS
25 puros (1/40)
20.64 (52) x 140
12.37 kg. millar

PALMITAS
25 puros (1/40)*
11.51 (29) x 135
3.86 kg. millar

CABINET SELECTION
No. I
25 puros (1/40)
16.67 (42) x 129
8.14 kg. millar

Bolivar

PETIT CORONA

25 puros (1/40)
16.67 (42) x 129
8.14 kg. millar

BOLIVARES

25 puros (1/40)
15.88 (40) x 126
7.29 kg. millar

ESPECIALES

25 puros (1/40)*
15.48 (39) x 125
6.21 kg. millar

REGENTES

25 puros (1/40)
13.49 (34) x 125
5.22 kg. millar

PRINCE CHARLES

50 puros (1/20)
19.84 (50) x 124
11.18 kg. millar

CORONAS EXTRA

BOLIVARES

Bolivar

CORONAS JUNIOR

25 puros (1/40)
16.67 (42) x 110
6.97 kg. millar

CHICOS

25 puros (1/40)*
11.51 (29) x 106
2.99 kg. millar

DEMI TASSE

25 puros (1/40)
11.91 (30) x 100
3.27 kg. millar

PETIT BOLIVAR

25 puros (1/40)
16.67 (42) x 95
6.03 kg. millar

Bolivar

GOLD MEDAL

CABINET SELECTION No. 1

CORONAS GRANDES

185

Hoyo De Monterrey

DOUBLE CORONA	LONGOS	SUPER SELECTION No. I	HUMIDORS No I	MONTERREYES
25 puros (1/40)	25 puros (1/40)	50 puros (1/20)	50 puros (1/20)*	5 puros (1/200)
19.45 (49) x 194	13.10 (33) x 178	16.67 (42) x 152	17.46 (44) x 145	21.83 (55) x 233
16.70 kg. millar	6.97 kg. millar	9.66 kg. millar	9.57 kg. millar	20.98 kg. millar

Hoyo De Monterrey

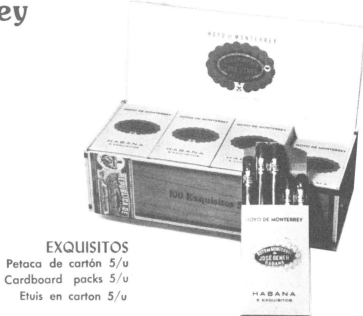

EXQUISITOS
Petaca de cartón 5/u
Cardboard packs 5/u
Etuis en carton 5/u

CORONAS

25 puros (1/40)
16.67 (42) x 142
8.97 kg. millar

PALMAS EXTRA

25 puros (1/40)*
16.67 (42) x 142
8.51 kg. millar

OBSEQUIOS

25 puros (1/40)
18.26 (46) x 137
9.34 kg. millar

EXQUISITOS

100 puros (1/10)*
15.88 (40) x 129
7.04 kg. millar

**GENERES
DE GENER**

25 puros (1/40)*
16.67 (42) x 129
7.77 kg. millar

Hoyo De Monterrey

PERFECTOS

25 puros (1/40)
17.46 (44) x 127
7.36 kg. millar

**SOUVENIRS
DE LUXE No. I**

50 puros (1/20)
15.88 (40) x 126
7.29 kg. millar

BELVEDERES

25 puros (1/40)*
15.48 (39) x 125
6.21 kg. millar

EPICURE No. 2

25 puros (1/40)
19.84 (50) x 124
11.18 kg. millar

MARGARITAS

25 puros (1/40)
10.32 (26) x 121
2.94 kg. millar

MARGARITAS

Hoyo De Monterrey

CORONATIONS
25 puros (1/40)*
16.67 (42) x 129
7.77 kg. millar

PETIT CORONATIONS
25 puros (1/40)*
16.67 (42) x 117
7.04 kg. millar

CORONATIONS
Tubo de aluminio
Aluminium tube
Tube en aluminium

PETIT CORONATIONS

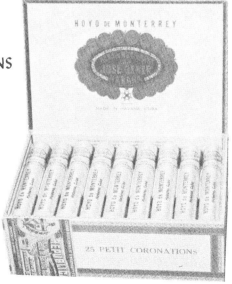

Hoyo De Monterrey

CRISTALES No. I
Jarra de cristal
Glass jar
Caraffe en cristal

GRACIELAS
25 puros (1/40)*
13.89 (35) x 110
4.60 kg. millar

PETIT HOYO
25 puros (1/40)
17.07 (43) x 106
6.99 kg. millar

BONITAS
25 puros (1/40)
15.88 (40) x 102
5.91 kg. millar

SHORT ONES
25 puros (1/40)
16.67 (42) x 110
6.97 kg. millar

CRISTALES No. I
25 puros (1/40)*
16.67 (42) x 142
8.51 kg. millar

Hoyo De Monterrey

PALMAS EXTRA

SHORT ONES
Petaca de cartón
Cardboard packs
Etuis en carton

Hoyo De Monterrey

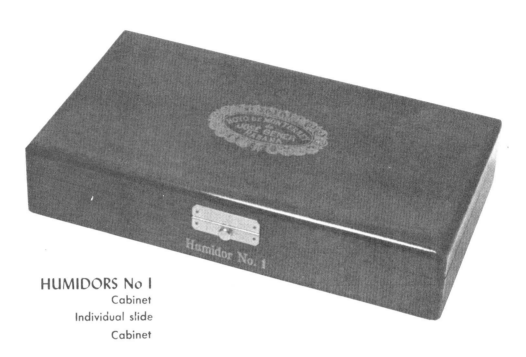

HUMIDORS No I
Cabinet
Individual slide
Cabinet

EPICURE No. 2

Por Larrañaga

MAGNUMS

25 puros (1/40)
19.84 (50) x 172
15.41 kg. millar

CETROS

25 puros (1/40)
16.67 (42) x 165
10.47 kg. millar

LARGOS
DE LARRAÑAGA

25 puros (1/40)*
13.89 (35) x 159
6.67 kg. millar

MONTECARLOS

25 puros (1/40)*
13.89 (35) x 159
6.67 kg. millar

CORONAS

25 puros (1/40)
16.67 (42) x 142
8.97 kg. millar

Por Larrañaga

PETIT CORONAS

25 puros (1/40)
16.67 (42) x 129
8.14 kg. millar

SYMBOLS

25 puros (1/40)*
15.88 (40) x 129
7.04 kg. millar

PICADORES

25 puros (1/40)
17.46 (44) x 127
8.86 kg. millar

POR LARRAÑAGA No. 10

25 puros (1/40)*
16.67 (42) x 125
7.54 kg. millar

SMALL CORONA

25 puros (1/40)
15.88 (40) x 110
6.37 kg. millar

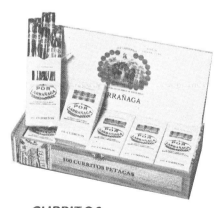

CURRITOS

Petaca de cartón 5/u
Cardboard packs
Etuis en carton

MAGNUMS

SUPER CEDROS

Lámina de cedro
Cedar sheet
Lamelle de cedre

194

Por Larrañaga

EDUARDOS

100 puros (1/10)
7.94 (20) x 109
1.47 kg. millar

CURRITOS

100 puros (1/10)*
11.51 (29) x 106
2.99 kg. millar

LOLAS EN CEDRO

25 puros (1/40)*
16.67 (42) x 129
7.77 kg. millar

SUPER CEDROS

25 puros (1/40)*
16.27 (41) x 127
8.28 kg. millar

SPORTSMAN

10 puros (1/100)*
16.67 (42) x 142
8.51 kg. millar

SPORTSMAN

Tubo de cristal
Glass tube
Tube en cristal

Jose L. Piedra

ROYAL PALMS

SUPERIORES

25 puros (1/40)
15.88 (40) x 146
8.46 kg. millar

ROYAL PALMS

25 puros (1/40)
11.91 (30) x 140
4.72 kg. millar

**PANETELITAS
DE HEBRA**

25 puros (1/40)
11.91 (30) x 111
3.68 kg. millar

SUPERIORES

Juan Lopez

EPICURES

25 puros (1/40)
15.08 (38) x 142
7.27 kg. millar

**PANETELAS
DE LUXE**

25 puros (1/40)
11.91 (30) x 140
4.60 kg. millar

PETIT CORONAS

25 puros (1/40)
16.67 (42) x 129
8.14 kg. millar

**TRES PETIT
CORONAS**

25 puros (1/40)
16.67 (42) x 122
7.73 kg. millar

PATRICIAS

25 puros (1/40)
15.88 (40) x 116
6.72 kg. millar

TITANIAS

25 puros (1/40)
15.88 (40) x 110
6.37 kg. millar

PANETELAS DE LUXE

Gispert

CORONAS

FANCY TALES
25 puros (1/40)
17.46 (44) x 171
11.22 kg. millar

PALMITAS
25 puros (1/40)
12.70 (32) x 152
5.52 kg. millar

CENADORES ONES
25 puros (1/40)
17.46 (44) x 150
10.44 kg. millar

CORONAS GRANDES
25 puros (1/40)
17.46 (44) x 143
9.94 kg. millar

Gispert

CORONAS

25 puros (1/40)
16.67 (42) x 142
8.97 kg. millar

**PETIT CORONA
DE LUXE**

25 puros (1/40)
16.67 (42) x 129
8.14 kg. millar

PANETELAS

25 puros (1/40)
13.49 (34) x 125
5.22 kg. millar

**HABANEROS
No. 2**

25 puros (1/40)
15.08 (38) x 120
6.44 kg. millar

VELAS

25 puros (1/40)
13.49 (34) x 117
4.85 kg. millar

Gispert

CORONAS GRANDES

TOLEDO CHICO
25 puros (1/40)
17.07 (43) x 106
6.99 kg. millar

MINIATURAS
25 puros (1/40)
11.91 (30) x 100
3.27 kg. millar

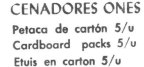

CENADORES ONES
Petaca de cartón 5/u
Cardboard packs 5/u
Etuis en carton 5/u

PETIT CORONA DE LUXE

H. Upmann

CORONAS

SIR WINSTON
25 puros (1/40)
18.65 (47) 178
14.08 kg. millar

EL PRADO
25 puros (1/40)*
13.89 (35) x 159
6.67 kg. millar

HUSSARS
25 puros (1/40)
12.70 (32) x 152
5.52 kg. millar

CORONAS
25 puros (1/40)
16.67 (42) x 142
8.97 kg. millar

ESPECIALES
25 puros (1/40)*
16.67 (42) x 142
8.51 kg. millar

H. Upmann

CRISTALES
Jarra de cristal
Glass jar
Caraffe en cristal

CRISTALES
25 puros (1/40)
16.67 (42) x 138
8.72 kg. millar

AROMATICOS
25 puros (1/40)*
16.67 (42) x 117
7.04 kg. millar

MEDIAS CORONAS
100 puros (1/10)
16.67 (42) x 129
8.14 kg. millar

EXCEPCIONALES DE ROTHSCHILDS
25 puros (1/40)
17.46 (44) x 127
8.86 kg. millar

BELVEDERES
25 puros (1/40)*
15.48 (39) x 125
6.21 kg. millar

H. Upmann

PETIT UPMANN
Petaca de cartón 5/u
Cardboard packs 5/u
Etuis en carton 5/u

PETIT UPMANN	DEMI TASSE	NATURALS	CORONAS MAJOR	SINGULARES
100 puros (1/10)*	25 puros (1/40)*	25 puros (1/40)*	25 puros (1/40)*	25 puros (1/40)*
12.30 (31) x 108	12.70 (32) x 100	14.68 (37) x 155	17.46 (44) x 132	16.27 (41) x 122
3.57 kg. millar	3.50 kg. millar	7.25 kg. millar	8.74 kg. millar	7.01 kg. millar

H. Upmann

CORONAS MAJOR

Tubo de aluminio
Aluminium tube
Tube en aluminium

CORONAS MINOR

25 puros (1/40)*
16.67 (42) x 117
7.04 kg. millar

SINGULARES
Tubo de aluminio
Aluminium tube
Tube en aluminium

CORONAS MINOR
Tubo de aluminio
Aluminium tube
Tube en aluminium

H. Upmann

SIR WINSTON
Cabinet
Individual slide
Cabinet

TRES TUBOS
Cajón mixto
Mixed box
Coffret mixte

Partagas

TOPPERS

FANCY TALES OF SMOKE

25 puros (1/40)
15.48 (39) x 171
8.92 kg. millar

TOPPERS

50 puros (1/20)*
15.48 (39) x 160
8.33 kg. millar

ALMIRANTES

25 puros (1/40)
14.68 (37) x 156
7.18 kg. millar

898 CABINET SELECTION

25 puros (1/40)
16.67 (42) x 152
9.66 kg. millar

CULEBRAS

25 puros (1/40)*
15.48 (39) x 146
6.67 kg. millar

Partagas

CULEBRAS

3 puros trenzados
3 braided Havana cigars
3 cigares tressés

SUPER PARTAGAS	CHARLOTTES	CORONAS	SEVILLA HUMIJAR	EMINENTES
25 puros (1/40)*	25 puros (1/40)	50 puros (1/20)	25 puros (1/40)	100 puros (1/10)*
16.27 (41) x 146	13.89 (35) x 143	16.67 (42) x 142	16.67 (42) x 138	17.46 (44) x 132
8.40 kg. millar	6.26 kg. millar	8.97 kg. millar	8.72 kg. millar	8.74 kg. millar

207

Partagas

**PETIT CORONAS
ESPECIALES**
10 puros (1/100)*
17.46 (44) x 132
8.74 kg. millar

ARISTOCRATAS
25 puros (1/40)*
15.88 (40) x 129
7.04 kg. millar

PETIT CORONAS
25 puros (1/40)
16.67 (42) x 129
8.14 kg. millar

PETIT PARTAGAS
25 puros (1/40)*
15.88 (40) x 129
7.04 kg. millar

PRINCESS
25 puros (1/40)*
13.89 (35) x 127
5.29 kg. millar

EMINENTES

Partagas

PALMAS REALES
Tubo de cristal
Glass tube
Tube en cristal

PALMAS REALES	CRISTALTUBOS	CUBANS	PARTAGAS DE LUXE	CORONAS SENÍOR
25 puros (1/40)*	10 puros (1/100)*	25 puros (1/40)*	25 puros (1/40)*	25 puros (1/40)*
15.48 (39) x 160	17.46 (44) x 145	13.89 (35) x 159	16.27 (41) x 146	17.46 (44) x 132
8.33 kg. millar	9.57 kg. millar	6.67 kg. millar	8.40 kg. millar	8.74 kg. millar

Partagas

PERFECTOS	CAPITOLS	DEMI TIP	HABANEROS
25 puros (1/40)*	100 puros (1/10)	25 puros (1/40)*	25 puros (1/40)*
17.46 (44) x 127	15.88 (40) x 126	11.51 (29) x 126	15.48 (39) x 125
7.36 kg. millar	7.29 kg. millar	3.68 kg. millar	6.21 kg. millar

CAPITOLS
Petaca de aluminio 5/u
Aluminium pack 5/u
Etuis en aluminium 5/u

Partagas

MILLE FLEURS

25 puros (1/40) *
16.67 (42) x 125
7.54 kg. millar

SEÑORITAS

20 puros (1/50)
7.94 (20) x 109
1.47 kg. millar

CHICOS

100 puros (1/10)*
11.51 (29) x 106
2.99 kg. millar

HALF-A-CORONA

25 puros (1/40)
16.67 (42) x 90
5.70 kg. millar

CUBANS

Tubo de aluminio
Aluminium tube
Tube en aluminium

CRISTALTUBOS

Tubo de cristal
Glass tube
Tube en cristal

Partagas

898 CABINET SELECTION

SEÑORITAS
Petaca de cartón 5/u
Cardboard packs 5/u
Etuis en carton 5/u

PETIT CORONAS ESPECIALES

Montecristo

MONTECRISTO A

25 puros (1/40)
18.65 (47) x 235
18.63 kg. millar

MONTECRISTO ESPECIAL

25 puros (1/40)
15.08 (38) x 192
10.03 kg. millar

MONTECRISTO
No. 1

25 puros (1/40)
16.67 (42) x 165
10.47 kg. millar

MONTECRISTO
No. 2

25 puros (1/40)
20.64 (52) x 156
12.19 kg. millar

Montecristo

MONTECRISTO TUBOS

MONTECRISTO
TUBOS
25 puros (1/40)
16.67 (42) x 155
9.89 kg. millar

MONTECRISTO
No. 3
25 puros (1/40)
16.67 (42) x 142
8.97 kg. millar

MONTECRISTO B
50 puros (1/20)
16.67 (42) x 135
8.56 kg. millar

MONTECRISTO
No. 4
25 puros (1/40)
16.67 (42) x 129
8.14 kg. millar

MONTECRISTO
No. 5
25 puros (1/40)
15.88 (40) x 102
5.91 kg. millar

Montecristo

MONTECRISTO SELECCION CAJON

Cajón mixto   Mixed box   Coffret mixte

MONTECRISTO B

MONTECRISTO A

215

Ramon Allones

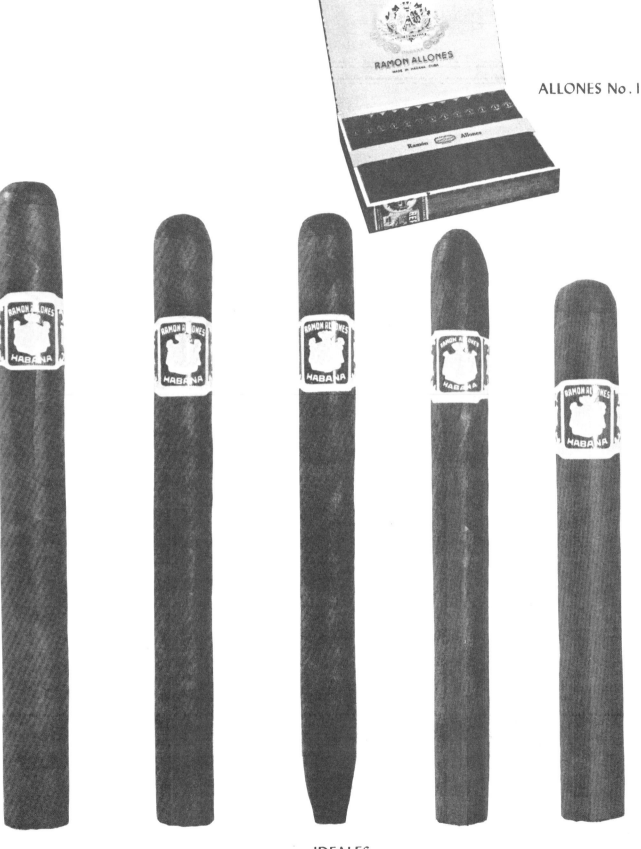

ALLONES No. 1

ALLONES No. 1	PRIVATE STOCK	IDEALES DE RAMON	TOPPERS	ALLONES EXTRA
25 puros (1/40)	25 puros (1/40)	25 puros (1/40)	25 puros (1/40)*	25 puros (1/40)
17.07 (43) x 170	15.87 (40) x 162	14.29 (36) x 161	15.48 (39) x 160	17.46 (44) x 143
11.07 kg. millar	9.29 kg. millar	7.59 kg. millar	8.33 kg. millar	9.94 kg. millar

Ramon Allones

898 CABINET SELECTION

CORONAS
25 puros (1/40)
16.67 (42) x 142
8.97 kg. millar

898
CABINET SELECTION
25 puros (1/40)
16.67 (42) x 142
8.97 kg. millar

CLUB CORONAS
25 puros (1/40)
16.67 (42) x 135
8.56 kg. millar

PALMITAS
25 puros (1/40)
11.51 (29) x 135
3.86 kg. millar

ARISTOCRATS
25 puros (1/40)
15.88 (40) x 129
7.04 kg. millar

Ramon Allones

PETIT CORONAS	PANETELAS	BELVEDERES	MILLE FLEURS	RAMONITAS	BITS OF HABANA
25 puros (1/40)	25 puros (1/40)*	25 puros (1/40)*	25 puros (1/40)*	25 puros (1/40)	25 puros (1/40)*
16.67 (42) x 129	13.89 (35) x 127	15.48 (39) x 125	16.67 (42) x 125	10.32 (26) x 121	11.51 (29) x 106
8.14 kg. millar	5.29 kg. millar	6.21 kg. millar	7.54 kg. millar	2.94 kg. millar	2.99 kg. millar

ALLONES EXTRA

PETIT CORONAS

Punch

NINFAS
25 puros (1/40)
13.10 (33) x 178
6.97 kg. millar

CLUB SELECTION
No. I
25 puros (1/40)
18.26 (46) x 143
10.90 kg. millar

DOUBLE CORONA
25 puros (1/40)
19.45 (49) x 194
16.70 kg. millar

DIADEMAS EXTRA
10 puros (1/100)
21.83 (55) x 233
20.98 kg. millar

Punch

CLUB SELECTION No. 1

Madera gruesa
Thick wood
Bois épais

PETIT CORONAS

Jarra de cristal
Glass jar
Caraffe en cristal

**PUNCH PUNCH
DE LUXE**

25 puros (1/40)
18.26 (46) x 143
10.90 kg. millar

CORONAS

25 puros (1/40)
16.67 (42) x 142
8.97 kg. millar

EXQUISITOS

25 puros (1/40)*
15.88 (40) x 129
7.04 kg. millar

CORONETS

25 puros (1/40)*
16.67 (42) x 129
7.77 kg. millar

Punch

SOUVENIRS DE LUXE

Petaca de aluminio 5/u
Aluminium pack 5/u
Etuis en aluminium 5/u

**PETIT CORONAS
DEL PUNCH**

25 puros (1/40)
16.67 (42) x 129
8.14 kg. millar

PETIT CORONAS

50 puros (1/20)
16.67 (42) x 129
8.14 kg. millar

**SOUVENIRS
DE LUXE**

50 puros (1/20)*
16.67 (42) x 129
7.77 kg. millar

TRIUNFOS

25 puros (1/40)*
16.67 (42) x 129
7.77 kg. millar

PERFECTOS

25 puros (1/40)*
17.46 (44) x 127
7.36 kg. millar

Punch

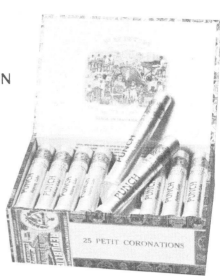

PETIT CORONATION
Tubo de aluminio
Aluminium tube
Tube en aluminium

MONARCAS
25 puros (1/40)
18.65 (47) x 178
14.08 kg. millar

ROYAL CORONATION
25 puros (1/40)
16.67 (42) x 142
8.97 kg. millar

CORONATIONS
25 puros (1/40)*
16.67 (42) x 129
7.77 kg. millar

PETIT CORONATION
25 puros (1/40)
16.67 (42) x 117
7.41 kg. millar

Punch

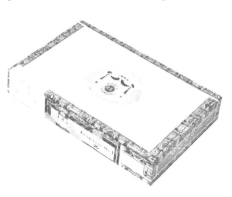

MARGARITAS	**EXHIBIT No. 5**	**PETIT PUNCH**	**AMBASSADOR No. I**	**PETIT CORONAS ONES**
25 puros (1/40)	25 puros (1/40)	100 puros (1/10)	25 puros (1/40)*	25 puros (1/40)
10.32 (26) x 121	15.88 (40) x 102	15.88 (40) x 102	16.67 (42) x 142	16.67 (42) x 129
2.94 kg. millar	5.91 kg. millar	5.91 kg. millar	8.51 kg. millar	8.14 kg. millar

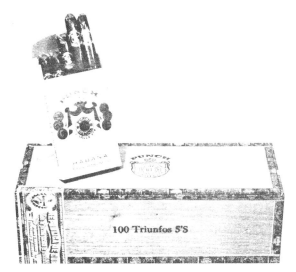

AMBASSADOR No. I
Lámina de cedro
Cedar sheet
Lamelle de cedre

TRIUNFOS
Petaca de cartón 5/u
Cardboard packs 5/u
Etuis en carton 5/u

100 Triunfos 5'S

Punch

MARGARITAS

PETIT CORONAS ONES

Petaca de cartón
Cardboard packs
Etuis en carton

ROYAL CORONATION

CORONATIONS

PETIT PUNCH

Petaca de cartón 5/u
Cardboard packs 5/u
Etuis en carton 5/u

Punch

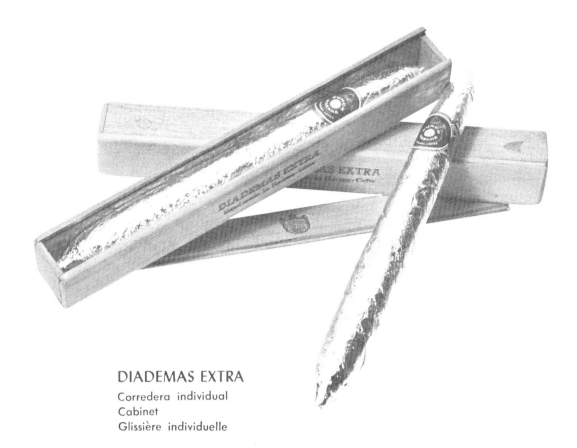

DIADEMAS EXTRA
Corredera individual
Cabinet
Glissière individuelle

LAS TRES PUNCH
Cajón mixto
Mixed box
Coffret mixte

225

Rafael Gonzalez

CORONAS EXTRA

SLENDERELLAS
50 puros (1/20)
11.11 (28) x 175
4.95 kg. millar

LONSDALES
25 puros (1/40)
16.67 (42) x 165
10.47 kg. millar

CONICALES
25 puros (1/40)
20.64 (52) x 156
12.19 kg. millar

CORONAS EXTRA
25 puros (1/40)
19.05 (48) x 140
11.59 kg. millar

Rafael Gonzalez

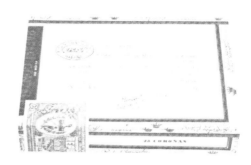

CORONAS

CORONAS CHICAS
25 puros (1/40)
16.67 (42) x 129
8.14 kg. millar

**CORONAS
LONSDALES**
25 puros (1/40)
17.46 (44) x 127
8.86 kg. millar

**TRES PETIT
LONSDALES**
25 puros (1/40)
15.87 (40) x 110
6.37 kg. millar

CIGARRITOS
50 puros (1/20)
7.94 (20) x 109
1.47 kg. millar

Rafael Gonzalez

SLENDERELLAS

LONSDALES

CORONAS LONSDALES

Saint Luis Rey

LONSDALES

CORONAS INMENSAS
25 puros (1/40)
19.05 (48) x 167
13.80 kg. millar

ENTRE PALMAS
25 puros (1/40)
15.08 (38) 166
8.60 kg. millar

LONSDALES
25 puros (1/40)
16.67 (42) x 165
10.47 kg. millar

SERIE B
25 puros (1/40)
19.05 (48) x 157
13.06 kg. millar

Saint Luis Rey

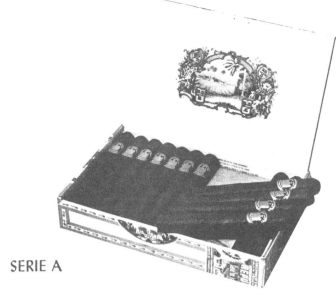

SERIE A

PYRAMIDES No. 1
25 puros. (1/40)
20.64 (52) x 156
12.19 kg. millar

CORONAS
25 puros (1/40)
18.26 (46) x 143
10.90 kg. millar

SERIE A
25 puros (1/40)
18.26 (46) x 143
10.90 kg. millar

REGIOS
25 puros (1/40)
19.05 (48) x 127
10.47 kg. millar

HAVANA CLUB
25 puros (1/40)
16.67 (42) x 122
7.73 kg. millar

Saint Luis Rey

CORONAS INMENSAS

PYRAMIDES No. I

SERIE B

Romeo Y Julieta

ARBOLADOS
Estuche tronco de árbol
Branch of a tree cabinet
Etuis sous la forme
de tronc d'arbre

CLEMENCEAUS
25 puros (1 40)
18.65 (47) x 178
14.08 kg. millar

CAZADORES
25 puros (1/40)
17.46 (44) x 162
11.27 kg. millar

ROMEOS
25 puros (1/40)
20.64 (52) x 162
13.23 kg. millar

AGUILAS
25 puros (1/40)
19.84 (50) x 143
11.80 kg. millar

ARBOLADOS
25 puros (1/40)
16.67 (42) x 142
8.97 kg. millar

Romeo Y Julieta

CORONAS
25 puros (1/40)
16.67 (42) x 142
8.97 kg. millar

CAPULETS
25 puros (1/40)*
15.88 (40) x 140
7.64 kg. millar

CELESTIALES FINOS
25 puros (1/40)
18.26 (46) x 137
9.34 kg. millar

CLUB KINGS
50 puros (1/20)
16.67 (42) x 129
8.14 kg. millar

CORONITAS
25 puros (1/40)*
15.88 (40) x 129
7.04 kg. millar

PETIT CORONAS
25 puros (1/40)
16.67 (42) x 129
8.14 kg. millar

CORONAS

Romeo Y Julieta

BULLY
25 puros (1/40)
19.05 (48) x 127
10.47 kg. millar

FAVORITAS
50 puros (1/20)*
15.48 (39) x 125
6.21 kg. millar

CLARINES
25 puros (1/40)*
16.27 (41) x 122
7.01 kg. millar

JULIETAS
25 puros (1/40)
15.87 (40) x 121
7.02 kg. millar

PANETELAS
25 puros (1/40)
13.89 (35) x 140
4.88 kg. millar

SPORTS LARGOS
25 puros (1/40)*
13.89 (35) x 117
4.88 kg. millar

CEDROS DE LUXE No. 2

Romeo Y Julieta

ROMEO No. I DE LUXE

Tubo de aluminio
Aluminium tube
Tube en aluminium

CHURCHILLS
25 puros (1/40)
18.65 (47) x 178
14.08 kg. millar

ROMEO No. 1 DE LUXE
25 puros (1/40)
16.67 (42) x 142
8.97 kg. millar

ROMEO No. 2 DE LUXE
50 puros (1/20)
16.67 (42) x 129
8.14 kg. millar

ROMEO No. 3 DE LUXE
25 puros (1/40)
15.88 (40) x 121
7.02 kg. millar

Romeo Y Julieta

CORONITAS EN CEDRO

Lámina de cedro
Cedar sheet
Lamelle de cèdre

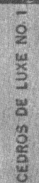

CEDROS DE LUXE
No. 1

25 puros (1/40)
16.67 (42) x 165
10.47 kg. millar

CEDROS DE LUXE
No. 2

25 puros (1/40)
16.67 (42) x 142
8.97 kg. millar

CEDROS DE LUXE
No. 3

25 puros (1/40)
16.67 (42) x 129
8.14 kg. millar

CORONITAS EN CEDRO

25 puros (1/40)*
15.88 (40) x 129
7.04 kg. millar

Romeo Y Julieta

CEDROS DE LUXE No. I

HALF A CORONA ONES

Petaca de cartón 5/u

Cardboard packs 5/u

Etuis en carton 5/u

HALF A CORONA ONES

25 puros (1/40)
16.67 (42) x 90
5.70 kg. millar

ROMEO No. 2 DE LUXE

Tubo de aluminio
Aluminium tube
Tube en aluminium

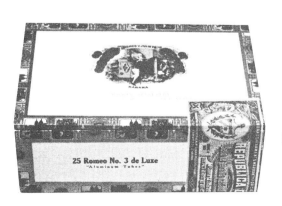

ROMEO No. 3 DE LUXE

Tubo de aluminio
Aluminium tube
Tube en aluminium

Romeo Y Julieta

LAS TRES JULIETAS
Cajón mixto
Mixed box
Coffret mixte

CHURCHILLS
Tubo de aluminio
Aluminium tube
Tube en aluminium

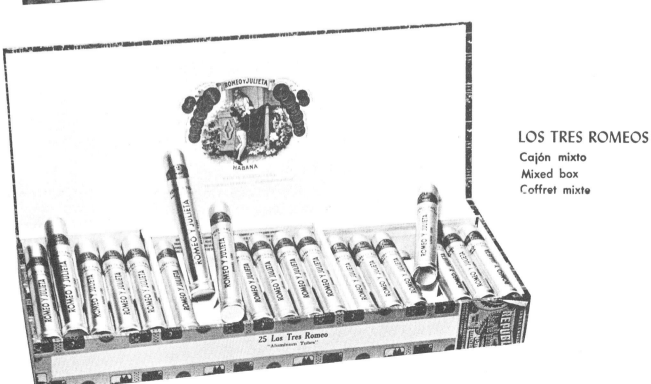

LOS TRES ROMEOS
Cajón mixto
Mixed box
Coffret mixte

238

Davidoff

DAVIDOFF No. 1	CHATEAU IQUEM	DAVIDOFF No. 2	CHATEAU LATOUR
25 puros (1/40)	25 puros (1/40)	25 puros (1/40)	25 puros (1/40)
15.08 (38) x 192	16.67 (42) x 152	15.08 (38) x 150	16.67 (42) x 142
10.03 kg. millar	9.66 kg. millar	7.82 kg. millar	8.97 kg. millar

Davidoff

AMBASSADRICE
Corredera de yagua
"Yagua" slide
Glissière en "yagua"

CHATEAU IQUEM
Corredera
Slide box
Glissière

CHATEAU MARGAUX

25 puros (1/40)
16.67 (42) x 129
8.14 kg. millar

CHATEAU LAFFITE

25 puros (1/40)
15.88 (40) x 116
6.72 kg. millar

AMBASSADRICE

50 puros (1/20)
10.32 (26) x 115
2.81 kg. millar

CHATEAU HAUT BRION

25 puros (1/40)
15.88 (40) x 102
5.91 kg. millar

Davidoff

DAVIDOFF No. 1

DAVIDOFF No. 2

241

Quintero

CORONAS SELECTAS

CHURCHILLS

25 puros (1/40)
16.67 (42) x 165
10.47 kg. millar

MIRAMAR

25 puros (1/40)
15.88 (40) x 146
8.46 kg. millar

CORONAS SELECTAS

10 puros (1/100)
16.67 (42) x 142
8.97 kg. millar

NACIONALES

25 puros (1/40)
15.88 (40) x 140
8.28 kg. millar

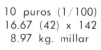

Quintero

MEDIAS CORONAS

BREVAS

BREVAS

25 puros (1/40)
16.67 (42) x 138
8.92 kg. millar

MEDIAS CORONAS

25 puros (1/40)
15.88 (40) x 126
7.29 kg. millar

CONCHAS No. I

25 puros (1/40)
15.08 (38) x 113
6.03 kg. millar

Quintero

CHURCHILLS

MIRAMAR

NACIONALES

244

La Gloria Cubana

MEDAILLE D'OR
No. 1

25 puros (1/40)
14.29 (36) x 185
8.56 kg. millar

TAINOS

10 puros (1/100)
18.65 (47) x 178
14.08 kg. millar

MEDAILLE D'OR
No. 3

25 puros (1/40)
11.11 (28) 175
4.95 kg. millar

MEDAILLE D'OR
No. 2

25 puros (1/40)
17.07 (43) x 170
11.07 kg. millar

La Gloria Cubana

MEDAILLE D'OR No. 3

CETROS
25 puros (1/40)
16.67 (42) x 165
10.47 kg. millar

GLORIAS
25 puros (1/40)
18.26 (46) x 162
12.33 kg. millar

FLECHAS
25 puros (1/40)
14.68 (37) x 156
7.18 kg. millar

MEDAILLE D'OR
No. 4
25 puros (1/40)
12.70 (32) x 152
5.52 kg. millar

SABROSOS
25 puros (1/40)
16.67 (42) x 152
9.66 kg. millar

La Gloria Cubana

TAPADOS
Corredera
Slide box
Glissière

CETROS

PINARES
25 puros (1/40)ˣ
16.67 (42) x 142
8.51 kg. millar

TAPADOS
10 puros (1/100)
16.67 (42) x 138
8.72 kg. millar

TRIUNFOS
25 puros (1/40)ˣ
17.46 (44) x 132
8.74 kg. millar

TURQUINOS
25 puros (1/40)ˣ
15.48 (39) x 125
6.21 kg. millar

MINUTOS
25 puros (1/40)
15.87 (40) x 110
6.37 kg. millar

Rey Del Mundo

CORONAS

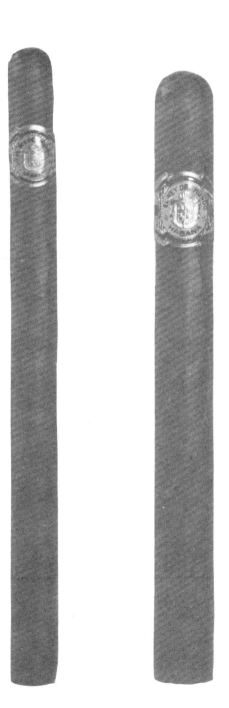

ELEGANTES
25 puros (1/40)
11.11 (28) x 175
4.95 kg. millar

LONSDALES
25 puros (1/40)
16.67 (42) x 165
10.47 kg. millar

CORONAS
25 puros (1/40)
16.67 (42) x 142
8.97 kg. millar

EPICURES
25 puros (1/40)
11.51 (29) x 130
3.91 kg. millar

ROYAL SERIES
No. 2
25 puros (1/40)
16.67 (42) x 129
8.14 kg. millar

Rey Del Mundo

CHOIX SUPREME
25 puros (1/40)
19.05 (48) x 127
10.47 kg. millar

PETIT LONSDALES
25 puros (1/40)
17.46 (44) x 127
8.86 kg. millar

ROYAL SERIES
No. 3
25 puros (1/40)
15.88 (40) x 110
6.37 kg. millar

DEMI TASSE
25 puros (1/40)
11.91 (30) x 100
3.27 kg. millar

PETIT LONSDALES

ROYAL SERIES No. 2

Rey Del Mundo

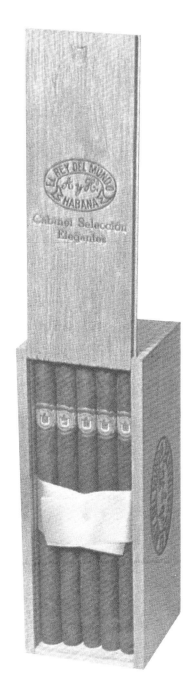

ELEGANTES

LONSDALES

CHOIX SUPREME

Sancho Panza

CORONAS GIGANTES

10 puros (1/100)
18.65 (47) x 178
14.08 kg. millar

PANETELA LARGA

25 puros (1/40)
11.11 (28) x 175
4.95 kg. millar

SANCHOS

10 puros (1/100)
18.65 (47) x 235
18.63 kg. millar

DULCINEAS

10 puros (1/100)
18.65 (47) x 232
18.17 kg. millar

Sancho Panza

QUIXOTES

CORONAS

MOLINOS

25 puros (1/40)
16.67 (42) x 165
10.47 kg. millar

CORONAS

25 puros (1/40)
17.46 (44) x 143
9.94 kg. millar

DULCINEAS

Sancho Panza

TRONQUITOS

25 puros (1/40)
16.67 (42) x 142
8.97 kg. millar

BELICOSOS

25 puros (1/40)
20.64 (52) x 140
12.37 kg. millar

QUIXOTES

25 puros (1/40)
17.46 (44) x 127
8.86 kg. millar

**CABINET
PETIT ROYALES**

25 puros (1/40)
18.26 (46) x 118
8.97 kg. millar

BACHILLERES

25 puros (1/40)
15.88 (40) x 116
6.72 kg. millar

TRONQUITOS

Estuche
Cabinet
Etuis

BELICOSOS

253

La Escepcion

GRAN GENER

10 puros (1/100)
21.83 (55) x 233
20.98 kg. millar

CORONAS
EXTRA LARGAS

25 puros (1/40)
17.46 (44) x 195
13.50 kg. millar

PALMAS REALES

25 puros (1/40)'
16.67 (42) x 142
 8.51 kg. millar

EXCEPCIONALES

50 puros (1/20)'
16.27 (41) x 127
 8.98 kg. millar

La Escepcion

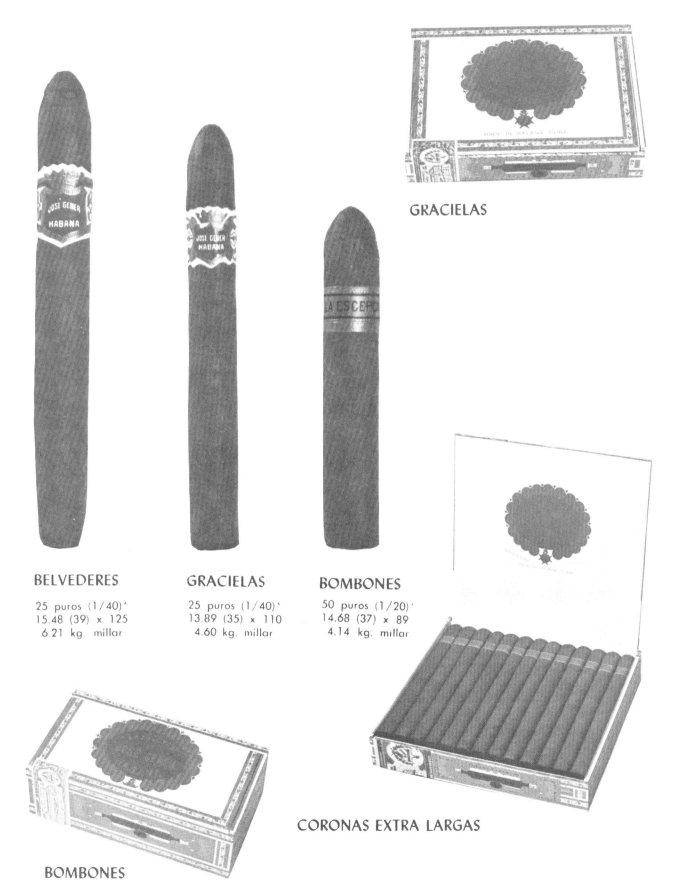

GRACIELAS

BELVEDERES

25 puros (1/40)'
15.48 (39) x 125
6.21 kg. millar

GRACIELAS

25 puros (1/40)'
13.89 (35) x 110
4.60 kg. millar

BOMBONES

50 puros (1/20)'
14.68 (37) x 89
4.14 kg. millar

CORONAS EXTRA LARGAS

BOMBONES

La Escepcion

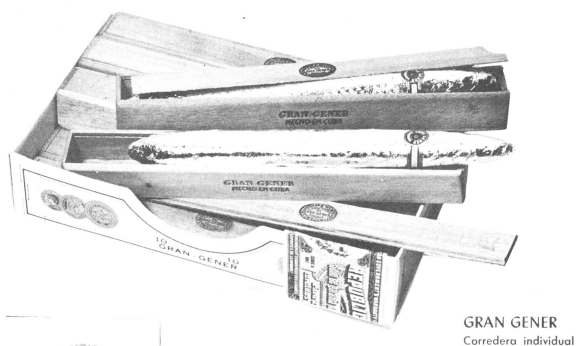

GRAN GENER
Corredera individual
Cabinet
Glissière individuelle

EXCEPCIONALES
Petaca de cartón 5/u
Cardboard packs 5/u
Etuis en carton 5/u

PALMAS REALES
Corredera
Slide box
Glissière